Human Rights, Sexual Orientation, and Gender Identity

How human rights principles, like the right to gender identity, freedom, integrity and equality, respond to the concerns of different groups of adults and children who experience gender harm due to the binary conception of sexuality and gender identity is the overall theme of this book. The Yogyakarta Principles on the Application of International Human Rights Law in Relation to Sexual Orientation and Gender Identity are analysed in the light of the dynamic jurisprudence of different human rights treaty bodies. Whether and how the status quo of gender duality is reproduced, in spite of international law's growing recognition of the multiplicity of sexualities and gender identities, is discussed. How transgender men, in countries that permit legal gender change, have been successfully prosecuted for gender fraud by female partners claiming to be unaware of their gender history is given attention. While human rights discourse related to LGBTI persons so far has been moulded on the experiences of adults this book gives voice to the concerns of gender non-conforming children. The jurisprudence of the Child Rights Committee, with focus on the complex social and legal issues faced by gender non-confirming children, is addressed. Through narratives, that give voice to these children's experiences, the book demonstrates how the legal gender assigned at birth impacts on their feeling of recognition, self-confidence, and self-respect in the private, social, and legal spheres.

This book was previously published as a special issue of the *Nordic Journal of Human Rights*.

Anne Hellum is Professor in the Department of Public and International Law, University of Oslo, Norway. Areas of teaching and research include women's law, equality and anti-discrimination law, human rights law, law and development, and sociology/anthropology of law. She is co-editor of *Human Rights of Women: CEDAW in International, Regional and National Law* (2014).

Human Rights, Sexual Orientation, and Gender Identity

Edited by
Anne Hellum

Routledge
Taylor & Francis Group
LONDON AND NEW YORK

First published 2017
by Routledge
2 Park Square, Milton Park, Abingdon, Oxon, OX14 4RN, UK

and by Routledge
711 Third Avenue, New York, NY 10017, USA

Routledge is an imprint of the Taylor & Francis Group, an informa business

British Library Cataloguing in Publication Data
A catalogue record for this book is available from the British Library

ISBN 13: 978-1-138-69850-5

Typeset in Times New Roman
by RefineCatch Limited, Bungay, Suffolk

Publisher's Note
The publisher accepts responsibility for any inconsistencies that may have
arisen during the conversion of this book from journal articles to book chapters,
namely the possible inclusion of journal terminology.

Disclaimer
Every effort has been made to contact copyright holders for their permission to
reprint material in this book. The publishers would be grateful to hear from any
copyright holder who is not here acknowledged and will undertake to rectify
any errors or omissions in future editions of this book.

Contents

Citation Information

The chapters in this book were originally published in the *Nordic Journal of Human Rights*, volume 33, issue 4 (November 2015). When citing this material, please use the original page numbering for each article, as follows:

Chapter 1: Editorial
Special Issue: Human Rights, Sexual Orientation, and Gender Identity
Anne Hellum
Nordic Journal of Human Rights, volume 33, issue 4 (November 2015), pp. 277–279

Chapter 2
The Yogyakarta Principles at Ten
Michael O'Flaherty
Nordic Journal of Human Rights, volume 33, issue 4 (November 2015), pp. 280–298

Chapter 3
Queering Gender [Identity] in International Law
Dianne Otto
Nordic Journal of Human Rights, volume 33, issue 4 (November 2015), pp. 299–318

Chapter 4
Enhancing LGBTI Rights by Changing the Interpretation of the Convention on the Elimination of All Forms of Discrimination Against Women?
Rikki Holtmaat and Paul Post
Nordic Journal of Human Rights, volume 33, issue 4 (November 2015), pp. 319–336

Chapter 5
The Rights of LGBTI Children under the Convention on the Rights of the Child
Kirsten Sandberg
Nordic Journal of Human Rights, volume 33, issue 4 (November 2015), pp. 337–352

Chapter 6
Legal Gender Meets Reality: A Socio-Legal Children's Perspective
Anniken Sørlie
Nordic Journal of Human Rights, volume 33, issue 4 (November 2015), pp. 353–379

Chapter 7

Sexual Intimacy, Gender Variance, and Criminal Law
Alex Sharpe
Nordic Journal of Human Rights, volume 33, issue 4 (November 2015), pp. 380–391

For any permission-related enquiries please visit:
http://www.tandfonline.com/page/help/permissions

Notes on Contributors

Anne Hellum is Professor in the Department of Public and International Law, University of Oslo, Norway.

Rikki Holtmaat is Professor in International Non-Discrimination Law at Leiden University, The Netherlands.

Michael O'Flaherty is Professor of Human Rights Law and Director of the Irish Centre for Human Rights, National University of Ireland, Galway, and Director of the European Union Fundamental Rights Agency.

Dianne Otto is Francine V McNiff Professor of Human Rights Law, Director of the Institute for International Law and the Humanities (IILAH), Melbourne Law School, The University of Melbourne, Australia.

Paul Post is a student at University College London, UK, and Student Assistant at the Department of European Law of Leiden University, The Netherlands.

Kirsten Sandberg is Professor in the Department of Public and International Law, University of Oslo, Norway.

Alex Sharpe is Professor of Law, Keele University, UK, and Adjunct Professor, Queensland University of Technology, Australia.

Anniken Sørlie is a PhD candidate in the Department of Public and International Law, University of Oslo, Norway.

Human Rights, Sexual Orientation, and Gender Identity

The articles presented in this Special Issue on Human Rights, Sexual Orientation, and Gender Identity are developed from papers presented at the international conference *Sexual Freedom, Equality and the Right to Gender Identity as a Site of Legal and Political Struggles* held in Oslo in December 2014.[1] LGBTI persons, unlike people who are discriminated against on grounds like sex and gender, race and ethnicity, or disability, lack a particular international convention which obliges states to ensure that their right to equality and non-discrimination is respected, protected, and fulfilled. An overall aim of the Oslo conference was to discuss recent developments in the field of human rights protection on the right to sexual orientation and gender identity without discrimination.

This Special Issue marks the 10th anniversary of the Yogyakarta Principles on the Application of International Human Rights Law in Relation to Sexual Orientation and Gender Identity. The Principles were drafted by a group of high level international experts in Yogyakarta in Indonesia in 2006 to fill the existing human rights gap. This declaration, which today constitutes an authoritative interpretation of general human rights principles, has been characterised as one of the most influential human rights documents of our time. It is against this background that this Special Issue seeks to situate the Yogyakarta Principles in a broader international and national legal landscape. A key question is how international, regional, and national law have responded to the wide range of human rights violations addressed by the Yogyakarta Principles. As regards law's growing recognition of the existing multiplicity of sexualities and gender identities a central query is whether, how, and to what extent the status quo of gender duality is reproduced.

As pointed out by Michael O' Flaherty in his article 'The Yogyakarta Principles at Ten', the drafters, through the Principles' definition, sought to avoid 'sexual orientation' and 'gender identity' as rigid binary categorisations. This effort, as O'Flaherty's article shows, has made its mark on the jurisprudence of a wide range of human rights treaty bodies, ranging from the Human Rights Committee, Council of Europe, the Court of Justice of the European Union, and the European Court of Human Rights, to domestic courts. The Yogyakarta Principles have, in many countries, along with other legal and political factors, led to a right to be assigned a legal gender in consonance with one's identity. Countries such as Denmark, Germany, New Zealand, Malta, India, and Nepal recognise a third gender. These Principles have, however, not been strong enough to extend the human right to marry and found a family to same-sex couples. Yet, many states like

[1] The conference was organised by the research group 'Individuals, Rights, Culture and Society' (RICS) and the Institute of Women's Law, Child Law and Discrimination Law at the Department of Public and International Law at the Faculty of Law, University of Oslo in cooperation with the Equality and Anti discrimination Ombud of Norway. The conference was part of the research project *Gender Identity and Sexual Orientation in International and National (Norwegian Law)* led by the Guest Editor and funded by the Research Council of Norway under the FRISAM programme.

Norway and the US do, with reference to changing social and legal circumstances, recognize same-sex marriage and as such reject the dual gender orthodoxy. In many countries where legislation allows transgender people to change their legal gender, such as the UK, US, and Israel, young transgender men have been prosecuted for gender fraud in situations where their female cisgender[2] partners claimed to be unaware of their gender history. The prosecutions from the UK, which are analysed in Alex Sharpe's article 'Sexual Intimacy, Gender Variance, and Criminal Law' were based on the assumptions that in these circumstances consent is lacking, harm is occasioned, and deception is present. Alex Sharpe discusses the imposition of a duty for transgender persons to disclose their gender identity from three legal angles. First, she questions the assumptions underlying the legal claim that non-disclosure of gender history serves to vitiate consent and cause harm. Secondly, she advances the argument that criminalisation of non-disclosure produces legal inconsistency and is potentially discriminatory. Thirdly, she argues that criminalisation is contrary to good public policy. Most importantly, Sharpe's analysis questions the underlying legal assumption that cisgender persons have a right to know and how this can be balanced against transgender persons' right to privacy and self-defined agency.

Human rights jurisprudence related to sexual orientation and gender identity has by and large been moulded on the experiences of adults. The Convention on the Rights of the Child (CRC) has been, as shown in Kirsten Sandberg's article in this issue, at the forefront in developing a human rights discourse that addresses the complex social and legal issues faced by children with a different sexual orientation or gender identity, and their parents, encountered at birth, during childhood and adolescence. The CRC Committee has recently taken the position that the medical practice of conducting genital surgery on children born with unclear genitals in order to have them labelled as boys or girls, often termed 'intersex genital mutilations', can be viewed as a harmful practice. The Committee emphasises the need for counselling and support to enable intersex children to live with their condition until they are able to make a decision themselves. In the article 'Legal Gender Meets Reality: A Socio-Legal Children's Rights Perspective', Anniken Sørlie provides an empirical case study from Norway. Through narratives she demonstrates how the legal gender assigned at birth impacts on gender non-confirming children's and adolescents' feeling of recognition, self-confidence, self-respect, and self-esteem in the private, social and legal spheres. Sørlie's analysis of how the Norwegian regulation of the assignment of gender and gender change, which is confined to the binary male/female dichotomy, leads to misrecognition in institutions like the family, the school, and social community where children grow up, is compelling reading. In the light of different children's experiences of misrecognition, she discusses different alternatives such as the recognition and introduction of a third gender, or the introduction of gender-neutral national identity numbers and identity documents.

The jurisprudence of the Convention on the Elimination of All Forms of Discrimination against Women (CEDAW) is analysed by Rikki Holtmaat and Paul Post. The text of CEDAW, particularly article 5(a) and (f), places a duty on state parties to take steps to eliminate or modify gender stereotypes. Against this background, the authors discuss whether CEDAW, in the light of its main purpose, to combat discrimination

---

[2]Cisgender is a concept that is used to refer to people who are comfortable with gender expectations and practices that follow normatively from sex designation.

against women, the legal potential to promote LGBTI rights. The authors argue that the Convention, in spite of its asymmetrical approach in addressing women, obliges states to enhance *de facto* equality of women by means of measures that eradicate the social, cultural, and religious structures that cause women's oppression, most importantly gender stereotypes that create, uphold, and reproduce the binary gender orthodoxy. Their study shows that CEDAW's commitment, with the exception of two General Recommendations that briefly mention sexual orientation and gender identity, remains limited to Concluding Observations to state reports. Emphasising the instrumentality of shadow reports for the work of the Committee, the authors call for contributions from civil society that document how discrimination of LGBTI persons is structurally connected to discrimination against women. Such a step-by-step approach may gradually lead to greater recognition by the CEDAW Committee that there is a crucial connection between discrimination against women and LGBTI persons.

Dianne Otto's article, 'Queering Gender [Identity] in International Law', offers a critical perspective on both the Yogyakarta Principles and CEDAW's definitions of gender identity. By associating gender identity with a 'deeply felt' individual destiny, the Yogyakarta Principles, Otto points out, exclude those who experience their gender as shifting or multiple, as well as those who identify some combination of blurring identities. This narrow approach, from the perspective of gender identity as a performative, fluid, flexible, and shifting category, re-naturalises the gender binary. Of the seven General Recommendations adopted by the CEDAW Committee since 2007, Otto observes that only two make reference to sexual orientation and gender identity. Seeing gender identity as an additional category in terms of intersectional discrimination, which can intensify discrimination against women, the Committee in effect precludes the insight that sex/gender/gender identity are all given substance by the same matrix of gendered social relations. To realise the transformative potential of article 5(a) and (f) of CEDAW, Otto concludes that the CEDAW Committee needs to entirely replace a (bio)logic conception with a performative conception of sex.

All in all, this Special Issue attempts to widen the perspective of the needs of different groups who experience gender harm due to the narrow binary conception of sexuality and gender identity. The issue hopes to contribute to the discussion on how these groups can take joint steps to realise the transformative potential of international human rights law.

Anne Hellum
Professor, Department of Public and International Law, University of Oslo

The Yogyakarta Principles at Ten

Michael O'Flaherty

Established Professor of Human Rights Law and Director of the Irish Centre for Human Rights, National University of Ireland, Galway; incoming Director of the European Union Fundamental Rights Agency.

ABSTRACT
From 6 to 9 November, 2006, a group of experts finalised the text of the Yogyakarta Principles on the Application of international Human Rights Law in relation to Sexual Orientation and Gender Identity. The Principles have garnered praise for enshrining the rights of persons of diverse sexual orientations and gender identities. Yet, they have also attracted critique as to their improvement beyond what some have described as radial and aspiration vision. The present article assesses the Principles in the light of almost a decade of experience. It seeks to determine the extent of the Principles impact, legal rigour, and engagement with actual lived experience. The article discusses the backdrop of the Principles, recalls their purpose and contents before moving on to a reflection on, inter alia, their influence at the national and regional levels in addition to that within the UN system. It concludes that a substantial revision of the text is not yet required, but rather, a better appreciation of the application of the Principles is needed.

From 6–9 November 2006, at Gadjah Mada University in Yogyakarta, Indonesia, a group of experts[1] finalised the text of the Yogyakarta Principles on the Application of

---

[1]Philip Alston (Australia), UN Special Rapporteur on extrajudicial, summary and arbitrary executions and Professor of Law, School of Law, New York University; Maxim Anmeghichean (Moldova), European Region of the International Lesbian and Gay Association; Mauro Cabral (Argentina), Universidad Nacional de Cordoba, International Gay and Lesbian Human Rights Commission; Edwin Cameron (South Africa), Justice, Supreme Court of Appeal, Bloemfontein, South Africa; Sonia Onufer Corre'a (Brazil), Research Associate at the Brazilian Interdisciplinary AIDS Association (ABIA) and Co chair of the International Working Group on Sexuality and Social Policy (Co chair of the experts' meeting); Yakin Erturk (Turkey), UN Special Rapporteur on violence against women, Professor, Department of Sociology, Middle East Technical University, Ankara; Elizabeth Evatt (Australia), former Member and Chair of the UN Committee on the Elimination of Dis crimination Against Women, former Member of the UN Human Rights Committee and Commissioner of the International Commission of Jurists; Paul Hunt (New Zealand), UN Special Rapporteur on the right to the highest attainable standard of health and Professor of Law, Department of Law, University of Essex; Asma Jahangir (Pakistan), Chairperson, Human Rights Commission of Pakistan; Maina Kiai (Kenya), Chairperson, Kenya National Commission on Human Rights; Miloon Kothari (India), UN Special Rapporteur on the right to adequate housing; Judith Mesquita (United Kingdom), Senior Research Officer, Human Rights Centre, University of Essex; Alice M Miller (United States of America), Assistant Professor, School of Public Health, Co director of the Human Rights Program, Columbia University; Sanji Mmasenono Monageng (Botswana), Judge of the High Court (The Republic of the Gambia), Commissioner of the African Commission on Human and Peoples' Rights, Chairperson of the Follow Up Committee on the implementation of the Robben Island Guidelines on prohibition and prevention of torture and other cruel, inhuman or degrading treatment (African Commis sion on Human and Peoples' Rights); Vitit Muntarbhorn (Thailand), UN Special Rapporteur on the human rights situation in the Democratic People's Republic of Korea and Professor of Law, Chulalongkorn University (Co chair of the experts' meeting); Lawrence Mute (Kenya), Commissioner of the Kenya National Commission on Human Rights; Manfred Nowak (Austria), Professor and Co director of the Ludwig Boltzmann Institute of Human Rights, Austria, and UN Human Rights Council Special Rapporteur on Torture and other Cruel, Inhuman or Degrading Treatment; Ana Elena Obando Mendoza (Costa Rica), feminist attorney, women's human rights activist, and international consultant; Michael O'Flaherty (Ireland), Member of the UN Human Rights Committee, Professor of Applied Human Rights and

International Human Rights Law in relation to Sexual Orientation and Gender Identity.[2] The Principles have been described as 'the most authoritative statement of what international human rights law obliges States to do and not do in promoting and protecting the rights of persons of diverse sexual orientations and gender identities and of intersex status'.[3] They have also attracted their share of controversy, ranging from constructive critique regarding how they could be improved,[4] to the unequivocal repudiation of what one author describes as 'an attempt by activists to present an aspirational, radical social policy vision'.[5]

In the role of rapporteur for development of the Yogyakarta Principles it was my function to propose textual language and to negotiate among the participating experts to find consensus formulations. The present article provides an opportunity to revisit that work and to assess the Principles in the light of almost a decade of experience. The primary interest is to determine the extent of their influence and to consider how well they have withstood the test of time in terms of legal rigour and engagement with actual lived experience. In order to lay a basis for that assessment, it is necessary first to briefly revisit the context for development of the Principles as well as to recall their intended purpose and their contents.

I. The Patterns of Human Rights Violation Lying behind the Yogyakarta Principles

The Yogyakarta Principles were developed against a backdrop of appalling human rights abuses perpetrated worldwide against persons on the basis of their actual or perceived sexual orientation or gender identity. Then as now, even the briefest of surveys would demonstrate a deeply disturbing degree of vulnerability and abuse.[6] Seven states maintain the death penalty for consensual same-sex practices, and reports are commonplace of persons who are killed because of their sexual orientation or gender identity.[7] Perpetrators often go unpunished. Trans and inter-sex persons are particularly likely to be targeted for violence. They are 'often subjected to violence in order to "punish" them for transgressing

---

Co director of the Human Rights Law Centre, School of Law, University of Nottingham, and Rapporteur for the development of the Yogyakarta Principles; Sunil Pant (Nepal), President of the Blue Diamond Society, Nepal; Dimitrina Petrova (Bulgaria), Executive Director, The Equal Rights Trust; Rudi Muhammad Rizki (Indonesia), UN Special Rapporteur on international solidarity, and Senior Lecturer and the Vice Dean for Academic Affairs, Faculty of Law, University of Padjadjaran, Indonesia; Mary Robinson (Ireland), Founder of Realizing Rights: The Ethical Globalization Initiative, former President of Ireland, and former United Nations High Commissioner for Human Rights; Nevena Vuckovic Sahovic (Serbia and Montenegro), Member of the UN Committee on the Rights of the Child, and President of the Child Rights Centre, Belgrade; Martin Scheinin (Finland), UN Special Rapporteur on counterterrorism, Professor of Constitutional and International Law, and Director of the Institute for Human Rights, Finland; Wan Yanhai (China), founder of the AIZHI Action Project and Director of Beijing AIZHIXING Institute of Health Education, China; Stephen Whittle (United Kingdom), Professor in Equalities Law, Manchester Metropolitan University; Roman Wieruszewski (Poland), Member of the UN Human Rights Committee, and Head of Poznan Centre for Human Rights; and Robert Wintemute (United Kingdom), Professor of Human Rights Law, School of Law, King's College London.
[2]Full text available at: http://www.yogyakartaprinciples.org/ (accessed 28 August 2015).
[3]C Sidoti, Asia Pacific Forum Manual for National Human Rights Institutions on Human Rights and Sexual Orientation, Gender Identity and Intersex Status, forthcoming 2016.
[4]D Brown, 'Making Room for Sexual Orientation and Gender Identity in International Human Rights Law: An Introduction to the Yogyakarta Principles' (2010) 31 *Michigan J of Int L* 821.
[5]P Tozzi, 'Six Problems with the Yogyakarta Principles', International Organisations Research Group Briefing Paper No 1. (C Fam, 2007) available at http://papers.ssrn.com/sol3/papers.cfm?abstract id=1551652 (last accessed 26 November 2015).
[6]For an extensive review of the forms of vulnerability, see M O'Flaherty and J Fisher, 'Sexual Orientation, Gender Identity and International Human Rights Law: Contextualising the Yogyakarta Principles' (2008) 8 *HRLR* 207.
[7]See http://76crimes.com/76 countries where homosexuality is illegal/ (accessed on 4 September 2015).

gender barriers or for challenging predominant conceptions of gender roles',[8] and trans-gender youth have been described as 'among the most vulnerable and marginalized young people in society'.[9] Violations directed against lesbians because of their sex are often inseparable from violations directed against them because of their sexual orientation. For example, the multiple rape of a lesbian was arranged by her family in an attempt to 'cure' her of her homosexuality.[10] Same-sex sexual relations between consenting adults are criminalised in some 77 states.[11] Some states apply laws against 'public scandals', 'immorality', or 'indecent behaviour' to punish people for looking, dressing, or behaving differently from what are considered to be the social norms.[12]

Serious problems have been identified regarding the enjoyment of economic, social, and cultural rights. For example, people have been denied employment or employment-related benefits or have faced dismissal because of their sexual orientation or gender identity.[13] In the context of the right to adequate housing, lesbian and transgender women are reported to be at a high risk of homelessness; discrimination based on sexual orientation or gender identity when renting accommodation has been experienced both by individuals and same-sex couples; and children have been thrown out of the family home by their families upon learning of their sexual orientation or gender identity.[14] Transgender persons often face obstacles in seeking access to gender-appropriate services at homeless shelters. Educational materials referencing issues of sexual orientation and gender identity have been banned from school curricula; student groups addressing sexual orientation and gender identity issues have been prohibited; students have faced high levels of bullying and harassment because of their actual or perceived sexual orientation or gender identity; and, in some cases, young persons who express same-sex affection have been expelled from school. In some countries, laws have prohibited the 'promotion of homosexuality' in schools.[15] Numerous health-related human rights violations based on sexual orientation and gender identity have been documented. People have been forcibly confined in medical institutions, subjected to 'aversion therapy', including electroshock treatment, and inter-sex people have been subjected to involuntary surgeries in an attempt to 'correct' their genitals.[16]

The persistence of the patterns of human rights violations that lay behind the development of the Yogyakarta Principles has been authoritatively demonstrated by a 2015 report of the United Nations High Commissioner for Human Rights.[17] This report observed,

---

[8]Report of the Special Rapporteur on the question of torture and other cruel, inhuman or degrading treatment or punishment, A/56/156 (3 July 2001) para 17.

[9]Report of the Special Rapporteur on the sale of children, child prostitution and child pornography, E/CN.4/2004/9 (5 January 2004) para 123.

[10]Report of the Special Rapporteur on violence against women, its causes and consequences, E/CN.4/2002/83 (31 January 2002) para 102.

[11]http://antigaylaws.org/ (accessed 12 September 2015).

[12]M O'Flaherty, 'Sexual Orientation and Gender Identity', in D Moekli et al (eds), *International Human Rights Law* (OUP, 2014) 305.

[13]Ibid.

[14]Ibid.

[15]Ibid.

[16]Ibid.

[17]Report of the Office of the High Commissioner for Human Rights, Discrimination and Violence Against Individuals Based on their Sexual Orientation and Gender Identity, A/HRC/29/23 (2015).

notwithstanding some positive developments (to which we will return in context of an assessment of the impact of the Principles), that:

> continuing, serious and widespread human rights violations [are] perpetrated, too often with impunity, against individuals based on their sexual orientation and gender identity. Since 2011, hundreds of people have been killed and thousands more injured in brutal, violent attacks … Other documented violations include torture, arbitrary detention, denial of rights to assembly and expression, and discrimination in health care, education, employment and housing.[18]

The global reach of violations was highlighted with the publication in 2014 of a report of the European Union Fundamental Rights Agency, indicating the degree to which members of sexual minorities within EU member states feel constrained to hide their sexuality – with 38 per cent indicating that they are never open on the matter and 66 per cent reporting that they would not show affection for a partner in public.[19]

II. The Purpose of the Yogyakarta Principles

Responding to human rights violations requires multi-faceted action from a range of national and international actors. To be effective, their efforts should be grounded in a strong and clear normative base in the form of international human rights law that is capable of and understood to apply for the full protection of the rights of members of sexual minorities.

As has been demonstrated elsewhere,[20] the application of international human rights law with regard to the particular situation of people of diverse sexual orientations and gender identities has long been identified. Fundamental principles, such as those of non-discrimination and of the universal application of general human rights standards, have been strongly affirmed. However, as has also been shown,[21] the courts, the treaty bodies, and the independent experts, limited as they are by the facts before them or their various mandates, have only indicated the actual application of these principles to a limited number of circumstances.

This is the context within which the Yogyakarta Principles were developed. The co-chairs of the process, in their introduction to the Principles, presented the exercise as follows:

> To address [the] deficiencies a consistent understanding of the comprehensive regime of international human rights law and its application to issues of sexual orientation and gender identity is necessary. It is critical to collate and clarify State obligations under existing international human rights law, in order to promote and protect all human rights for all persons on the basis of equality and without discrimination.[22]

In seeking to reflect the application of existing international human rights law, the Principles have a tripartite quality.[23] In the first place, they 'map' the human rights violations

[18]Ibid, para 3.
[19]European Union Agency for Fundamental Rights, LGBT Survey (2014) 12.
[20]See O'Flaherty in Moekli (n 12).
[21]O'Flaherty and Fisher (n 7).
[22]Sonia Onufer Corrêa and Vitit Muntarbhorn 'Introduction to the Yogyakarta Principles' The Yogyakarta Principles (2007) 6 7.
[23]Address of the Rapporteur, launch event of the Principles (March 2007).

experienced by people of diverse sexual orientations and gender identities. Secondly, the application of international human rights law to such experiences is articulated. Finally, the Principles spell out the nature of the obligation on states for implementation of each of the human rights.

III. Definitions

All of the Yogyakarta Principles are framed with reference to the categorisations of 'sexual orientation' and 'gender identity'. Sexual orientation is defined as, 'each person's capacity for profound emotional, affectional and sexual attraction to, and intimate sexual relations with, individuals of a different gender or the same gender or more than one gender'.[24] 'Gender identity' is described as 'each person's deeply felt internal and individual experience of gender, which may or may not correspond with the sex assigned at birth, including the personal sense of the body (which may involve, if freely chosen, modification of bodily appearance or function by medical, surgical or other means) and other expressions of gender, including dress, speech and mannerisms'.[25]

The categories of sexual orientation and gender identity establish a personal scope of application for the Principles. They were chosen rather than such usages as 'homosexual', 'lesbian', 'gay', 'bi-sexual', 'transgender', 'intersex', etc. in order to better reflect the universal reach and application of human rights law. As an interpretive guide to the Principles put it:

> The Yogyakarta Principles articulate universal rights for all people, but they do not suggest specific standards for particular groups. In the wording of the Principles themselves, the drafters sought to uphold the universal nature of human rights by avoiding wording that would limit rights to particular groups. Thus, instead of speaking about the rights of heterosexuals, homosexuals, lesbians, gay men, bisexuals, or transgender people, each Principle is said to apply to all people regardless of the characteristic of actual or perceived sexual orientation or gender identity. By expressing the rights in this way, the drafters have also sought to avoid the necessity of requiring individuals to absolutely categorise themselves by identity labels that may not be appropriate for all cultural contexts. The notions of sexual orientation and gender identity are fluid. Requiring a person to subscribe to a particular identity group would only perpetuate the oppression that the rights are seeking to combat. None of the rights in the Principles can be considered particular or unique to one group, but rather are enjoyed by all.[26]

IV. Content of the Yogyakarta Principles

There are 29 Principles. Each comprises a statement of the law, its application to a given situation, and an indication of the nature of the state's duty to implement the legal obligation. Principles 1–3 address the universality of human rights and their application to all persons without discrimination, as well as the right of all people to recognition before the law. The experts placed these elements at the beginning of the text in order to recall the

---

[24]Preamble to the Yogyakarta Principles.
[25]Ibid.
[26] *An activists' guide to the Yogyakarta Principles* (2010) 23, at www.ypinaction.org/content/activists guide (accessed 1 September 2015).

primordial significance of the universality of human rights and the scale and extent of discrimination against people because of their actual or perceived sexual orientation or gender identity, as well as the manner in which they are often rendered invisible within society and its legal structures. Principles 4 – 11 deal with the fundamental rights to life, freedom from violence and torture, privacy, access to justice, and freedom from arbitrary detention. Principles 12–18 address non-discriminatory enjoyment of economic, social, and cultural rights, including accommodation, employment, social security, health, and education. Principles 19 – 21 concern the importance of the freedom to express oneself, one's identity, and one's sexuality, without discriminatory or otherwise undue state interference, including the rights to participate peaceably in public assemblies and events and otherwise associate in community with others. Principles 22 and 23 address the right to seek asylum from persecution based on sexual orientation or gender identity. Principles 24 – 26 deal with the rights to participate in family life, public affairs, and the cultural life of the community, without discrimination based on sexual orientation or gender identity. Principle 27 recognises the right to defend and promote human rights without discrimination based on sexual orientation and gender identity, and the obligation of states to ensure the protection of human rights defenders. Principles 28 and 29 affirm the importance of holding rights violators accountable and of ensuring redress for those whose rights are violated.

A notable feature of the Principles is the manner in which they spell out in some detail the legal obligations of the state with regard to each of the rights that are affirmed. Drawing on well-established international law and practice[27] a general typology for the obligations can be observed. States must: (1) take all necessary legislative, administrative, and other measures to eradicate impugned practices; (2) take protection measures for those at risk; (3) ensure accountability of perpetrators and redress for victims; and (4) promote a human rights culture by means of education, training, and public awareness-raising.

Although the Principles are addressed to states, as the principal duty-bearers in international law, the experts were of the view that recommendations should also be delivered to other relevant actors. There are 16 of these recommendations directed to the UN High Commissioner for Human Rights, treaty monitoring bodies, international and regional governmental and non-governmental bodies, national human rights institutions, commercial organisations and others.

The Principles exist in six 'official' linguistic versions, English, French, Spanish, Russian, Chinese, and Arabic (the six United Nations official languages).[28] They are also available in numerous 'unofficial' translations. A 2010 report[29] identified versions either completed or in process of translation in Portuguese, Indonesian, Japanese, Nepali, Bengali, Romanian, Hungarian, Dutch, German, Polish and Macedonian, as well as in the South American indigenous languages, Quechua, Aymara and Guarania.

---

[27]See General Comment 3, Article 2 Implementation at the National Level, Human Rights Committee UN Doc HRIGEN1REV. 1 at 4 (1994; General Comment 3, The Nature of States Parties' Obligations, Committee on Economic Social and Cultural Rights (2003) UN Doc HRI/GEN/1/REV.6 at 14; See also Frédéric Mégret, 'Nature of Obligations' in Moecklli (n 12) 96.

[28]N 2 above.

[29]P Ettelbrick, Z Trabucco, 'The Impact of the Yogyakarta Principles on International Human Rights Law Development: A Study of November 2007 June 2010   Final Report' (10 September 2010).

Other versions since then include Catalan, Euskara (Basque), Filipino, Lithuanian, Persian (Farsi), Sinhala, Slovak, and Tamil.[30]

V. Dissemination of the Principles

From the outset, the Yogyakarta Principles benefited from a vigorous and ambitious dissemination campaign led by such organisations as Human Rights Watch, International Service for Human Rights, ARC International and the International Commission of Jurists.[31] They were launched in Geneva on 26 March 2007 at a public event that coincided with a session of the United Nations Human Rights Council. They were then discussed at a side-event of that session, attended by numerous diplomats and civil society representatives. An additional launch took place at UN headquarters in New York on 7 November 2007, hosted by the governments of Brazil, Argentina, and Uruguay on the sidelines of a session of the General Assembly's Third Committee (the committee that deals with human rights matters). Briefings were also held for UN human rights treaty monitoring bodies, Human Rights Council special procedures mandate holders and others.[32]

There were numerous further launch-like and awareness-raising events worldwide. The most significant regional initiative was the convening by the Asia–Pacific Forum – the coordinating body for national human rights institutions of that region – of a major awareness-raising workshop that was attended by the NHRIs of nine states.[33] Some inter-governmental regional events also occurred. For instance, in Latin America, a working group of MERCOSUR was briefed on the principles[34] and, in Europe, they were introduced at a working group of the Council of Europe's Committee of Ministers.[35] There were additional launches at the national and local levels, usually organised by civil society groups. Although a comprehensive list of these does not seem to be maintained at any central location, signatories to the principles either initiated or participated in numerous such events. For instance, I attended launches in three national capitals and at a number of other more local venues (including private homes) and recall the spirited participation of central and local government officials, activists, parliamentarians and community organisers. Dissemination across the range of relevant stakeholder groups was facilitated by the publication of supporting materials including an activists' guide[36] and a set of jurisprudential annotations to the Principles.[37] Other materials were developed locally, including promotional films, animations and songs – with many of these still accessible following a search of the term 'Yogyakarta Principles' on the website YouTube.[38]

---

[30]Available at http://www.ypinaction.org/content/Principles Unofficial Translation (accessed on 28 August 2015).
[31]See the Williams Institute note Yogyakarta Principles Working Group Meeting Summary, The Williams Institute, UCLA School of Law, Global Art of Justice Conference, Los Angeles, California (11 12 March 2009).
[32]O'Flaherty and Fisher (n 7).
[33]Ettelbrick and Trabucco (n 29) 45.
[34]Ibid, 27
[35]Ibid, 54.
[36] An Activists' Guide to the Yogyakarta Principles 2010, available in English, French, German and Spanish, is at www.ypinaction.org/content/activists guide (last accessed 26 November 2015).
[37]The Jurisprudential Annotations to the Yogyakarta Principles' (2007) available at http://www.sxpolitics.org/wp content/uploads/2009/05/yogyakarta principles jurisprudential annotations.pdf (accessed on 9 September 2015).
[38]https://www.youtube.com/results?q=the+yogyakarta+principles (accessed on 2 September 2015).

VI. Influence

The ultimate test of the Yogyakarta Principles is their impact for the better protection of human rights. An assessment of that type, concentrating on the actual experience of rights-holders, is beyond the scope of this article. Instead, attention is paid to the extent to which a measurable positive influence can be discerned on the actions of governments, inter-governmental bodies, judiciaries, and other relevant actors. (Inevitably, this evaluation will be inadequate, since it will fail to capture forms of remote causality where the Principles have played an unacknowledged role in helping to shape some good outcome).

Writing in 2008, John Fisher and I[39] had already identified some notable developments:

- Within days of the Geneva launch 30 states spoke in at the Human Rights Council in favour of enhanced human rights protection in the context of sexual orientation and gender identity, with seven favourably citing the Principles;
- The then UN High Commissioner for Human Rights, Louise Arbour, delivered a supportive statement to the New York launch event;
- The annual meeting of the heads of UN human rights field operations welcomed the Principles and the UN supported at least one national level launch, in Nepal;
- Two other UN entities, the UN Office on Drugs and Crime and UN AIDS endorsed the Principles;
- The Netherlands stated that 'the Yogyakarta Principles are seen by the government as a guideline for its policy' and there were further supportive statements of policy from such states as Canada, Uruguay, Brazil and Argentina;
- The European Parliament's Intergroup on Gay and Lesbian Rights endorsed the Principles;
- Local successes included a call by a representative of a city council – that of Johannesburg in South Africa – for the Principles to 'become accepted by all members of our increasingly diverse communities'; and
- Worldwide, civil societies groups were referencing the Principles in their advocacy.

That article also attempted to convey the extent to which the Principles were empowering members of sexual minority groups. It cited one on-line commentator who wrote at the time of their launch, 'I am now, under International Human Rights Law, officially human. And yesterday, I wasn't'.[40] The Principles also seemed to provide a context in which states could undertake critical self-examination. As Ireland's delegate to a session of the UN Human Rights Council put it in 2008:

> One of our well known Irish writers once posed the question: Why have our differences been so unfruitful? In our society, which was for a long time less open than at present to such differences, we have discovered in recent decades that the celebration of difference can be of benefit to all in society. In that regard, it would be a valid goal for States to seek to ensure that the obligations as defined in the Yogyakarta Principles be reflected in domestic law.[41]

---

[39]O'Flaherty and Fisher (n 7).
[40]Report on the Launch of the Yogyakarta Principles, ARC International, available at http://www.ypinaction.org/files/45/Report on Launch of Yogyakarta Principles.pdf (accessed on 9 September 2015) 5.
[41]Ettelbrick and Trabucco (n 29).

The following years have witnessed a notable growth in the indications of direct impact at international, regional, and national levels. Among the most significant developments has been the manner in which the Yogyakarta categories of 'sexual orientation' and 'gender identity', with their respective definitions, have been embraced. They were explicitly adopted by a treaty monitoring body, the Committee on Economic, Social and Cultural Rights, in a General Comment it issued on non-discrimination.[42] Subsequently other treaty bodies have increasingly framed issues on the basis of the two categories.[43] Multiple other actors, including the UN High Commissioners for Human Rights and Refugees, have employed the definitions in significant reports and policy positions. The definitions have also been relied on in a number of judgments of higher court at the national level.[44] Ettelbrick and Trabucco, in a report published in 2010, captured the significance of the wide adoption of the terms:

> The importance of this cross cultural and cross disciple consensus ... on these basic terms cannot be overstated. Agreement as to who is included in the social grouping that is the subject of the law and its application is the necessary first step to actually interpreting and applying the law. These definitions   devoid of the morally and medically stigmatising con notations often found in the law   have started already to build an important link among States and other authorities that have already adopted or referenced them in the context of legislative, judicial or executive level law making, reporting or debate. Should this trend continue the Yogyakarta Principles themselves will have made one of the more significant contributions to date to the development of international human rights norms as applied to the lives of LGBT people.

VII. Influence at the Level of the United Nations

Impact has extended well beyond invocation of the definitions. In 2008, the first ever statement at the General Assembly in support of full protection of human rights for persons of diverse sexual orientations and gender identities was delivered on behalf of 66 states.[45] The authors of the statement acknowledged the extent to which its contents were informed by the Yogyakarta Principles.[46] In what Stephanie Farrior describes as, 'a sad display of ignorance'[47] a 'counter-statement' was issued on behalf of 57 other states[48] which argued, *inter alia*, that the statement could lead to the 'social normalisation, and possibly the legitimating, of many deplorable acts including paedophilia'.

---

[42]General Comment 20, Non Discrimination in Economic, social and Cultural Rights, Committee on Economic, Social and Cultural Rights (2009) E/C.12/GC/20.

[43]Concluding Observation of the Committee Against Torture, Mongolia, adopted on 20 January 2011, CAT/C/MNG/CO/1, para 25; Concluding Observation of the Committee Against Torture, Finland, adopted on 29 June 2011, CAT/C/FIN/CO/5 6, para 24; Concluding Observation of the Committee on the Elimination of Discrimination against Women, Panama 5 February 2010, CEDAW/C/PAN/CO/7, para 22.

[44] *Naz Foundation v Government of NCT of Delhi* (Delhi High Court, 2 July 2009; *Blue Diamond Society, et al v Nepal Govern ment*, Writ No 917 of the year 2064 (BS) (2007 AD) (Supreme Court of Nepal, 21 December 2007). *Ang Ladlad LGBT Party v Commission on Elections* (COMELEC) (Philippines Supreme Court (8 April 2008).

[45]UN General Assembly, *Statement on Human Rights, Sexual Orientation and Gender Identity*, 18 December 2008, available at: http://www.refworld.org/docid/49997ae312.html (accessed 9 September 2015).

[46]Statement of Argentina (18 December 2008) video archived (at 2 hours, 25 mins) at: http://www.un.org/webcast/ga.html (last accessed 26 November 2015).

[47]Stephanie Farrior, 'Human Rights Advocacy on Gender Issues: Challenges and Opportunities', (2009) 1 *J of Human Rights Practice* 89.

[48]Statement of Syria (18 December 2008), video archived (at 2 hours, 32 mins) at: http://www.un.org/webcast/ga.html (last accessed 26 November 2015.

With regard to the Human Rights Council reference has already been made to the welcoming remarks of a number of states.[49] In addition, some special procedures of the Council have also made use of the Principles. Notable among these have been the Special Rapporteur on the rights of everyone to the enjoyment of the highest attainable standard of physical and mental health, the Special Rapporteur on torture and other cruel, inhuman or degrading treatment or punishment, and the Special Rapporteur on the promotion and protection of human rights and fundamental freedoms while countering terrorism.[50] The latter rapporteur, Martin Scheinin, reported that the Principles, 'identify that States must ensure that procedures exist whereby all State-issued identity papers which indicate a person's gender/sex … reflect the person's profound self-defined gender identity'.[51] In defending this view, he subsequently stated, 'on the use of sources, the Yogyakarta Principles is introduced as comparison and as a soft-law document, which enriches the discussion on human rights legislation'.[52]

Another Human Rights Council mechanism, the Universal Periodic Review procedure – the framework in which the Council peer-reviews the human rights record of UN member states – has frequently invoked the Principles. Ettelbrick and Trabucco cite 17 instances in the period 2007–2010 in which states recommended to a state under review that it should implement them.[53] Of these, five either explicitly or implicitly accepted the recommendation, eight either did not respond or gave unclear answers and four rejected the recommendation.[54] A study of UPR recommendations, undertaken in 2015, demonstrates a notable drop-off in explicit reference to the Principles in recent years, albeit the raising of sexual orientation and gender identity related recommendations has become commonplace.

Ettelbrick and Trabucco consider the Principles to be the inspiration for the growing attention to the human rights of LGBTI persons by the Office of the High Commissioner for Human Rights (OHCHR).[55] They correctly observe a prioritisation of the issues starting with the OHCHR 2010–2011 Strategic Plan.[56] Indeed, in the period since Ettelbrick and Trabucco published their study, there has been a further intensification of attention in the framework of OHCHR's impressive global campaign, 'Born Free and Equal: Sexual Orientation and Gender Identity in International Human Rights Law'.[57] However, this development will not be explored further here since neither OHCHR nor successive High Commissioners have expressly drawn a connection with

---

[49] Joint Statement Delivered by Norway on Behalf of Nordic States Denmark, Finland, Iceland, Norway and Sweden, UN Human Rights Council (2007); Statement of the Minster of Foreign Affairs of the United Kingdom of the Netherlands, H.E. Mr Maxime Verhagen, UN Human Rights Council (2008); Statement of Czech Republic (during interactive dialogue with the Special Rapporteur on Freedom of Expression, UN Human Rights Council (2007); Statement of Ireland, UN Human Rights Council (2008); statement of Slovenia on behalf of the EU (5 March 2008), considered as the first affirmation of the Yogyakarta Principles by the EU, see Ettelbrick and Zeran (n 29) 19.

[50] Report of the Special Rapporteur on the Right of Everyone the Enjoyment of the Highest Attainable Standard of Physical and Mental Health (27 April 2010) A/HRC/14/20 5; Report of the Special Rapporteur on the Promotion and Protection of Human Rights and Fundamental Freedoms while Countering Terrorism (3 August 2009) 8.

[51] Report of the Special Rapporteur (n 50) para 48.

[52] Ibid.

[53] Ettelbrick and Trabucco (n 29).

[54] Ibid.

[55] Ibid v11.

[56] Ibid.

[57] Born Free and Equal: Sexual Orientation and Gender Identity in International Human Rights Law, United Nations Office of High Commissioner for Human Rights (2012) available at http://www.ohchr.org/Documents/Publications/BornFreeAndEqualLowRes.pdf (accessed 9 Sep. 2015).

the Principles. It may be added that the Principles are only paid slight attention in OHCHR reports and other publications.[58]

It is to the other UN High Commissioner – for refugees (UNHCR) – that we turn for the most notable invocation of the Principles by any major UN organ. In 2008, the UNHCR published a 'Guidance Note on Refugee Claims Related to Sexual Orientation and Gender Identity'.[59] The document contains several references to the Principles in the guidance it offers to states and it observes that, 'it is now well established that LGBT persons are entitled to all human rights on an equal basis with others … The Yogyakarta Principles reflect binding international legal standards with regard to sexual orientation which are derived from key human rights instruments'.[60] UNHCR has also included the Principles in its compendium of instruments relevant to sexual orientation and gender identity to be used in cases of refugee claims.[61] The embracing of the Principles by UNHCR is of great significance because of its impact for the determination of refugee status at the national level.

The final cluster of UN entities to be mentioned is that of the treaty monitoring bodies. Other than in the definitional context addressed above, they appear to have only occasionally explicitly invoked the Principles. Two rare instances, both from the Committee Against Torture, and both in 2011, were the delivery to states (Mongolia and Finland) concerning recommendations for reforms to be undertaken in compliance with the Principles.[62] There is also some evidence that, on occasion, the Principles implicitly inform recommendations delivered to states.[63]

The Principles have also played a role, albeit unacknowledged, in at least one important case decided under the Human Rights Committee's individual complaint procedure, *Fedotova v Russian Federation* (2012).[64] Having participated in the Committee's consideration of the case, I can attest to the influence of the Principles in informing the reasoning.

Ms Fedotova had complained of a violation of the right of freedom of expression (article 19, International Covenant on Civil and Political Rights) because of her arrest for having demonstrated near a school in Moscow while displaying posters that read 'I am proud of my homosexuality' and 'homosexuality is normal'. The Committee had no difficulty in finding that the Covenant had been violated and further observed:

> the Committee is of the view that, by displaying posters that declared 'Homosexuality is normal' and 'I am proud of my homosexuality' near a secondary school building, the author has not made any public actions aimed at involving minors in any particular

---

[58]See eg 2011 report at para 75.
[59]UN High Commissioner for Refugees (UNHCR), *UNHCR Guidance Note on Refugee Claims Relating to Sexual Orientation and Gender Identity*, 21 November 2008, available at: http://www.refworld.org/docid/48abd5660.html (accessed 13 September 2015.).
[60]Ibid, 6.
[61]UNHCR Guidelines on International Protection No 9 Claims to Refugee Status based on Sexual Orientation and/or Gender Identity within the context of Article 1A(2) of the 1951 Convention and/or its 1967 Protocol relating to the Status of Refugees available at http://www.unhcr.org/50ae466f9.pdf (accessed 13 September 2015).
[62]See Concluding Observation on Mongolia and Finland (n 43).
[63]See recommendations of the Human Rights Committee to Bolivia, contained in concluding observations adopted in 2015, CCPR/C/BOL/CO/3.
[64] *Irina Fedotova v Russian Federation*, CCPR/C/106/D/1932/2010, Human Rights Committee, Views adopted by the Committee at its 106th Session (15 October 2 November 2012).

sexual activity or at advocating for any particular sexual orientation. Instead, she was giving expression to her sexual identity and seeking understanding for it.[65]

Fedotova is significant not only for extending the Committee's jurisprudence on sexual orientation beyond matters of discrimination and privacy but also for the introduction of language recognising the need to respect individual identity in all its diversity. This position echoes and was informed by Yogyakarta Principle 3 which states, 'Each person's self-defined sexual orientation and gender identity is integral to their personality and is one of the most basic aspects of self-determination, dignity and freedom'.

VIII. Impact at the Regional Level

At the regional level, the impact of the Principles can be observed primarily in Europe. The European Parliament, as well as other entities of the European Union, most recently its Fundamental Rights Agency, have relied on, endorsed, or otherwise cited the Principles.[66]

The Council of Europe, for its part, has also undertaken a number of initiatives. In 2010, its Committee of Ministers adopted a recommendation on discrimination based on sexual orientation and gender identity.[67] While it does not mention the Principles, they were an important resource during the drafting process (I can attest to this since I had the occasion to brief the drafting group). The Council of Europe Commissioner for Human Rights has been a powerful advocate for and invoker of the Principles. In 2007, the then Commissioner, Thomas Hammarberg, described the Principles as 'an important tool in identifying the obligations of States to respect, protect and fulfil the human rights of all persons, regardless of their sexual orientation or gender identity'.[68] He and his successor have referenced the principles, including in commentary on the human rights situation within member states of the Council of Europe.

The Principles have been invoked in both the European Court of Human Rights (ECtHR) and the Court of Justice of the European Union (ECJ). In *Hämäläinen v Finland* (2014), the ECtHR considered whether a law which made the recognition of the applicant's new gender conditional on the transformation of her marriage into a registered partnership violated relevant provisions of the European Convention on Human Rights,[69] while the majority held that the law did not violate the Convention. In a joint dissent, Judges Sajó, Keller, and Lemmens referred to Yogyakarta Principle 3, which provides for the right to recognition before the law, in their analysis of the scope of article 12 of the Convention (the right to marry and found a family). In their view, Principle 3 supported the argument that article 12 guarantees the right to remain married unless there is a compelling reason to dissolve a marriage that both spouses wish to continue.[70] The ECJ in *Minister voor Imigratie en Asiel v X, Y and Z* (2013) determined whether homosexuals

---

[65] Ibid, para 10.7.

[66] See (n 19).

[67] Council of Europe Recommendation CM/Rec(2010) 5 of the Committee of Ministers to member states on measures to combat discrimination on grounds of sexual orientation or gender identity available at https://wcd.coe.int/ViewDoc. jsp?id=1606669 (accessed 12 September 2015).

[68] Human Rights and Gender Identity, Issue Paper by Thomas Hammarberg, Council of Europe Commissioner for Human Rights available at https://wcd.coe.int/ViewDoc.jsp?id=1476365 (accessed 13 September 2015).

[69] *Hämäläinen v Finland* (App No 37359/09) ECHR 16 July 2014.

[70] Joint Dissenting Opinion of Judge Sajo, Keller and Lemmens, paras 15 16.

form a particular social group under the EU Directive establishing guidelines for the assessment of refugee status.[71] The court adopted the position of its Advocate General who had relied upon the definition of sexual orientation in the Principles to submit that homosexual asylum seekers may form a particular social group entitled to protection under the Directive.[72]

The Inter-American human rights system has invoked the Principles on a number of occasions. Notably, the Inter-American Commission on Human Rights (IACHR) Rapporteurship on the Rights of LGBTI person has made multiple references[73] and the IACHR, in *Homero Flor Freire v Ecuador*, cited the Principles' definition of 'sexual orientation', referred to Principle 25 as 'international doctrine' and quoted it in full.[74] One might have expected judicial citations in the ground-breaking case in 2011 of *Atala Riffo and Daughters v Chile*,[75] concerning the custody rights to her own children of a woman in a same-sex partnership. However, the Inter-American Court of Human Rights found for the applicant but made no reference to the principles. This absence of mention in the *Atala* judgment, in as much as the expert pleadings in the case are silent with regard to the Principles, suggests an advocacy strategy rather than any particular judicial resistance.[76]

IX. Influence at the National Level

A 2015 study indicates that the Principles have been cited in just 17 domestic court proceedings.[77] This seemingly paltry number belies the significance of some of the cases. In *Pant v Nepal Government*, the Nepalese Supreme Court explicitly relied on the Yogyakarta definitions of 'sexual orientation' and 'gender identity' in ordering the government to recognise trans-gendered persons as a third gender.[78] In *Naz Foundation v Government of NCT of Delhi*,[79] the High Court of Delhi, India, struck down a statute that criminalised same-sex sexual activity and extensively cited the Principles as well as the commentary on them by John Fisher and me.[80] The Indian Supreme Court overturned this judgment but did not impugn reasoning related to the significance of the Principles.[81] Indeed, a 2014 decision of the Indian Supreme Court, *National Legal Services Authority v Union of India*,[82] extensively cited the Principles in its finding that trans-gender persons have a right to be registered as a third gender. The Court also referred to the Principles when discussing the harmonisation of international law with domestic constitutional law:

---

[71] *X, Y, Z v Minister voor Immigratie en Asiel*, C 199/12   C 201/12, European Union: Court of Justice of the European Union (7 November 2013).
[72] Ibid, para 18.
[73] See for instance www.oas.org/en/iachr/lgbti/links/, last visited on 24 November 2015.
[74] *Homero Flor Freire v Ecuador*, Report No 81/13, IACHR 4 November, 2013. See also *Angel Alberto Duque v Colombia*, Report No 5/14, IACHR 2 April 2014.
[75] *Atala Riffo and Daughters v Chile*, Inter American Court of Human Rights (Judgement of 24 February 2012).
[76] See e.g. http://arc international.net/wp content/uploads/2011/08/El Escrito de amicus curiae en ingles.pdf (accessed on 2 September 2015).
[77] See Review of the Use of the Yogyakarta Principles in Domestic and International Litigation, Freshfields Bruckhaus Derin ger, for the International Service for Human Rights (28 January 2015).
[78] *Pant v Nepal Government* (2007) Writ No 917, translated in (2008) 2 Nat Jud Acad L J 261.
[79] *Naz Foundation v Government of NCT of Delhi* (2009) 160 DLT 277 (High Court of Delhi).
[80] Ibid.
[81] *Koushal v NAZ Foundation* (2013) (Supreme Court of India).
[82] *National Legal Services Authority v Union of India* (2014) 5 SCC 438.

'Principles ... including [the] Yogyakarta Principles, which we have found not inconsistent with the various fundamental rights guaranteed under the Indian Constitution, must be recognized and followed'.[83]

On occasion, the Principles have been the subject of judicial critique. In the Philippines Supreme Court case of *Ang Ladlad LGBT Party v Commission on Elections* (2010), the petitioner invoked the Principles as binding rules of international law.[84] The Court rejected this submission on the grounds that the Principles: (i) are not a source of international law; (ii) could be recognised as *de lege ferenda* at best; and (iii) do not constitute binding obligations for the Philippines.[85]

The Principles have also been invoked in odd and potentially dangerous contexts. In at least two cases, the Australian Refugee Review Tribunal decided against the appellant, holding that the adoption of the Principle at Yogyakarta in Indonesia has been considered to be indicative of an improved level of tolerance of homosexuality in that country.[86] In similar fashion, the same tribunal took account of the participation in the negotiation of a Kenyan expert as a relevant consideration in assessing the levels of acceptance of lesbianism in Kenya – albeit in that case the tribunal found for the appellant.[87]

This brief review of the domestic cases demonstrates the considerable potential role of the Principles in influencing domestic jurisprudence. However, the number of cases indicates the extent to which this potential is unrealised, no doubt due to very low levels of awareness among lawyers and the judiciary. The *Ang Ladlad* case also indicates the need for the Principle to be cited appropriately, as indicative of – rather than in themselves – constituting international law. Finally, the practice of the Australian Refugee Review Tribunal is both abusive and a further reminder of the need for the delivery at national levels of enhanced and nuanced awareness-raising.

With regard to impact beyond jurisprudence, the Ettelbrick and Trabucco study contains a wealth of data.[88] In a 2015 a draft report that I prepared for the UN briefly summarised the impact of the Principles for state practice at the domestic level:

- National legislatures in such states as Argentina, Brazil, Canada, Uruguay, and Mexico have introduced or passed bills citing the Yogyakarta Principles as relevant resources.[89]
- Provincial legislatures in Buenos Aires and El Chaco (Argentina) have drawn on the Principles in enacting laws addressing issues of gender identity.
- Government departments, including Brazil's Ministry of Education, Bolivia's Justice Ministry, Spain's Social Affairs Ministry and the Foreign Ministries of Belgium, the Netherlands, Ireland and the UK have favourably cited the Principles.[90]
- In Ecuador, the National Police Human Rights Training Course cites the Yogyakarta Principles in explaining the rights of imprisoned transgender persons and highlighting the fact that gender identity and sexual orientation are basic aspects of human dignity.

---

[83]Ibid, para 53.
[84]*Ang Ladlad LGBT Party v Commission on Elections* (2010) GR No 190582.
[85]Ibid, para. 52.
[86]*Case No 071263822* (2007) RRTA 115 (Australian Refugee Review Tribunal); *Case No 1000927* (2010) RRTA 444 (Australian Refugee Review Tribunal), para 48.
[87] *Case No 1204063* (2012) RRTA 694 (Australian Refugee Review Tribunal), para 78.
[88]Ettelbrick and Trabucco (n 29).
[89]Ettelbrick and Trabucco (n 29) 30 34.
[90]Ibid, 33, 58, 57, 58.

The final exam of the course includes a question regarding the meaning and application of the Principles.[91]

- Germany, Brazil,[92] and Montenegro[93] have funded the translation and publication of the Yogyakarta Principles in their national languages.[94]

An experience of mine with regard to the invocation of the Principles within the Irish parliament may be of anecdotal interest. In early 2015, the parliament was debating a bill on the subject of gender recognition. The first draft was problematic from a human rights point of view. The bill failed to respect self-determination and privacy by adopting a medical model whereby recognition of a new gender would only be possible following medical certification and the undergoing of surgical 'gender re-assignment'. It was also proposed that a change of gender, once recognised, would be irreversible and that no child under the age of 16 would be permitted to seek recognition of changed gender. An opinion piece of mine on the matter in an Irish national newspaper, *The Irish Times*, referred to the human rights concerns and extensively referenced the Yogyakarta Principles.[95] Subsequently, when the bill came before the upper house of parliament, the Senate, a number of senators cited the article and made specific reference to the Principles.[96] The relevant government minister responded that the principles did not constitute international law.[97] Nevertheless, a short time later, a revised bill was published that addressed each of the human rights issues. This bill has now been enacted into law and is a model of good practice that is fully consistent with the relevant Principles.[98]

X. The Quality of the Yogyakarta Principles

Quality is a matter of both legal accuracy and appropriateness. Each requires a brief examination. On the matter of accuracy, as rapporteur for the text, I was comfortable in 2007 that the Principles did not go beyond the then prevailing state of international law. The indications of impact discussed above suggest wide agreement with that view. Furthermore, the large literature on the Principles has not convinced me that any significant mistakes were made.

One of the most comprehensive legal examinations of the Principles is by David Brown, published in 2010.[99] He is of the view that, while the Principles are broadly compliant with

---

[91] Ibid, 34.

[92] Ibid, 57, 32.

[93] 'Implementation of the Yogyakarta Principles: Key Factors for Implementation in Montenegro and Achievements in Implementation in Other Parts of the World' Presentation at "Promotion and Importance of Yogyakarta Principles" Round table, Ministry of Foreign Affairs and European Integration (17 July 2014) http://williamsinstitute.law.ucla.edu/wp content/uploads/IntegratingYYPMontenegro.pdf (last accessed 26 November 2015).

[94] Draft report submitted to the United Nations Office of the High Commissioner for Human Rights. On file with the author.

[95] Michael O'Flaherty, 'Gender recognition Bill is in Violation of International Human Rights Law', *Irish Times* (10 February 2015), available at http://www.irishtimes.com/opinion/gender recognition bill is in violation of international human rights law 1.2097289 (accessed on 15 September 2015).

[96] Seanad (Senate) debate on the Gender Recognition Bill 2014, Tuesday 17 February 2015: http://oireachtasdebates. oireachtas.ie/debates%20authoring/debateswebpack.nsf/takes/seanad2015021700002?opendocument#CC00200 (accessed on 15 September 2015).

[97] Ibid.

[98] Gender Recognition Bill, Department of Social and Family Affairs (2014) available at https://www.welfare.ie/en/downloads/Gender Recognition Bill 2014.pdf (accessed on 17 September 2015).

[99] D Brown, 'Making Room for Sexual Orientation and Gender Identity in International Human Rights Law: An Introduction to the Yogyakarta Principles' (2010) 31 *Michigan J of Int L*.

the law, on occasion they 'push the limits' of existing law and they contain some errors.[100] On the former point perhaps he overlooks a large part of the purpose of the Principles which is to apply existing law to a diversity of circumstances, something that the experts were particularly well qualified to do. He proposes two 'major errors of law': (a) that the principles fail to acknowledge the progressive realisation principle regarding economic, social and cultural rights, and (b) they erroneously derive a right of same-sex couples to found a family.[101] On the first point, he seems to be of the view that the Principles' unqualified acknowledgement of a right to health care or to housing disregards the progressive realisation principle. In so doing, he may be overlooking the established doctrine of the Committee on Economic, Social and Cultural Rights on a state's minimum core obligations regarding the substantive elements of all rights contained in the Covenant on Economic, Social and Cultural Rights.[102] Concerning the right to found a family, Brown conflates issues of marriage and family – a distinction which the Principles were assiduous in maintaining. His view, also, is at odds with the direction of jurisprudence of the European Court of Human Rights. The Court in *Schalk and Kopf v Austria*,[103] reversing previous findings, observing that, 'a cohabiting same-sex couple living in a stable *de facto* partnership, falls within the notion of "family life", just as the relationship of a different-sex couple in the same situation would'.[104] The Inter-America Court of Human Rights adopted similar reasoning in the *Atala Riffo and Daughters* case.[105]

Conversely to Brown, Joke Swiebel has written that the Principles' failure to identify a right of same-sex marriage, 'does not contribute to the credibility of the Principles'.[106] She does not argue her position and I remain of the view that it was not possible to identify such a right as of 2006–2007. Circumstances have changed considerably since then. Contemporary arguments for the identification of such a right on grounds of non-discrimination[107] as well as the 2015 ruling on the matter by the US Supreme Court[108] have made the identification of such an internationally recognised human right a plausible proposition. Any such articulation will, of course, have to overcome the contrary ruling of the Human Rights Committee in *Joslin v New Zealand*[109] as well as the European Court of Human Rights which, in *Schalk and Kopf*, found that there is not as yet sufficient state practice to identify an obligation to grant a same-sex couple access to marriage.[110]

Turning to issue of appropriateness, there is a considerable literature concerning the framing of the principles within the categories of 'sexual orientation' and 'gender identity'. Aeyal Gross observes[111] that not all non-western humanity frames identity on the basis of gender or sexual orientation and he considers that the Principles 'represent an attempt at

---

[100]Ibid, 878.

[101]Ibid, 863 867.

[102]Ibid, 862.

[103]*Schalk and Kopf v Austria*, Application No 30141/04, Judgement of 24 June 2010.

[104] Ibid, para 94. See also, *P.B. and J.S. v. Austria* (No. 1898/02), Judgment of 22 July 2010.

[105]*Atala Riffo and Daughters v Chile* (n 72).

[106]J Swiebell, 'Lesbian, Gay, Bisexual and Transgender Human Rights: the Search for an International Strategy' (2009) 15 *J of Cont Pol* 29. See also A Gross, 'Sex Love and Marriage: Questioning Gender and Sexuality Rights in International Law' (2008) 21 *Leiden J of Int L* 253.

[107]P Gerber, 'Marriage: A Human Rights for All?' (2014) 36 *Sydney L Rev* 643.

[108] *James Obergefell v Hodges* 576 U.S.   (2015), No. 14 556. Argued April 28, 2015   Decided June 26, 2015.

[109]*Ms Juliet Joslin et al v New Zealand*, Communication No 902/1999, UN Doc A/57/40 at 214 (2002).

[110]*Schalk and Kopf* (n 103) at para 63.

[111]See Gross (n 104).

offering freedom of, but not freedom from, sexual orientation and gender identity'. In so doing, suggests Gross, the Principles buy into binary and hierarchical categories of gender and sexuality. Tom Dreyfus comments that, 'it appears that to be intelligible to the Principles, subjects must fix their "gender identity", ensuring that it matches one of the non-conforming identities alluded to in the Principles Preamble. This presents particular difficulties to people of diverse sexes and genders, whose multiplicities and individual experiences of sex and gender may resist definition altogether'.[112]

Such concerns as these are reasonable, pointing as they do to the inevitable inadequacy of and the risk of cultural specificity in categorisations and definitions. Gross, however, also provides a response to the critique when he observes that the approach of the Principles is grounded in the context of a, 'world where LGBT individuals suffer from discrimination based on their sexual orientation or gender identity'.[113] This was indeed the rationale for the reliance on these categories. Experience, also, has shown that the definitional approach of the Principles has not impeded them from supporting non binary gender assumptions, as witnessed in the decisions cited above of the Nepalese and Indian Supreme Courts. Matthew Waites suggests a reasonable route forward when he writes, 'switch[ing] from unproblematised, undefined uses of "sexual orientation" and "gender identity", to taking the opportunities that arise to offer careful, explicit definitions of the concepts that are compatible with the diversity of sexual and gender subjectivities … This might generally include use of the definitions in the Yogyakarta Principles, but perhaps with additional notes or commentary'.[114]

One further issue of appropriateness has to do with the targets of the Principles – those with the role or duty to promote and protect human rights. The Principles identify the state as the duty-bearer and only engage other actors in the short list of recommendations that appear almost as an appendix to the document. This approach is unimpeachable as a matter of law. However, it can be considered to pay inadequate attention to the extent to which human rights abuse and protection engage non-state actors. In the years since the adoption of the Principles, there has been considerable reflection in this area, with particular focus on the role as duty-bearer of the business sector.[115] There has also been increasing appreciation of the manner in which such non-state entities as national human rights institutions can be the champions of human rights.[116] It may be concluded that were the Principles to be adopted today considerably greater attention would be warranted to the role, for good and ill of actors other than the state.

XI. How Best to Mark the 10th Anniversary

When the Yogyakarta Principles were adopted, it was acknowledged in the preface to the text that:

---

[112]T Dreyfus, The "Half Invention" of Gender Identity in International Human Rights Law: from CEDAW to the Yogyakarta Principles' (2014) 37 *Australian Feminist L J* 45.

[113]Gross (n 104) p 250.

[114]M Waites, 'Critique of "Sexual Orientation" and "Gender Identity" in Human Rights Discourse: Global Queer Politics Beyond the Yogyakarta Principles' (2009) 15 *J of Cont Pol* 153.

[115]UN Guiding Principles on Business and Human Rights (2011).

[116]K Linos and T Pegram, *Integrating Form and Function: Designing Effective National Human Rights Institutions*, The Danish Institute for Human Rights (2015).

> (T)his articulation must rely on the current state of international human rights law and will require revision on a regular basis in order to take account of developments in that law and its application to the particular lives and experiences of persons of diverse sexual orientations and gender identities over time and in diverse regions and countries.[117]

Ten years later, on my own review of the Principles in light of changed circumstances, I conclude that they have withstood the test of time and remain of considerable relevance in efforts to secure compliance with existing international human rights law to the benefit of people regardless of and in full respect for their diverse sexual orientations and gender identities. It does not seem to me that the moment has yet come when any form of substantial revision of the text is required.

However, it is equally evident that there is a need for a better appreciation of the application of the Principles. It is also clear that they would benefit from a new programme of dissemination. These conclusions suggest an appropriate set of actions to be undertaken – or at least initiated – on the 10th anniversary of the adoption of the principles.

It is timely now to prepare a detailed guidance note with regard to the application of the Principles. This would not seek to re-open or to compete with the adopted text. Instead, I propose an authoritative commentary, not unlike the 'general comments' that, from time to time, are adopted by UN human rights treaty bodies regarding aspects of the treaties they oversee.[118] Drawing on emerging good practice for the development of treaty body general comments,[119] the commentary should benefit from wide-ranging consultations with relevant civil society groups and be drafted over a period, during which interested parties have the opportunity to comment on the text. It should also integrate reference to good and promising practice for implementation of the human rights at issue.

The commentary itself would best be authored by a high level group of experts including participants with experience regarding international human rights law as well as with a deep appreciation of the lived experience of LGBTI persons across the world. At least some of these experts should have already participated in the adoption of the Principles themselves. The commentary would take account of contemporary understanding of issues of sexual orientation and gender identity as well as of relevant developments in international human rights law. In such a context the opportunity would be provided, for instance, to clarify the scope and the appropriates of the categories and definitions of 'sexual orientation' and 'gender identity' as well as to take account of recent legal discourse and practice on such matters as marriage entitlements.

The production of a commentary would also afford the opportunity to expand considerably on the recommendations to non-state actors, including the business community and national human rights institutions, making the best possible use of the myriad good practice initiatives and tools developed in recent years.

Completion of a commentary would afford the timely moment to undertake a new programme of dissemination of the Principles and the commentary. A lesson to be learned from the efforts of 10 years ago, might, I suggest, be that of the need for sustained efforts over a considerable number of years, rather than reliance on an intensive but short-lived effort on initial launch of the materials. Reflection on the earlier experience

---

[117] Preamble to the Yogyakarta Principles.
[118] M O'Flaherty, 'Freedom of Expression: Article 19 of the General Comment on Civil and Political Rights and the Human Rights Committee's General Comment No 34' (2012) 12 *Human Rights L Rev* 627.
[119] Ibid.

might also suggest that a special effort is needed to heighten awareness among lawyers, the judiciary, diplomats, and a range of international actors, as well, of course, among the range of others addressed in the recommendations.

It is to be hoped that the champions of the Yogyakarta Principles, not least the civil society groups that supported their development, will rise to the challenge of this important anniversary moment. Ten years ago they showed initiative and vision; again now they need to lead the way towards realisation of what the co-chairs of the Yogyakarta process described as, '[the] promise a different future where all people born free and equal in dignity and rights can fulfil that precious birth-right'.[120]

Acknowledgements

My thanks to Mesenbet Assefa Tadeg for assistance with the referencing of this article as well as to the two anonymous reviewers whose comments were extremely helpful.

---

[120]Onufer Corrêa and Vitit Muntarbhorn (n 22).

Queering Gender [Identity] in International Law

Dianne Otto

Francine V McNiff Professor of Human Rights Law, Director of the Institute for International Law and the Humanities (IILAH), Melbourne Law School, The University of Melbourne, Australia

ABSTRACT

In a growing number of countries, developments in domestic law concerning transgendered people are moving towards a more social approach to recognising and regulating gendered bodies. International developments – illustrated here by the Yogyakarta Principles - appear to be taking a different course in which (bio) logic and heteronormative family forms are uncritically embraced. This article provides examples from the Committee on the Elimination of Discrimination against Women which illustrate a reluctance to fully pursue the opportunities opened by new understandings of sex/gender and the related unwillingness to address gendered discrimination suffered by men and other genders. To counter the reinstatement of biology as foundational in gender, the article argues for more feminist and queer coalitional work and the adoption of a performative understanding of 'sex'. A more liberatory and inclusive conception of gender should be pursued, without obscuring the specificity and diversity of the human rights abuses felt by those who are, or who are perceived as, transgendered.

In recognition of the multitude of possible gender identities, Facebook provides its members with a list of 56 options, in addition to male and female, from which they can choose up to ten to have recorded in their profiles.[1] For those who are uncertain or confused or just plain curious, another enterprising cyber forum provides an on-line quiz, offering the reassurance of instant diagnosis of your gender identity after a series of questions have been answered about such matters as what makes you cry and whether you need someone else's constant attention.[2] My own result was that I was 'male' with higher stereotypically female traits than stereotypically male traits; clearly lacking was the vast range of options offered by Facebook.

Grateful thanks to both Candice Parr and Kalia Laycock Walsh for their invaluable research assistance. Thanks also to two anonymous referees for their thoughtful comments on an earlier draft. All internet websites were last accessed on 17 November 2015.

[1]'Here Are All the Different Genders You Can Be on Facebook', *Future Tense: The Citizen's Guide to the Future* (New York, 13 February 2014) http://www.slate.com/blogs/future tense/2014/02/13/facebook custom gender options here are all 56 custom options.html. The gender identity choices are not provided as a full list, but a drop down menu of options is provided once you type the first letter into an empty text field. Interestingly, there is no option to craft your own gender identity if it is not on the list, nor can you leave the field blank.

[2]See 'Wild Quiz: What's your Gender Identity', at UnBoxifyMe, http://unboxifyme.com/wild quiz whats your gender identity/.

Following Facebook's lead, I argue in this article that it is important to recognise that everyone has a 'gender identity' – including those who identify as cisgendered[3] – and that there is a dynamic relationship between the body and identity which gives rise to multiple possible alignments, which can change over time, or even from moment to moment. Consequently, the tendency for gender identity to be understood as dualistic (m/f) and treated as a category that applies only to transgendered people (and sometimes perhaps to intersex people) needs to be resisted, but without obscuring the specificity and diversity of the human rights abuses more likely to be suffered by those who are, or who are perceived to be transgendered, such as trans-phobic violence and the denial of individual freedom to define and redefine one's own gender identity as life unfolds.[4] I am concerned that feminist and queer human rights advocates have been working in isolation and at odds with each other on issues of gender [identity],[5] and my argument is that this needs to change if we are ever to develop a more liberatory and inclusive conception of gender in international (and domestic) law.

My genealogy of recent developments in international human rights law, associated with gender identity, starts with an account of the crucial role that feminists played in challenging the biological determinism that underpins international law's historical treatment of women and men. This challenge led eventually, despite virulent opposition, to the admission of the language of 'gender' into the lexicon of international law in the mid-1990s, which distinguished between immutable sex (biology) and malleable gender (socially constructed). [6] I go on, in part 2, to examine the reluctance of many feminists to fully pursue the opportunities opened by this new understanding of sex/gender and, in particular, the failure to question the male/female dualism and biological base of sex/gender orthodoxy, and the related unwillingness to address gendered discrimination suffered by men and other genders, often including even transgendered women. I use the work of the Committee on the Elimination of Discrimination against Women (CEDAW Committee) to illustrate the constraining effects of this reluctance.

Nevertheless, the sex/gender distinction, as newly described, paved the way for other feminists and queer activists to denaturalise sex, as well as gender; to understand that neither sex or gender exists prior to regulatory discourses which make certain permutations of gender intelligible (normal) and dismiss others that fall outside the m/f binary, in various ways, as abnormal. [7] Rather than being anchored in biology, sex and

---

[3]'Cisgender' refers to those whose sex assignment at birth conforms to their self identity as a man or woman. The term is often used to mean the opposite of 'transgender'. See, for example, Paula Blank, 'Will "Cisgender" Survive?' *The Atlantic* (Washington, 24 September 2014) http://www.theatlantic.com/entertainment/archive/2014/09/cisgenders linguistic uphill battle/380342/. However, this understanding relies on a separation of body and mind, which is inconsistent with performative understandings of gender, and continues to treat gender as a binary system, rather than as plurality and fluidity. Thanks to an anonymous reviewer for drawing my attention to this important point.

[4]See further, 'The International Bill of Gender Rights', as adopted at the International Conference on Transgender Law and Employment Policy (ICTLEP), Houston, Texas, 17 June 1995, http://www.transgenderlegal.com/ibgr.htm.

[5]My use of the square brackets signals a challenge to those who would distinguish 'gender' from 'gender identity' some thing that I shall later explain in more detail. The separation between feminist and queer work is also of concern in advo cacy for sexuality rights. See Dianne Otto, 'Between Pleasure and Danger: Lesbian Human Rights' (2014) *European Human Rights L Rev* 618.

[6]See, for example, Commission on Human Rights, 'Report of the Expert Group Meeting on the Development of Guidelines for the Integration of Gender Perspectives into United Nations Human Rights Activities and Programmes', UN Doc E/CN.4/1996/105 (20 November 1995) Annex [13]: 'The term "gender" refers to the ways in which roles, attitudes, values and relationships regarding women and men are constructed by all societies all over the world . . . while the sex of a person is determined by nature, the gender of that person is socially constructed'.

[7]Judith Butler, 'Gender Regulations' in *Undoing Gender* (Routledge, 2004) 40 42.

gender should both be understood as the effects of performative and reiterative gender norms (legal, social, symbolic . . .) which materialise, naturalise, regulate, and discipline sexed bodies and identifications. Yet, as I argue in part 3, although advocates for gay, lesbian, bisexual, transgender, and intersex (GLBTI) rights have been more eager than many feminists to explore the new openings for recognition and inclusion presented by the language of gender, their efforts have floundered. While more recent developments in domestic law concerning transgendered people are slowly shifting from a purely '(bio)logic' approach, which determines sex at birth,[8] towards a more social approach to recognising and regulating gendered bodies,[9] international developments appear to be taking a different course. To illustrate this problem, I examine the definition of 'gender identity' offered by the Yogyakarta Principles on the Application of International Human Rights Law in relation to Sexual Orientation and Gender Identity (Yogyakarta Principles), drafted in 2007 by a group of human rights experts and activists, which ignores social context and appears to rely, instead, on biology.[10] My fear is that the Yogyakarta Principles, despite their queer historiography, step away from hard-won social constructivism and threaten to uncritically embrace (bio)logic and heteronormative family forms as normative for everyone. They are in need of a queer-feminist coalitional revision.

In the fourth and final section, I urge for more feminist and queer coalitional work and the adoption of a performative understanding of 'sex', in order to counter the reinstatement of biology as foundational, which merely shifts the boundaries of acceptable dualistic and heteronormative gender identities, rather than, following Facebook's example, dispensing with the gender binary and its biological moorings all together. I urge rejection of the idea that any of the categories – sex/gender/gender identity – is natural and thus immutable.[11] To accept the idea of a sex–gender distinction that is reflective of a nature–nurture divide, as in the official United Nations (UN) definitions, is to limit the manifold creative possibilities for the expression of identity, desire, and sexuality that would be opened up by completely releasing the category of sex from its biological foundations. To accept the definition of gender identity offered in the Yogyakarta Principles is to limit these possibilities even further. As Judith Butler has observed, '[t]here is no gender identity behind the expressions of gender; that identity is performatively constituted by the very "expressions" that are said to be its result'.[12] Thus my bracketing of identity in the title of this article is not meant to suggest skepticism about the idea of identity, but to indicate that gender is already an identity.

---

[8]See Andrew N Sharpe, *Transgender Jurisprudence: Dysohoric Bodies of Law* (2nd edn, Routledge Cavendish, 2006) 9. For common law systems, the (bio)logic approach was set out by Ormond J of the former English Probate Division in *Corbett v Corbett* [1971] 2 All ER 33. He held that, in the context of marriage, sex is a biological matter determined at birth by chromosomes, gonads and genitals. This approach was confirmed by the House of Lords as recently as 2003 in *Bellinger v Bellinger* [2003] 2 AC 467, 473.

[9]See, for example, *AB v Western Australia* (2011) 244 CLR 390, where the High Court of Australia interpreted legislation regulating when sex recorded on a birth certificate could be changed, to depend on external rather than internal physical characteristics (genital surgery was not a requirement) and on identification as such by 'other members of society'.

[10]'Yogyakarta Principles on the Application of International Human Rights Law in Relation to Sexual Orientation and Gender Identity' (International Commission of Jurists, 2007) (Yogyakarta Principles).

[11]For a persuasive development of this position see Margaret Davies, 'Taking the Inside Out: Sex and Gender in the Legal Subject' in Ngaire Naffine and Rosemary J Owens (eds), *Sexing the Subject of Law* (North Ryde, LBC Information Service and Sweet and Maxwell 1997) 25.

[12]Judith Butler, *Gender Trouble: Feminism and the Subversion of Identity* (Routledge 1990) 25.

I. Feminist Work to Denaturalise Sex

In international law, sex has traditionally been treated in a rigidly deterministic fashion as male/female (m/f) dichotomy, and the privileged status of men vis-à-vis women (m>f) has been understood as the natural order. [13] Congruent with medical science, customary practices and religious prescriptions, this biologically anchored dualistic and hierarchical understanding of sex was affirmed and instantiated by the law. Women were largely constituted as family property, making crimes against them, such as military rape or forced prostitution, an abuse of the honour of the family – a violation of the rights of the male family head – rather than an abuse of the woman's dignity and autonomy. [14] To the extent that women were granted a measure of autonomous legal subjectivity, the law's approach was protective, denying agency (as in the anti-trafficking conventions) or limiting it (by promoting restrictive employment practices, for example).

International law's historical approach to sex/gender: *legitimated by (bio)logic*		
m/f (dualism)	nature	
m>f (hierarchy/asymmetry)	nature	

The belief that sex/gender characteristics are biologically determined and therefore immutable is also reflected in some strands of feminist thought, which seek to revalue the feminine rather than disrupt dualistic conceptions of gender.[15]

Yet, while the advent of universal human rights law in 1945, with its core principles of equality and non-discrimination, made it possible to challenge the assumed hierarchy of gender (m>f), the understanding of sex/gender as dualistic (m/f) remained unquestioned.[16] The adoption of the Convention on the Elimination of All Forms of Discrimination Against Women (CEDAW) in 1979,[17] did little to change this state of affairs. As indicated by its appellation, CEDAW takes an asymmetrical approach by prohibiting sex discrimination suffered by only one gender group (women).[18] Men are the only other gender [identity] recognised in CEDAW, and they primarily serve as the comparator against which women's (in)equality is to be measured. Paradoxically this arrangement, whereby men's experience sets the universal standard for everyone, reaffirms the tradition of both gender duality and hierarchy in an instrument that seeks to promote women's full humanity. As a result, protective responses to women's disadvantage have continued to proliferate where women's experience is not directly comparable with men's, with extra intensity in relation to women from the global south[19] – notably in the fields of

---

[13]My thanks to Janet Halley who adopted these abbreviated forms to describe current US feminist projects. Janet Halley, *Split Decisions: How and Why to Take a Break from Feminism* (Princeton University Press, 2006) 17 18.

[14]Brussels Declaration Concerning the Laws and Customs of War 1874 art XXXVIII; Manual of the Laws and Customs of War on Land 1880 art 49; Convention Respecting the Laws and Customs of War on Land 1899, 32 Stat 1803 art XLVI; Convention Respecting the Laws and Customs of War on Land 1907 (entered into force 26 January 1910) 36 Stat 2277 art XLVI.

[15]See, for example, Sara Ruddick, *Maternal Thinking: Towards a Politics of Peace* (Boston: Beacon Press 1989).

[16]Dianne Otto, 'International Human Rights Law: Towards Rethinking Sex/Gender Dualism' in Margaret Davies and Vanessa Munro (eds), *A Research Companion to Feminist Legal Theory* (Ashgate Companion Series, 2013) 19.

[17]Convention on the Elimination of All Forms of Discrimination Against Women (adopted 18 December 1979, entered into force 3 September 1981) 1249 UNTS 13 (CEDAW).

[18]For discussion, see Darren Rosenblum, 'Unsex CEDAW, or What's Wrong with Women's Rights' (2011) 20(2) *Columbia J of Gender and L* 98.

[19]Ratna Kapur, 'The Tragedy of Victimisation Rhetoric: Resurrecting the "Native" Subject in International/Postcolonial Feminist Legal Politics' (2001) 10 *Columbia J of Gender and L* 333.

reproductive health and employment – which re-entrenches women's inequality, rather than fundamentally challenging it. On this reading of CEDAW, as founded on the biological m/f binary, it is doubtful whether a transgendered (m-f) woman would qualify as a 'woman' who can therefore be a victim of 'sex' discrimination. The dualistic framework of CEDAW makes it likely that the CEDAW Committee might eventually follow recent reforms in some domestic legal systems and predicate recognition on invasive sex reassignment surgeries, [20] which would still keep the m/f binary intact. Clearly other instances of sex discrimination – experienced by men and those whose sex/gender expressions and identities do not even claim to fit neatly into the m/f binary – remain outside CEDAW's register of gender harms.

Yet, on closer reading, it is apparent that CEDAW's treatment of sex is not entirely as a natural category. It is also recognised that sex has social dimensions, which must be challenged and changed if women's equality is ever to be realised. This recognition creates a foothold for interpretations of CEDAW that refuse the binary assumption of gender and its attendant (bio)logic. The starting point lies in the preambular recognition 'that a change in the traditional role of men as well as the role of women in society and in the family is needed to achieve full equality between men and women',[21] which is an important acknowledgement that sex/gender is socially produced and regulated, and that change in one set of dyadic gendered social expectations necessarily involves change in the other, although the binary arrangement is not questioned. Article 2(f) underlines the need for social change by making it clear that state parties' obligations are not confined to changing laws and regulations that discriminate against women, but extend to modifying or abolishing discriminatory customs and practices. The obligation to support and foster meaningful social change, in relation to men as well as women, is made clear in article 5(a) which requires states parties to 'modify . . . social and cultural patterns . . . with a view to achieving the elimination of prejudices and customary and all other practices which are based on the idea of the inferiority or superiority of either of the sexes or on stereotyped roles for men and women'.

While the sexed language of CEDAW article 5(a) remains dualistic, fully recognising the social and cultural nature of gender practices and stereotypes seems to me to lead inexorably to the conclusion that gender [identity] can be experienced and/or perceived as fluid and potentially multiplicitous, constrained only by its historical and cultural context. In other words, it is possible to interpret CEDAW as prohibiting all forms of sex discrimination, including those forms experienced by men and other genders, such as intersex and transgendered people, gender transients, multi-gendered people, androgynes, butch lesbians, transvestites, cross-dressers, those identify as an 'in-between,' sex 'non-specific,' third sex and any others.[22] Rikki Holtmaat describes this as the 'transformative' potential of CEDAW, whereby the obligation to modify gender stereotypes and fixed parental roles should enable everyone to express their gender identity in the way they choose, without suffering adverse discriminatory consequences.[23] Yet, the transformations

---

[20]Sharpe (n 8), 58 75.

[21]CEDAW (n 17), preamble [14].

[22]Surya Monro, 'Transgender: Destabilising Feminisms?' in Vanessa Munro and Carl F Stychin (eds), *Sexuality and the Law: Feminist Engagements* (Routledge Cavendish, 2007) 125.

[23]Rikki Holtmaat, 'The CEDAW: a Holistic Approach to Women's Equality and Freedom' in Anne Hellum and Henriette Sinding Aasen (eds), *Women's Human Rights: CEDAW in International, Regional and National Law* (Cambridge University Press, 2013) 95, 115 116.

envisaged by Holtmaat all take place in the social/cultural sphere, leaving the underlying (bio)logic of the law still unchallenged.

Two developments occurred in the 1990s, which strengthened the potential for the CEDAW Committee to treat sex/gender as, in large part if not totally, socially constituted. The first was the acceptance of the language of 'gender' into the international legal lexicon. In 1995, after a protracted struggle, a distinction between 'sex' (understood as biologically determined) and 'gender' (understood as the result of social practices and interactions) was formally accepted by states at the Fourth World Conference on Women in Beijing,[24] although there were some notable dissenters including the Vatican and (most) members of the Organization of Islamic Conference, who have remained intransigent on this point ever since.[25] Nevertheless, this moment marked a critical turning point for feminist (and queer) engagement with international law because the acceptance of gender as a social category provided the means to fundamentally challenge the tradition of masculine superiority (m>f) and disrupt (bio)logic (m/f) by admitting the possibility of more than two sexes, just as the Vatican feared in Beijing.[26] This shift also opened the potential to challenge 'natural' conceptions of the (heteronormative) family and humanise a host of so-called unnatural forms of gender identity and expression, including transgender and intersex, as well as those that resist normative definition altogether. Unfortunately however, the subsequently adopted official UN definitions impose limits on these possibilities by continuing to anchor social constructions of 'gender' in a biological base of 'sex',[27] which still leaves space for those who insist dualistic gender is the natural order because the m/f binary of physiological sex is treated as the bedrock for gendered social arrangements.[28] While feminists disagree about how far to take social constructivism, the result has nevertheless rendered biological explanations for unequal treatment of women and men highly suspect – thus de-naturalising the gender hierarchy (m>f).

Linked to the introduction of the new language of gender was the second development – the adoption of the strategy of 'gender mainstreaming' across the entire UN system, which was first endorsed at the 1993 Vienna World Conference on Human Rights and reaffirmed in 1995 at the Beijing World Conference on Women. This development prompted the chairpersons of the human rights treaty committees to commit to fully integrating gender perspectives into their working methods.[29]As a result, several treaty bodies adopted gender mainstreaming General Comments (authoritative interpretations) which seek to mainstream women's experience of human rights abuses into the interpretation of universal human rights norms. For example, the Human Rights Committee, which

---

[24]Dianne Otto, 'Holding Up Half the Sky but for Whose Benefit? A Critical Analysis of the Fourth World Conference on Women' (1996) 6 *Australian Feminist LJ* 7, 11 12.

[25]See, for example, the Final Statement of the Holy See made at the Concluding Ceremony of the Fourth World Conference on Women; 'The term "gender" is understood by the Holy See as grounded in biological sexual identity, male or female': Holy See (Fourth World Conference on Women, Beijing, 15 September 1995) http://www.its.caltech.edu/~nmcenter/women cp/beijing3.html. See also Vanja Hamzic, 'The Case of "Queer Muslims": Sexual Orientation and Gender Identity in International Human Rights Law and Muslim Legal and Social Ethos' (2011) 11/2 *Human Rights L Rev* 237, 245 247.

[26]Otto (n 24).

[27]Commission on Human Rights (n 6). More recently, see 'UNESCO's Gender Mainstreaming Implementation Framework (GMIF) for 2002 2007' (UNESCO, 2003) annex 2: baseline definitions of key concepts and terms, 17 http://unesdoc.unesco.org/images/0013/001318/131854e.pdf.

[28]Wendy O'Brien, 'Can International Human Rights Law Accommodate Bodily Diversity?' (2015) 15 *Human Rights L Rev* 1, 2.

[29]'Report of the Sixth Meeting of Persons Chairing the Human Rights Treaty Bodies' (4 October 1995) UN Doc A/50/505 [34] (a) (f).

monitors implementation of the International Covenant on Civil and Political Rights (ICCPR),[30] recognises that domestic violence may be a form of torture or cruel inhuman and degrading treatment (violating article 7),[31] and that a state's failure to provide access to safe methods of abortion may be a violation of the right to life (violating article 6).[32] This approach, which interprets existing human rights so they are more inclusive of women's experience, transforms the universal standard so that it is no longer based solely on men's lives. As women's specific experience becomes included in the universal, there is less need for women's rights advocates to rely so heavily on a non-discrimination framework, which requires comparisons with men. Thus, gender mainstreaming has the potential to reduce the need for comparing women and men, decreasing reliance on gender dualism and hierarchy to frame and assess human rights abuses specific to women and making protective responses less likely.

Taking gender mainstreaming a step further, the Committee on Economic, Social and Cultural Rights, which monitors implementation of the International Covenant on Economic, Social and Cultural Rights (ICESCR),[33] recognises men, as well as women, as potential victims of sex discrimination by, for example, interpreting the right to social security to guarantee 'adequate maternity leave for women, paternity leave for men, and parental leave for both men and women'.[34] More boldly, the Committee that monitors implementation of the Convention Against Torture and Other Cruel, Inhuman and Degrading Treatment or Punishment (CAT)[35] recognises gender as 'a key factor' that can intersect with other characteristics of a person to make them more vulnerable to torture or ill-treatment,[36] and goes on to identify violations that are experienced solely or primarily by men, and transgendered people, as well as by women, 'on the basis of their actual or perceived non-conformity with socially determined gender roles'.[37] These developments vastly extend our capacity to challenge the social practices of dualistic gender, although the (bio)logic of m/f, which has such a firm historical grip on the international legal imagination, has not yet been explicitly challenged. The shift can be illustrated as follows:

International law's 'feminist' approach to sex/gender: *social contructivism acts upon biological base*
maintain m/f (duality)   nature
challenge m>f (hierarchy)   nurture

---

[30]International Covenant on Civil and Political Rights (adopted 16 December 1966, entered into force 23 March 1976) 999 UNTS 171 (ICCPR).

[31]Human Rights Committee, 'General Comment 28: Article 3 (The equality of rights between men and women)' (2000) UN Doc HRI/GEN/1/Rev.9 (Vol I) 228 [11].

[32]Ibid [10].

[33]International Covenant on Economic, Social and Cultural Rights (adopted 16 December 1966, entered into force 3 January 1976) 999 UNTS 3 (ICESCR).

[34]Committee on Economic, Social and Cultural Rights, 'General Comment 16: The Equal Right of Men and Women to the Enjoyment of All Economic, Social and Cultural Rights (Art. 3 of the Covenant)' (2005) UN Doc E/C.12/2005/4 [26]. Note, unlike CEDAW, the wording of ICESCR does not limit its prohibition of sex discrimination to discrimination against women.

[35]Convention Against Torture and Other Cruel, Inhuman and Degrading Treatment or Punishment (adopted 10 December 1984, entered into force 26 June 1987) 1465 UNTS 85 (CAT).

[36]Committee Against Torture, 'General Comment 2: Implementation of Article 2 by State Parties' (2007) UN Doc HRI/GEN/1/ Rev.9 (Vol II) 376 (27 May 2008) [22].

[37]Ibid.

I.i *Feminist reluctance to challenge gender duality*

Yet, while these developments have been promoted and supported by feminists, there has also been a reluctance to pursue all the potential for rethinking gender that they open, for fear that this will undermine the feminist project. Many feminists worry that the coherence of the category of 'women' as an organising focus will be threatened if gender is understood as mobile and plural, and especially if its biological anchor is questioned. They are anxious that women's specific disadvantage may again be marginalised if gender discrimination experienced by men and other genders is included in the struggle for women's rights.[38] Others put this reluctance down to the vestiges of biological determinism that continue to linger in feminist thinking,[39] or to homophobia and trans-phobia, and to the associated fear that expanding feminist demands to include those whose gender expression falls outside the m/f dualism and heteronormativity might threaten the fragile 'respectability' of feminism and limit its effectiveness.[40] As a result, most feminist efforts have been limited to emphasising the social contingency of gender hierarchy, without questioning the assumed biological base of gender dualism. Even within the confines of the social, so understood, feminist efforts have seldom extended to conceiving of gender as shifting and multiple. While this failure to fully exploit the liberatory potential of the language of gender may in some contexts be pragmatically defensible,[41] at least as a short-term measure, it has had enduring effects and resulted in a rift between much feminist and queer work on gender in the law,[42] especially when the latter seeks to challenge the assumption of m/f duality.

In questioning the natural foundation of both gender dualism and gender hierarchy, I do not want to deny the patterns of gender disadvantage that impact on every woman's life, although the picture is vastly complicated by the many differences among women because of intersecting systems of discrimination. Rather, the question that weighs increasingly heavily is whether dualism and asymmetry provide the *best* way to pursue the emancipatory possibilities for everyone, including ciswomen, that are opened up by the recognition that gender is primarily (if not entirely) a social category. One problem is that such a relentlessly dualistic understanding of sex/gender is so easily recolonised by naturalised accounts of biological sex which completely fail to acknowledge the dynamic and interwoven performative relationships between sexed bodies and identities. Another is that the asymmetrical reproduction of injured and vulnerable representations of women casts men in the role of perpetrators or protectors, which reconstitutes the

---

[38]Titia Loenen, 'Rethinking Sex Equality as a Human Right' (1994) 12 *Netherlands Quarterly of Human Rights* 253; Bertha Esperanza Hernandez Truyol, 'Unsex CEDAW? No! Super Sex It!' (2011) 20 *Columbia J of Gender and L* 195; Nalini Persram, 'Politicizing the Feminine, Globalizing the Feminist' (1994) 19 *Alternatives* 285, 287.

[39]Sally Baden and Anne Marie Goetz, 'Who Needs [Sex] When You Can Have [Gender]? Conflicting Discourses on Gender at Beijing', in Cecile Jackson and Ruth Pearson eds, *Feminist Visions of Development: Gender Analysis and Policy* (1998) 19.

[40]Alice M Miller, 'Sexuality, Violence Against Women, and Human Rights: Women Make Demands and Ladies Get Protection' (2004) 7 *Health and Human Rights* 17, 36 39; Cynthia Rothschild et al, *Written Out: How Sexuality is Used to Attack Women's Organizing* (rev edn, IGLHRC and CWGL, 2005).

[41]IGLHRC, *Equal and Indivisible: Crafting Inclusive Shadow Reports for CEDAW* (IGLHRC 2008) 3, http://www.iglhrc.org/sites/default/files/287 1.pdf. The authors acknowledge that many feminists and queer theorists have moved away from the sex/gender binary arguing they are both given meaning socially, but maintain that for pragmatic reasons, in work with CEDAW, the binary remains useful.

[42]See for example, Halley (n 13), who suggests the need to 'take a break' from feminism in order to see important dimensions of sexuality that feminism does not make visible. The same argument can be made with regard to feminist myopia about the links between their struggles for women's rights and the human rights struggles of other gender identities.

traditional imaginary of m>f gender hierarchies.[43] A third problem is the exclusionary and disciplinary effect of understanding sex/gender as always tied to a biological base, which prevents a full understanding of the way that sex/gender operates as a technology of power, regulating populations so they are more compliant and easily governable.[44]

This feminist reluctance is evident in the unwillingness of the CEDAW Committee to address discrimination on the basis of gender identity as a form of discrimination against women. On the few occasions that the Committee has used the term, it has mostly been coupled, and often conflated, with sexual orientation. An examination of 181 Concluding Observations adopted between 2007 (when the Yogyakarta Principles were adopted) and 10 March 2014 reveals that issues relating to sexual orientation, gender identity and/or lesbians were raised in only 38 of them (20.9 per cent). One third of these 38 references are in the 'positive aspects' of the Concluding Observations, where the Committee 'welcomes' information about new anti-discrimination legislation or same-sex partner recognition that was provided in state parties' reports.[45] In these instances, the CEDAW Committee does not go beyond merely repeating the information the state party has provided, so it cannot be credited with raising the issue and, despite being given the opportunity, notably fails to discuss any aspects of these developments that may need improvement. It is likely that the remaining, more critical references are based on information provided by NGOs in shadow reports. [46] Yet, despite drawing attention to serious human rights abuses,[47] the references are brief, and the state party concerned is not seriously taken to task. For example, in the case of criminalisation of 'same-sex relationships', as in Sri Lanka, which the Committee admits leaves women 'completely excluded from legal protection' and at risk of arbitrary detention, it merely expresses its 'concern'.[48] 'Sexual orientation' and 'gender identity' are not even routinely included in standard lists of prohibited grounds of discrimination when they appear in the Committee's Concluding Observations, despite other human rights treaty bodies adopting this practice.

When examined through the single lens of gender identity (detached from sexual orientation), it is clear that the CEDAW Committee, notorious for its 'slowness' to engage with issues of sexuality,[49] is even more resistant to facing up to the challenges presented by the concept of gender identity. Indeed, a member of the CEDAW Committee has observed that the term 'gender identity' is anathema to many Committee members because it is

---

[43]Dianne Otto, 'The Exile of Inclusion: Reflections on Gender Issues in International Law over the Last Decade' (2009) 10 *Melbourne J of Int L* 11.

[44]Michel Foucault, Graham Burchell, Colin Gordon and Peter Miller. *The Foucault Effect: Studies in Governmentality* (University of Chicago Press, 1991).

[45]See, for example, Committee on the Elimination of Discrimination Against Women, 'Concluding Observations: Bosnia and Herzegovina' (30 July 2013) UN Doc CEDAW/C/BIH/CO/4 5 [4(a)], where anti discrimination legislation that includes 'sexual expression' and 'sexual orientation' as prohibited grounds of discrimination is welcomed; and Committee on the Elimination of Discrimination Against Women, 'Concluding Observations: Chile' (12 November 2012) UN Doc CEDAW/C/CHL/CO/5 6 [46], where it is 'noted' that 'a bill on de facto unions, which includes same sex relationships, is before the Senate'.

[46]Guidelines were developed in 2008 by the International Gay and Lesbian Human Rights Commission (IGLHRC), to help NGOs prepare shadow reports for the CEDAW Committee, which include human rights issues related to sexual orientation, gender identity and gender expression. See IGLHRC (n 41).

[47]These references can be grouped into five main areas of concern: violence against women, health issues, failure to prohibit discrimination, harmful stereotypes, and particularly disadvantaged or vulnerable women.

[48]Committee on the Elimination of Discrimination Against Women, 'Concluding Observations: Sri Lanka' (8 April 2011) UN Doc CEDAW/C/LKA/CO/7 [24].

[49]Mindy Jane Roseman and Alice M Miller, 'Normalizing Sex and its Discontents: Establishing Sexual Rights in International Law' (2011) 34 *Harvard J of L and Gender* 313, 353.

seen as 'watering down' CEDAW obligations to women.[50] More than half of the 38 references in my sample of Concluding Observations are substantively concerned only with issues of sexuality (sexual orientation discrimination, same sex relationship recognition, violence against lesbians, and lesbian reproductive rights). All but three of the remaining references either couple gender identity with sexual orientation (SOGI), or include transgender in a list with lesbian, bi-sexual, and intersex (LBTI). As Jena McGill argues, the treatment of gender identity and transgender issues as if they converged with issues of sexuality, runs the risk that the specificity of human rights issues related to gender identity will be marginalised or disappear altogether.[51] The CEDAW Concluding Observations are a good example of such a disappearance. On only three occasions does the Committee refer to issues that are unique or of primary concern to the transgendered community. Twice, the Committee expresses concern about the compulsory sterilisation that transgendered people must undergo to get birth certificates changed, [52] and once it notes the difficulties faced by transgendered asylum seekers due to the narrow construction of gender-related persecution.[53] When it does use the term gender identity to refer to specific violations, it is understood to apply only to transgendered people, indicating that the CEDAW Committee does not consider women and men to be gender identities.

Clearly, members of the CEDAW Committee are divided on how to incorporate issues of sexual orientation and gender [identity] into their work. While earlier making sporadic references to sexual orientation, the Committee was completely silent on issues of sexuality between 2002 and late 2008, falling out of step with most other UN human rights mechanisms.[54] Following the 1995 Beijing World Conference on Women, it took the Committee another 15 years to reach agreement about its understanding of the distinction between sex and gender. This was finally clarified in 2010 in General Recommendation 28: that 'sex' refers to 'biological differences between men and women' and 'gender' to 'socially constructed identities, attributes and roles for women and men'.[55] Accepting this distinction is a necessary prerequisite to grasping the idea that discrimination may be suffered on the basis of social conceptions of gender identity or gender expression, even though the continued mooring of sex in (bio)logic is problematic, as I have already discussed. At the same time, reflecting the concerns of feminist human rights advocates who are reluctant to question gender dualism, the CEDAW Committee makes it clear that its task is to challenge the 'hierarchical relationships between women and men' and the 'distribution of power and

---

[50]Comments made by Violetta Neubauer (Slovenia), former member of the CEDAW Committee (Sexual Freedom, Equality and Rights to Gender Identity Conference, Oslo, 11 12 December 2014) (notes on file with author).

[51]Jena McGill, 'SOGI . . . So What? Sexual Orientation, Gender Identity and Human Rights Discourse at the United Nations' (2014) 3/1 *Canadian J of Human Rights* 1, 23 25.

[52]Concluding Observations of the Committee on the Elimination of Discrimination against Women: Finland (10 March 2014) UN Doc CEDAW/W/C/FIN/CO/7 [28]; Concluding Observations of the Committee on the Elimination of Discrimination against Women: The Netherlands (5 February 2010) UN Doc CEDAW/C/NLD/CO/5, [46] [47], also expressing concern about the non reimbursement by health insurance of the cost of surgical breast implants.

[53]Concluding Observations of the Committee on the Elimination of Discrimination against Women: Norway (23 March 2012) UN Doc CEDAW/C/NOR/CO/8 [35].

[54]Grace Poore, '30 Years of CEDAW: Achievements and Continuing Challenges Towards the Realization of Women's Human Rights', International Gay and Lesbian Human Rights Commission (3 September 2009) http://iglhrc.org/content/30 years cedaw achievements continuing challenges towards realization women%E2%80%99s human rights.

[55]Committee on the Elimination of Discrimination Against Women, 'General Recommendation 28: The Core Obligations of States Parties under Article 2 of the Convention on the Elimination of All Forms of Discrimination against Women' (16 December 2010) UN Doc CEDAW/C/GC/28 [5].

rights favouring men and disadvantaging women'.[56] Questioning the duality of sex/gender and its biological assumptions is clearly not on its agenda.

Of the seven General Recommendations adopted by the CEDAW Committee since 2007, only two make reference to 'sexual orientation and gender identity,' and neither refers to the Yogyakarta Principles.[57] Both references treat the two categories as aspects of intersectional discrimination that can compound or intensify discrimination against women based on sex or gender, which treats gender identity as an additional category of prohibited discrimination, rather than a form of sex/gender discrimination. In refusing the insight that sex/gender/gender identity are all given substance by the same matrix of gendered social relations, the CEDAW Committee completely fails to recognise the transformative potential of CEDAW, as conceived by Holtmaat. Further, the Committee's approach denies the reality that everyone has a gender identity and refuses to 'see' the multiple subjectivities performatively constituted in and through daily practices of sex/gender/gender identity.

While the feminist fear of losing the precarious spaces that have been carved out for addressing women's human rights abuses is not without substance, it is my view, as a feminist, that those spaces can be better protected by relinquishing the view of gendered power as always dualistic (m/f) and only ever hierarchically organised in men's favour (m>f), and jettisoning the fiction of a biological foundation. Instead, gender should be understood queerly as performative, as constituted and made intelligible by regulatory social norms, which govern the naturalisation of bodies and the assumption of sexed identities, while also providing the means of their contestation.[58] As Brenda Cossman argues, '[performativity] would allow us to tell a story of marginality that has not yet been told'.[59] If the CEDAW Committee were to embrace the transformative opportunities presented by articles 2(f) and 5(a), and entirely replace (bio)logic with performative conceptions of sex, while staying alert to the multiple arrangements of unequal power that can result, it would make a powerful contribution to a truly liberatory social transformation. Interpreting CEDAW in this way would provide a better means of troubling the persistent reproduction of protective and victimised representations of women that continue to proliferate in international law, as well as develop a fuller account of the diversity of gendered relations of power and the heteronormative interests they serve.

II. Queer Utilisations of the Language of Gender

Compared with the reluctance of the CEDAW Committee and many feminists, and indeed the cautiousness of the other human rights treaty bodies in the context of women's rights and gender mainstreaming, human rights advocates in the context of promoting GLBTI rights have been more open to exploring the new openings for recognition and inclusion presented by the language of gender. Many of the Special Procedures of the Human Rights Council (HRC) (and its predecessor, the Commission on Human Rights)

---

[56]Ibid.

[57]Committee on the Elimination of Discrimination Against Women, 'General Recommendation 27: Older Women and Protection of Their Human Rights' (16 December 2010) UN Doc CEDAW/C/GC/27 [13]; 'General Recommendation 28', (n 55) [18].

[58]Butler (n 7).

[59]Brenda Cossman, 'Gender Performance, Sexual Subjects and International Law' (2002) 15 *Canadian J of L and Jurisprudence* 281, 289.

have moved intrepidly to break free from the orthodoxies of dualistic (m/f) sex/gender in addressing human rights abuses related to sexual orientation and gender identity. The first formal references to human rights abuses suffered by transgendered people were made in 2001 by the Special Rapporteur on the question of torture[60] and the Special Rapporteur on extrajudicial, arbitrary and summary executions.[61] In the following years, other Special Procedures have also expressed concern about gender-based discrimination outside the (bio)logic of m/f.[62] This work has been heavily reliant on human rights NGOs[63] and activists from affected communities who have provided detailed evidence of abuses, often at great personal risk.[64] One of my activist informants told me recently that GLBTI advocacy at the HRC has become as ubiquitous as advocacy for the rights of indigenous peoples[65] – courage indeed given the hostility that many HRC members continue to express. Supporting these developments, the Office of the High Commissioner for Human Rights released a report in 2012 that sets out the core obligations that states have towards LGBT people[66] and launched a global campaign in 2013 to promote awareness of discrimination based on sexual orientation and gender identity.[67] Even the World Bank has extended its social inclusion agenda to address exclusion based on sexual orientation and gender identity.[68] But we have yet to see a Special Procedures report devoted specifically to human rights violations that are associated with gender identity, which would provide the opportunity to acknowledge and draw links between the experiences, not only of transgendered people around the world, but also those many others who suffer violence and discrimination because of their gender performativity, including

---

[60]'Report of the Special Rapporteur on the question of torture and other cruel, inhuman or degrading treatment or punish ment, UN General Assembly' (3 July 2001) UN Doc A/56/156[17], concerned that transgendered people are 'often sub jected to violence . . . in order to "punish" them for transgressing gender barriers or for challenging predominant conceptions of gender roles'.

[61]'Report of the Special Rapporteur on extrajudicial, arbitrary and summary executions' (2001) UN Doc E/CN.4/2001/9 [50], condemning threats against LGBT defenders.

[62]See 'Report of the Special Representative of the Secretary General on the situation of human rights defenders' (22 March 2006) UN Doc E/CN.4/2006/95/Add.1 [290], highlighting particular dangers faced by human rights defenders 'associated with lesbian, gay, transgendered, bisexual and HIV Aids issues in Jamaica'; 'Report of the Special Rapporteur on the right of everyone to the highest attainable standard of physical and mental health' (16 February 2004) UN Doc E/CN.4/2004/49 [33], [38], [39], expressing concern about violence, discrimination and stigma that threatens the sexual and reproductive health of sexual minorities, making specific reference to 'men who have sex with men, lesbians, and transgendered and bisexual people'; 'Report of the Independent Expert on minority issues' (6 January 2004) UN Doc E/CN.4/2006/74 [28], [42], drawing attention to 'multiple forms of exclusion' of members of minority communities, including on the basis of 'sexual orientation or gender expression that challenges social or cultural norms'.

[63]Amnesty International, 'Crimes of Hate, Conspiracy of Silence. Torture and Ill treatment Based on Sexual Identity' (AI Index ACT 40/016/2001, Amnesty International 2001); Human Rights Watch (HRW), 'In A Time of Torture: The Assault on Justice in Egypt's Crack down on Homosexual Conduct' (HRW 2004); Human Rights Watch, 'Hated to Death: Homophobia, Vio lence and Jamaica's HIV/AIDS Epidemic' (HRW 2004); Human Rights Watch, 'More than a Name: State Sponsored Homo phobia and its Consequences in South Africa' (HRW 2003).

[64]'Report of the Special Rapporteur on the situation of human rights defenders' UN Doc A/HRC/13/22 (30 December 2009) [49].

[65]Conversation with Cynthia Rothschild, New York, 24 October 2014 (notes on file with author). See further, Dodo Karsay 'How far has SIGII advocacy come at the UN and where is it heading? Assessing sexual orientation, gender identity, and intersex activism and key developments at the UN 2003 2014' (ARC International 2014) http://arc international.net/wp content/uploads/2013/09/How far has SOGII for web.pdf.

[66]Office of the High Commissioner for Human Rights, Born Free and Equal: Sexual Orientation and Gender Identity in Inter national Human Rights Law HR/PUB/12/06 (UN, New York and Geneva 2012) http://www.ohchr.org/documents/publications/bornfreeandequallowres.pdf.

[67]Free and Equal, Press Release, 'UN Human Rights Office Launches Unprecedented Global Campaign for Lesbian, Gay, Bisexual and Transgender Equality' (Cape Town, 26 July 2013) http://www.ohchr.org/EN/NewsEvents/Pages/DisplayNews.aspx?NewsID=13583.

[68]World Bank Panel, 'Addressing Exclusion Based on Sexual Orientation and Gender Identity', 20 May 2015, http://www.worldbank.org/en/events/2015/05/18/addressing exclusion based on sexual orientation and gender identity.

cismen and ciswomen. Such a report would provide an important opportunity to confront the (un)realities of (bio)logic in international law.

Even so, controversy has plagued these developments, which quickly came to symbolise a geo-political divide between the purported liberality of the west and illiberalism of the (Muslim) non-west.[69] (It is worth noting here that all three instances of the CEDAW Committee raising concern about transgender issues in Concluding Observations, mentioned earlier, involved western European states). The first official use of the term 'gender identity' by a collectivity of states (rather than human rights experts) in a UN document was in 2006, in a Joint Statement to the HRC, made on behalf of 54 states (18 were HRC members).[70] In 2008, a group of 66 states made another Statement on 'Human rights, sexual orientation and gender identity' to the General Assembly calling for decriminalisation and protection from discrimination and violence',[71] which prompted an opposing Statement read by Syria, on behalf of 57 states, completely rejecting the 'so-called notions' of sexual orientation and gender identity which 'have no legal foundations in any international human rights instruments'.[72]

It was not until 2011 that the HRC managed to adopt its first resolution (by a narrow margin) which expressed 'grave concern' about violence and discrimination directed at individuals based on their sexual orientation or gender identity and called for a global study of such discriminatory laws and practices,[73] which was completed later that year.[74] In 2014, the still deeply divided HRC adopted a follow-up resolution calling for an update of its 2011 report,[75] although the group of states opposing its adoption tried, through a series of proposed amendments, to remove all references to 'sexual orientation' and 'gender identity', continuing to argue that they were notions not known to international law.[76] The updated report found that, since the previous report, 'hundreds of people have been killed and thousands more injured in brutal, violent attacks' and documented many other violations 'including torture, arbitrary detention, denial of rights to assembly and expression, discrimination in health care, education, employment and housing'.[77]

---

[69]Dianne Otto, 'Transnational Homo Assemblages: Reading "Gender" in Counter terrorism Discourses' (2013) 4(2) *Jindal Global Law Review, Special Double Issue   Part II: Law, Culture and Queer Politics in Neoliberal Times* 79.

[70]Human Rights Council, 'Joint Statement on Human Rights Violations based on Sexual Orientation and Gender Identity', delivered by H E Wegger Chr Strommen (Norway), (3rd Session, 1 December 2006).

[71]Joint Statement read by Argentina in the General Assembly on behalf of 66 states, 'Human rights, sexual orientation and gender identity', 18 December 2008, http://arc international.net/global advocacy/sogi statements/2008 joint statement/.

[72]Statement read by Syria in the General Assembly on behalf of 57 states, predominantly Organization of Islamic Confer ence members, 'Human rights and the so called notions of "sexual orientation" and "gender identity"', 18 December 2008, http://iglhrc.org/content/united nations general assembly statement affirming human rights protections include sexual. The Statement argues there is 'no legal foundation' for the notions of 'sexual orientation' and 'gender identity' and asserts the right of states to enact laws that meet 'just requirements of morality, public order, and the general welfare in a democratic society'

[73]Human Rights Council, 'Human rights, sexual orientation and gender identity', UN Doc A/HRC/RES/17/19 (15 June 2011), adopted 23/19 with 3 abstentions.

[74]'Discriminatory laws and practices and acts of violence against individuals based on their sexual orientation and gender identity', UN Doc A/HRC/19/41 (17 November 2011).

[75]Human Rights Council, 'Human rights, sexual orientation and gender identity', UN Doc A/HRC/27/32 (26 September 2014).

[76]Proposed amendments to draft resolution UN Doc A/HRC/27/L.27/Rev.1: UN Doc A/HRC/27/L.45 (25 September 2014), UN Doc A/HRC/27/L.46 (25 September 2014), UN Doc A/HRC/27/L.47 (25 September 2014), UN Doc A/HRC/27/L.48 (25 Sep tember 2014), UN Doc A/HRC/27/L.49 (25 September 2014), UN Doc A/HRC/27/L.50 (25 September 2014), UN Doc A/HRC/27/L.51 (25 September 2014).

[77]Report of the Office of the United Nations High Commissioner for Human Rights, 'Discrimination and violence against individuals based on their sexual orientation and gender identity', UN Doc A/HRC/29/23, para 6 (4 May 2015).

In the midst of these developments, seeking to consolidate the work of the various human rights procedures and NGOs in the face of hostility, the Yogyakarta Principles were launched in 2007.[78] Supported by the International Commission of Jurists and the International Service for Human Rights, [79] the human rights advocates who drafted them set out to 'collate and clarify State obligations under existing international human rights law' in its application to issues of 'sexual orientation' and 'gender identity'. [80] The aim of the exercise was deliberately conservative in seeking to articulate the 'current state' of international human rights law, while acknowledging that the law continues to develop and therefore that 'revision' will be required 'on a regular basis'.[81] Given the organised opposition, the tactic of fostering inclusion by progressive interpretation of existing human rights was strategic. It mirrors the feminist strategy of gender mainstreaming by promoting more inclusive interpretations of mainstream human rights, rather than relying too heavily on anti-discrimination protections or hoping for the recognition of new human rights.

The Yogyakarta Principles offer the following definition of gender identity:

> Gender identity is understood to refer to each person's deeply felt internal and individual experience of gender, which may or may not correspond with the sex assigned at birth, including the personal sense of the body (which may involve, if freely chosen, modification of bodily appearance or function by medical, surgical or other means) and other expressions of gender, including dress, speech and mannerisms.[82]

Importantly, the definition sets out to be inclusive by acknowledging that *everyone* has a gender identity, although those who do not experience gender as an 'identity', or feel they have no gender or are 'gender neutral,' are excluded.[83] Perhaps use of the more open term 'gender expression', preferred by some of the drafters,[84] would have helped to alleviate this problem. The other aspect of the definition that I welcome is its insistence that any bodily modifications, by way of surgeries and other medical interventions, must be 'freely chosen'. In other words, there is no necessary correspondence between 'bodily appearance or function' and a person's gender identity. These two elements of the definition contribute to a transformative understanding of gender [identity] in two ways. First, gender identity is not treated as something unique to transgendered people but as a universal characteristic and, second, gender identity is not defined by – or even reliant upon – any particular (bio)logic configuration of bodily/physiological features. It follows that 'women' and 'men' are but two of the gender identities possible in a world of gender diversity, although it would have been helpful if the drafters had made this point explicitly.

Yet other aspects of the definition still hold onto the idea of a physiological base. The description of gender identity as a 'deeply felt internal . . . experience', suggests it is an

---

[78]'Yogyakarta Principles (n 10).
[79]Michael O'Flaherty and John Fisher, 'Sexual Orientation, Gender Identity and International Human Rights Law: Contextualising the Yogyakarta Principles' (2008) 8(2) *Human Rights Law Review* 207.
[80]Yogyakarta Principles (n 10), introduction [7].
[81]Ibid, preamble [9].
[82]Ibid, preamble [5].
[83]Aeyal Gross raises similar concerns about the notion of 'sexual orientation'. See Aeyal Gross, 'Queer Theory and International Human Rights Law: Does Each Person have a Sexual Orientation?' [2007] *Proceedings of the American Society of International Law* 129.
[84]Matthew Waites, 'Critique of "sexual orientation" and "gender identity" in human rights discourse: global queer politics beyond the Yogyakarta Principles' (2009) 15/1 *Contemporary Politics* 137, 147.

inherent characteristic – both innate and unitary. This approach excludes those who experience their gender as shifting or multiple, as well as those who identify as some combination or blurring of male and female, for example, gender transients, multi-gendered, gender 'in-between' or 'non-specific', and many others. It is telling that all the excluded gender subjectivities challenge the stability of the m/f binary. This indicates that the definition's understanding of gender as a 'deeply felt, internal and individual experience' serves to reinstate (bio)logic which, in turn, re-naturalises the gender binary. To the extent that the definition recognises that gender has expressive dimensions, by way of 'dress, speech and mannerisms', it is assumed that such expressions are freely chosen and that they arise from and are consistent with the 'deeply felt' foundation of gender [identity].

Equally alarming, the definition in the Yogyakarta Principles completely fails to acknowledge the influence of social context on the way that gender is understood and expressed, including on the way individuals understand and articulate what is experienced as 'deeply felt'. The representation of gender identity as an individual's (deeply felt) destiny, without reference to the way that social context continuously de-limits the choices available to every individual, stands in stark contrast to the standard 'feminist' UN definition of gender as a social category:

> The term 'gender' refers to the ways in which roles, attitudes, values and relationships regard ing women and men are constructed by all societies all over the world . . . while the sex of a person is determined by nature, the gender of that person is socially constructed.[85]

Both definitions anchor gender in a dualistic biological (deeply felt) base, but they diverge on the question as to whether gender is also a social category. The hard-won feminist understanding of gender [identity] as, in large part if not totally, socially constituted has disappeared in the context of promoting the rights of transgendered people.

Yogyakarta Principles approach to sex/gender [identity]: *reinstatement of (bio)logic*
m/f dualistic gender [identity]　nature
trans 'deeply felt' m/f gender identity　nature

The most important advance made by the definition of gender identity in the Yogyakarta Principles is that we all have a gender identity. This creates a foothold for more complex and dynamic understandings of gender as a performative construct that affects everyone. Yet, the treatment of gender identity in the body of the Yogyakarta Principles immediately forecloses this promised inclusivity and its transformative potential. Like the CEDAW Committee, they treat 'gender' as if it has a meaning distinct from gender identity by referring to it as an aspect of intersectional discrimination, as a characteristic like 'race, age, religion, disability, health and economic status' that that may compound discrimination on the basis of gender identity.[86] I struggle to imagine how this distinction would work in practice, even in the case of someone who identifies as transgendered. Consider, for example, discrimination experienced by a trans (m-f) woman because she is not allowed to use the female bathroom at work. Compare this to a ciswoman who is not allowed to use the male bathroom at work, which is much closer to her workstation than the female bathroom. Both cases could be defended on some combination of

---

[85]Commission on Human Rights (n 6).
[86]Yogyakarta Principles (n 10), P 2.

biological and social grounds and, while there may be some differences in the rationale for different treatment, the grounds of the discrimination complained of are the same. Each complainant is basing their claim on sex/gender. The notion of gender identity adds nothing more. It makes no difference whether their claim is assessed by reference to their membership of a sub-group of 'women' or as a member of the transgendered group whose gender identity is that of 'women'. Further, the example illustrates that drawing a distinction between sex (biology) and gender (culture) serves no useful purpose, as the discrimination complained of is based on social understandings and perceptions of biology intertwined with expression. As the Canadian judge in the *Sheridan* case,[87] which considered the question of access of a trans woman to women's bathrooms in public places, said:

> I am satisfied that discrimination against a transsexual constitutes discrimination on the basis of sex. Whether the discrimination is regarded as differential treatment because the transsex ual falls outside the traditional man/women dichotomy . . . or because male to female trans sexuals are regarded as a subgroup of females (and vice versa) . . . the result is the same . . .[88]

The promised universality of the definition of gender identity in the Yogyakarta Principles is completely undercut as they go on to elaborate states' obligations under existing human rights law. The only specific human rights issues associated with gender identity that are drawn attention to are those that apply solely to transgendered people – without even the self-consciousness of providing an explanation for failing to include cisgender and other gender identities. For example, the elucidation of the right to recognition before the law (Principle 3) asserts that everyone's 'self-defined . . . gender identity . . . is one of the most basic aspects of self-determination' and maintains that legal recognition must never be predicated on medical interventions, marital, or parenthood status. There is no doubt that this is an important interpretation of the right, but its coverage is limited to transgendered people, ignoring completely, for example, the still widespread practice of denying full legal personality to those whose gender identity is that of a 'woman'. This, I fear, confines the category of gender identity to trans people, closing down its transformative possibilities for everyone. This fear is compounded by the CEDAW Committee's failure to engage with the new terminology of 'gender identity' in its work on challenging women's inequality and harmful gender stereotypes.

While mainstreaming can have powerfully inclusionary effects, the attempt to 'fit' diverse sexual and gender practices into existing dualistic and heteronormative sexual and gender categories in human rights law requires embracing those categories rather than challenging them.[89] The failure of the Yogyakarta Principles to challenge the tradition of m/f dualism and its biological base can be explained in this way. More evidence of the limiting effect of the strategy can be seen in the treatment of the family. The Yogyakarta Principles recognise that everyone has the right to found a family, 'regardless of sexual orientation or gender identity' and that families 'exist in diverse forms'.[90] However, the list of states obligations identified as necessary to implement the right,

---

[87] *Sheridan v Sanctuary Investments Ltd (No 3) (1999)* 33 CHRR D/467.
[88] Ibid [93]. quoted in Sharon Cowan, "'Gender is no Substitute for Sex": A Comparative Human Rights Analysis of the Legal Regulation of Sexual Identity' (2005) 13 *Feminist Legal Studies* 67, 82 83.
[89] Wayne Morgan, 'Queering International Human Rights Law' in Carl Stychin and Didi Herman (eds), *Sexuality in the Legal Arena* (Athlone Press, 2000) 208.
[90] Yogyakarta Principles (n 10), P 24.

merely reconfigure, rather than contest the heteronormative family model. They assume, for example, that the primary purpose of the family is to procreate, that the foundational family relationship is a monogamous couple and that the interests of children will be a primary concern.[91] This reinstates what Butler has called the 'heterosexual matrix' which she describes as

> a hegemonic discursive/epistemic model of gender intelligibility that assumes . . . there must be a stable sex expressed through a stable [dualistic] gender that is oppositionally and hier archically defined through the compulsory practice of heterosexuality.[92]

Feminist concerns about the abuses of power in this kind of family arrangement are nowhere apparent, which would warrant, at the very least, the affirmation of the equal rights and responsibilities of family members in intimate relationships. There is also no reference to sexual rights and freedoms (in a pleasurable sense) in the context of the family or anywhere else in the document. This is surely a significant watering down, if not betrayal, of the radical sexual politics of queer and sex positive feminist theory and activism.

Simply trying to press diverse gender (and sexuality) subjectivities into the dominant grid of binary gender and heterosexual normativity as reflected in mainstream international law, merely installs the heterosexual matrix in a particular new form.[93] It is what Tom Dreyfus has described as the 'half-invention' of gender identity, whereby people to whom the new category applies must find a way to fit themselves into the definition now found in law.[94] The result is to re-normalise heterosexuality and re-biologise everyone's gender identity. In this process, the Yogyakarta Principles establish a new asymmetry whereby the gender disadvantage of gender [identity] minorities is measured against the heteronormative standard of dualistic gender, which serves to reinforce the normative power of the m/f status quo, rather than challenge it.

III. The Need for Queer and Feminist Coalitional Work

Feminist and queer human rights advocates need to work in coalition if they are ever to challenge fundamentally the discursively produced m/f dualism along with its claimed biological foundations, and dislodge the heterosexual family as the universal model for normative sexuality, household and caring arrangements. This means giving up the 'gender territorialisation' that has characterised advocacy of women's and GLBTI rights in recent years, resulting in competing conceptions of gender and disconnected advocacy channels.[95] This does not have to mean forsaking feminism's long-standing commitments to exposing the gendered violence of the heteronormative family and improving the status of women, and nor does it necessarily mean diluting the radical sexual history of queer politics. In fact, it is my view that bringing these two bodies of activism and critique together will help to resist some of the

---

[91]Ibid, A G.
[92]Butler (n 12), 5.
[93]Waites (n 84), 139.
[94]Tom Dreyfus, 'The "Half Invention" of Gender Identity in International Human Rights Law: From CEDAW to the Yogyakarta Principles' (2012) 37 *Australian Feminist L J* 33, 48.
[95]Roseman and Miller (n 49), 362.

depoliticising and domesticating effects of engaging with mainstream institutions of law and politics.

The 2009 gender mainstreaming report of the Special Rapporteur on the protection of human rights while countering terrorism, Martin Scheinin, provides a positive example of such a coalitional effort.[96] Drawing on a number of human rights documents to support his approach, including CEDAW General Recommendations and the Yogyakarta Principles, [97] Scheinin explains three times in his report that:

> Gender is not synonymous with women but rather encompasses the social constructions that underlie how women's and men's roles, functions and responsibilities, including in relation to sexual orientation and gender identity, are defined and understood.[98]

Unlike the CEDAW Committee and the Yogyakarta Principles, the Special Rapporteur does not confine his understanding of gender identity to transgendered people, but acknowledges that 'gender' refers to the social expectations of women and men, including their gender identity. He goes on to say that, as a consequence, 'gender is not static; it is changeable over time and across contexts'.[99]

Despite still holding onto gender dualism, this approach enables the Special Rapporteur to discuss a broad range of ignored and under-reported human rights violations that result from measures aimed at countering terrorism by highlighting, in turn, the negative effects that counter-terrorism measures are having on women's rights,[100] on the rights of sexual and gender minorities[101] and on men's rights, particularly the rights of male terrorist suspects.[102] Importantly, this broad coverage enables him to highlight a number of inter-relationships and convergences between rights violations experienced by women and sexual and gender minorities, such as the 'bartering' of their rights in efforts to appease terrorist or extremist groups as in Pakistan and Egypt,[103] the impact of restrictive immigration controls on women and transgendered people,[104] and the criminalisation and stigmatisation of women's and GLBTI human rights defenders as 'terrorists'.[105] The report shows how identifying patterns of gender-based discrimination by tracing their effects

---

[96]'Report of the Special Rapporteur on the promotion and protection of human rights and fundamental freedoms while countering terrorism', UN Doc A/64/211, sect III (3 August 2009).

[97]Ibid [21]. In addition to the Yogyakarta Principles, the Special Rapporteur cites the UNHCR 'Guidelines on International Protection No 1: Gender Related Persecution Within the Context of Article 1A(2) of the 1951 Convention and/or its 1967 Protocol relating to the Status of Refugees' (7 May 2002) UN Doc HCR/GIP/02/01; Committee on the Elimination of Discrimination Against Women 'General Recommendation No 25' (2004) UN Doc A/59/38 (Supp.) annex 1; UN Committee on Economic, Social and Cultural Rights, 'General Comment No 20: Non discrimination in economic, social and cultural rights' (2009) UN Doc E/C.12/GC/20 [32].

[98]Ibid [20]. See further summary and [52] (conclusions).

[99]Ibid [20].

[100]Ibid, for example, checkpoint delays which have increased the risks associated with childbirth for Palestinian women and the impact of counter terrorism measures on the economic, social and cultural rights of Chechnyan women: Report of the Special Rapporteur 2009 [18]; the targeting of women for attack and repression by many groups involved in conflict as in Iraq [23]; the risks to the security and liberty of women related to male terrorism suspects as in Uganda [31]; and the penalisation of women who wear particular forms of religious clothing as in the Maldives and parts of Europe [38].

[101]Ibid, for example, he condemns vague definitions of 'terrorism' that have justified measures that target those individuals who do not conform to traditional gender roles, such as attacks on meti (effeminate males or transgendered people) in Nepal, ibid [23]; and the arrests and persecution of 'suspected homosexuals' in Egypt [27].

[102]Ibid, for example, the use of gender stereotypes in profiling male terrorist suspects, ibid [37]; and the use of gender specific interrogation techniques which exploit perceptions of Muslim men's homophobia and seek to induce feelings of emasculation [44].

[103]Ibid [36].

[104]Ibid [48].

[105]Ibid [27].

on a diversity of gender groups, can deepen our understanding of the technologies of gendered power and enable more informed, coalitional and, hopefully, more effective responses to be crafted. Importantly, the Special Rapporteur's application of a socially based and fluid conception of gender does not result in the marginalization of women's human rights. Instead, it provides a consistently rights-based analysis that avoids sliding into protectionism when it refers to women. The report also promotes increased gender and sexual freedom by seeking to enhance freedom of movement and freedom of expression for all gender identities, in keeping with the sexual and gender radicalism of queer politics. The Special Rapporteur carries a brief for everyone whose human rights are violated because of their gender identity, which would also be possible for the CEDAW Committee and a revised version of the Yogyakarta Principles to do. The Special Rapporteur's approach looks to the specifics of the situation in order to identify the nature of the gender disadvantage and its victims and crafts remedies accordingly, rather than relying on the automatic assumptions of gender duality and asymmetry. It gives me hope that it may yet be possible to defeat the tenacity of biological determinism and its attendant protective representations of women and dehumanising insistence on gender duality; to move the law from (bio)logic to performative understandings of gender.

However, this move will require the complete rejection of the idea that there is an immutable, natural biological foundation for the social experiences of gender. As Simone de Beauvoir observed in her pioneering work, one is not born a woman [or any other gender] but rather becomes one.[106] In her development of this idea, Butler argues that sex, like gender, is a performative category; that the 'naturalness' of sex is produced culturally and discursively.[107] While these are not new insights, they remain deeply unacceptable to some feminist and GLBTI rights advocates, as well as to social and religious conservatives. (Although the refusal of the Organization of Islamic Conference to use the language of 'sexual orientation' and 'gender identity' in their efforts to deny human rights obligations owed to those who might fall into these categories seems to rely on precisely the insight that there is no prediscursive natural human subject.)[108] Those feminists who remain committed to biology as the anchor for women's solidarity in the struggle for women's equality and rights need to understand that this not only impedes the struggle, but continually gives sustenance to conservatives who argue that women's inequality is the natural order. They also need to recognise that gender is a technology of power that privileges only elite masculine interests and that there are others, besides women, who experience gendered injuries. At the same time, queer activists must learn from the long feminist struggle with issues of gender, resist the respectability that claiming a biological (deeply felt) base for transgendered identities promises, and broaden their own gaze to be inclusive of the diverse ways in which gender operates to enforce gendered hierarchies and heteronormativity in everyone's lives.

This movement to completely jettison (bio)logic, and instead treat gender as a wholly performative category, relies on feminist and GLBTI human rights advocates finding ways to draw productively on the synergies of their intersecting gender concerns. They/we need to stand together in solidarity in the face of taunts of perversion and promiscuity, rather

---

[106]Simone de Beauvoir, *The Second Sex* (H M Parshley ed and tr, Vintage Books 1974) 295.
[107]Butler (n 12), 140 141.
[108]See further, Otto, n 69.

than surrender the radical aspirations of our grass roots communities and founding movements. They/we need to draw on our coalitional strength to challenge the (bio)logic that continues to underpin international human rights law, unshaken by the arrival of the new category of gender identity. They/we need each other to resist inclusion by way of being fitted into the *status quo* of gender duality and heteronormative marriage, which merely shifts the boundaries of acceptable gender identities, rather than erasing them. The solution is to foster coalitional strategies, linking feminist and queer ways of thinking,[109] in order to resist assimilation and present a united challenge to dualistic gender (and sexuality) hierarchies that, supported by international law, help to normalise and maintain an international order that is deeply unjust.

Conclusions

I have opened the question of what work we want the term 'gender identity' to do through its codification as a prohibited ground of discrimination in international law. I have argued that we need to promote its use it in such a way that its liberatory potential is maximised. Just as conflating 'gender' with 'women' limits our ability to make visible all forms of gendered harm, so the conflation of 'gender identity' with 'transgendered people' limits our ability to treat gender as a fully social and performative category that plays a key role in shaping everyone's access to resources and opportunities in life. If international (human rights) law is ever to realise the potential it has to operate as an inclusive language of emancipation and justice, feminist and queer human rights advocates must find ways to work together in the project of queering gender [identity] in international law. Understanding sex/gender/gender identity as performative brings the coalitional project into focus, as a struggle against the same restrictions on the performance of gender, within a hegemonic heterosexual matrix, that requires stable, dualistic and disciplined sexed bodies. One pressing coalitional task is to revise the Yogyakarta Principles so that they are inclusive of all gender identities and informed by feminist perspectives. Another is to encourage the CEDAW Committee to overcome its resistance to embracing sex/gender/gender identity as a fully social category in its work. The shift to a performative understanding in international law, of how bodies come to be sexed and thus are made vulnerable to gendered human rights abuses, has barely begun.

---

[109]Dianne Otto, 'Sexualities and Solidarities: Some Thoughts on Coalitional Strategies in the Context of International Law' (1999) 8 *Australasian Gay and Lesbian L J* 27.

Enhancing LGBTI Rights by Changing the Interpretation of the Convention on the Elimination of All Forms of Discrimination Against Women?

Rikki Holtmaat[a] and Paul Post[b]

[a]Professor in International Non-Discrimination Law at Leiden University, The Netherlands; [b]Student at University College London, UK, and Student Assistant at the Department of European Law of Leiden University, The Netherlands

ABSTRACT

At first sight, it seems clear that the Convention on the Elimination of All Forms of Discrimination against Women (CEDAW) aims to eliminate discrimination against (only) *women*. However, a legal analysis of the object and purpose of the Convention reveals that CEDAW, in particular article 5a (which requires modification of 'cultural patterns of conduct'), could be instrumental in addressing at least some aspects of LGBTI rights. Nevertheless, an analysis of Concluding Observations adopted by the Committee since 2010 reveals that the Committee, the body entrusted both with monitoring the implementation of the Convention and acting as its principal interpreter, does not yet use the possibility offered under article 5a to interpret the Convention in such a way. This article argues that the most realistic (albeit slow) way to enhance LGBTI rights within the framework of the CEDAW Convention seems to be to encourage state parties and non-governmental organisations to include discussions of discrimination against LGBTI persons in their Country Reports and Shadow Reports to the Committee, thereby inviting the Committee to reflect on LGBTI discrimination.

I. Introduction

In contrast to other non-discrimination grounds like sex, race/ethnicity, and disability, there is no one particular international legal instrument that expressly and explicitly obliges state parties to respect the human rights of lesbian, gay, bisexual, transgender, and intersex (LGBTI) persons and prohibits all forms of discrimination against these persons.[1] How then can the enhancement of the human rights of LGBTI persons be

---

We thank members of the Dutch Feminist Legal Theory Reading Group and the anonymous reviewers of this paper for their constructive comments. All websites were last accessed 15 September.

[1]A recent overview of existing legal and non legal instruments that do address the human rights of LGBTI persons can be found in M O'Flaherty's contribution in this special issue. See also Gemma MacArthur, 'Securing Sexual Orientation and Gender Identity Rights within the United Nations Framework and System: Past, Present and Future' (2015) 15 *Equal Rights Rev* 25 54; available at: http://www.equalrightstrust.org/ertdocumentbank/Securing%20Sexual%20Orientation%20and %20Gender%20Identity%20Rights%20within%20the%20United%20Nations%20Framework%20and%20System%20Past %2C%20Present%20and%20Future.pdf.

advanced, and, in particular, their rights to sexual freedom and gender identity? This question was at the heart of the discussions at the conference held in Oslo in December 2014.[2] The right to sexual freedom and gender identity are of crucial importance for each and every human being, regardless of his or her sexual orientation or gender identity, but are most fiercely contested when it concerns LGBTI persons.[3] *Sexual freedom* refers to the freedom of people to choose with which other person(s) they want to establish relationships of a sexual nature and whether or not they can or should formalise these relations in any legal construction provided for by the state.[4] *Gender identity*, on the other hand, refers to the freedom of people to express the way they experience a particular gendered identity.[5] Gendered, in this context, means that the sense of self (identity) is co-determined (among many other factors) by the biological or genetic 'sex' features that persons have, in interaction with the socially and culturally constructed meanings and normative regulations of sex and sexuality that are attached to this 'sex'. Sex, sexuality, and gender, therefore, come together in the notion of gender identity. The question we address in our contribution to this special issue is whether the UN Convention on the Elimination of All Forms of Discrimination against Women (CEDAW) can in some way be instrumental to the goal of enhancing the rights to sexual freedom and gender identity of LGBTI persons. We shall approach this question primarily from a positivist legal perspective. Section II contains a legal analysis of the object and purpose of the Convention in so far as it relates to the issue of LGBTI rights. Wr argue that, in particular, article 5a, which requires modification of 'cultural patterns of conduct', could in theory be instrumental in addressing at least some aspects of LGBTI rights.[6] But, as will be shown in section III on the basis of a systematic analysis of Concluding Observations communicated since 2010, while the CEDAW Committee gives considerable attention to LGBTI issues, article 5a has thus far not been the road taken by the Committee in its authoritative interpretations of the Convention to expand the interpretation therein. Although some people have set high hopes on the CEDAW as a possible way of enhancing the human rights of LGBTI people, we are therefore not particularly optimistic about the Convention's actual contribution in this respect.

---

[2] University of Oslo, 'Sexual Freedom and the Right to Gender Identity as a Site of Legal and Political Struggle', Oslo, House of Literature, 11 12 December 2014.

[3] Sexual freedom and gender identity are not catalogued in any of the existing international human rights treaties and therefore formally do not exist as explicitly guaranteed and established human rights. Rather, as the title of the Oslo Conference indicates, these (normative) concepts are sites of legal and political debate, over their very existence as rights, over their meaning, as well as over their consequences.

[4] In so far as this freedom is recognised as a right, it is immediately restricted to being only applicable to adult human beings who (can) give their free and conscious consent to having particular sexual relationships. Pedophilia, bestiality, sexual assault, and rape are not deemed to be protected by this (presumed) freedom to have sexual relationships of one's own choice. It is also contested whether persons have the freedom to choose to engage in sexual relationships of a purely commercial or economic nature, either as a provider, as a customer, or both.

[5] The right to gender identity, therefore, is not only about something that people experience 'internally', but in fact is most contested when people express their gender identity, in particular, when this identity deviates from what are perceived as 'normal' expressions along the bipolar axes of the 'male' and 'female' sexes and of heterosexuality.

[6] In this article, we have chosen to focus on the potential of article 5a CEDAW. Other substantive articles in this Convention could (and should) also be investigated as regards their potential to contribute to the enhancement of the human rights of LGBTI persons. The same applies for the potential of other international and regional human rights instruments, eg the UN ICCPR and the European Convention on Human Rights, which include substantive rights, like the right to marriage and the right to private life that have great relevance for LGTI persons. However, time and space are too limited to include all such possibilities for progressive interpretation and implementation of these instruments in this article.

The question raised at the Conference in Oslo also calls for a theoretical and strategic analysis of the pros and cons, or the opportunities and obstacles, of using this Convention to enhance LGBTI (human) rights.[7] In the concluding section IV, we briefly raise some of the most important concerns regarding these problems. We argue that the most realistic (albeit slow) way forward seems to be to urge state parties and NGOs to include discussions of discrimination against LGBTI persons in Country Reports and Shadow Reports to the Committee and thus invite the Committee to reflect on LGBTI discrimination.

II. The Object and Purpose of the CEDAW Convention: A Holistic Approach to Equality[8]

In order to answer the question of whether CEDAW can be instrumental in enhancing LGBTI rights, it is necessary to consider the object and purpose of the Convention. At first sight it seems clear that the Convention aims to eliminate discrimination against *women*, ie discrimination on the ground of the female sex (and not sexuality or gender identity). The object and purpose of the Convention are, however, less clear-cut and more contested than may be expected on the basis of its name. In this section, we shall consider whether there are any theoretical pegs on which to hang claims that move beyond that understanding of the Convention as exclusively aimed at women's equality. We first discuss the main object of the Convention, which is to provide international legal standards to combat all forms of discrimination against *women*. Subsequently, the Convention's definition of *discrimination* against women is considered. Thirdly, we shall analyse *the three main objectives of CEDAW* and assess whether there is – at least in theory – space for including LGBTI rights within the scope of this Convention.

II.i. *For women only? CEDAW's asymmetrical approach to equality*

The preamble of CEDAW expressly recognises that, despite the international obligations to put an end to discrimination between men and women that were laid down in the previously adopted human rights treaties,[9] extensive discrimination against women continues to exist. The drafters recognised that in reality it is predominantly women who suffer from sex discrimination and that therefore a Convention specifically aiming at the elimination of this discrimination was necessary.[10] In the view of some commentators, CEDAW's asymmetrical nature is seen as a great advantage over sex-equality laws that are symmetrical, ie those which protect both sexes equally from differential treatment.[11] In the words of Brown, referring to McKinnon: 'the more gender-neutral or gender-blind a particular

---

[7]These issues are also addressed in Dianne Otto's contribution to this issue.

[8]For a more detailed discussion see R Holtmaat, 'CEDAW: A Holistic Approach to Women's Equality and Freedom', in A Hellum and H Sinding Aasen (eds), *Women's Human Rights: CEDAW in International, Regional and National Law* (Cambridge University Press, 2013).

[9]Universal Declaration of Human Rights, articles 2 and 7; International Covenant on Civil and Political Rights, articles 2, 3 and 26; International Covenant on Economic, Social and Cultural Rights, article 3.

[10]See for a critical assessment D Otto, 'International Human Rights Law: Towards Rethinking Sex/Gender Dualism and Asymmetry', in M Davies and V Munro (eds), *A Research Companian to Feminist Legal Theory* (Ashgate, 2013), available as Melbourne Legal Studies Research Paper No 620, available at http://papers.ssrn.com/sol3/papers.cfm?abstract id=2178769http://papers.ssrn.com/sol3/papers.cfm?abstract id=2178769.

[11]This consequences of this difference are explained in more detail in R Holtmaat and C Tobler, 'CEDAW and the European Union's Policy in the Field of Combating Gender Discrimination' (2005) 12 *Maastricht J of Eur and Comparative L* 399.

right (or any law or public policy) is, the more likely it is to enhance the privilege of men and eclipse the needs of women as subordinates.'[12] This is also applicable to the right to equality: 'The person who has the power of definition, who succeeds at defining discrimination against women as sex discrimination, takes the sting out of the matter and at the same time does not have to fear much from it anymore.'[13] CEDAW's asymmetrical approach fits well with its substantive approach to equality:[14] it means that the ultimate aim of non-discrimination law is not only to put an end to unfair or unjustifiable classifications of individuals on the basis of a particular characteristic, but also to put an end to oppression and exclusion of groups that are subordinated in society.[15] Although the Convention in most of its substantive articles provides that women have rights of 'on a basis of equality between men and women', it clearly includes the obligation of state parties to enhance *de facto* equality of women by means of both special measures and eradicating the causes of women's oppression and violence against women.[16]

The women-only approach of the CEDAW Convention has also been fiercely criticised. First, it is argued that the Convention falls into the trap of essentialising 'women', thereby neglecting the fact that the unequal relations between the sexes are socially constructed. The Convention, in other words, (supposedly) fails to address or redress *gender* inequality. Secondly, it is argued that the effect of the asymmetrical approach is that women are further stigmatised as victims *per se* of discrimination and of (sexual) violence. Thirdly, the approach is said to disregard the possibility that men too may be victims of gender discrimination, such as gender stereotypes and fixed parental roles.[17] The solution to these problems would, at least in theory, be to expand the scope of the Convention to also cover men. While some arguments have been presented in favour of such an interpretation, it is still commonly understood that it is a 'women's only' Convention.[18]

The asymmetrical approach of CEDAW is also debated in relation to LGBTI rights. In 2011, Rosenblum proposed that the Convention should be 'unisexed', ie that it would be

---

[12]W Brown, 'Suffering Rights as Paradoxes' (2000) 7 *Constellations* 230, 231.

[13]H van Maarseveen, 'Internationaal vrouwenrecht. Een afzonderlijk rechtsgebied?', in H. van Maarseveen et al (eds), *Inter nationaal recht en vrouwen* (Tjeenk Willink, 1987) at 74 75 (translation RH). See also C Smart, *Feminism and the Power of Law* (Routledge, 1989) at 2.

[14]In other words, that the general abstract equality of all human beings is not the starting point for the construction of legal norms, but the fact that, in reality of social life, large differences in power and differences in the actual situation and capacities of human beings exist. The goal of realising more *de facto* equality is therefore the core of the substantive approach to legal equality.

[15]This refers to the difference between non discrimination as an anti classification or as an anti subordination principle. See J Balkin and R Siegel, 'The American Civil Rights Tradition: Anticlassification or Antisubordination?' (2003) 58 *U of Miami L Rev* 9; A McColgan, *Discrimination, Equality and the Law* (Hart Publishers, 2014).

[16]This is evidently from the way the Convention conceives of temporary special measures and the way the Committee in General Recommendation 19 has elaborated on women's right to be free from violence. See I Boerefijn et al (eds), *Temporary Special Measures. Accelerating De Facto Equality of Women Under Article 4(1) UN Convention on the Elimination of All Forms of Discrimination Against Women* (Intersentia, 2003); F Raday, 'Article 4' and C Chinkin, 'Violence Against Women', both in M. Freeman et al (eds), *The Convention on the Elimination of All Forms of Discrimination Against Women: A Commentary* (Oxford University Press, 2012).

[17]See eg D Otto, 'Lost in Translation: Re sexing the Sexed Subjects of International Human Rights Law', in A Orford (ed), *International Law and its Others* (Cambridge University Press, 2006), and D Otto (n 10).

[18]The Convention's focus on women (instead of the neutral category 'sex') is expressed in its title and in the definition of discrimination in article 1. See A Byrnes, 'Article 1', in M Freeman et al (eds) (n 16). For an argument in favour of expand ing the Convention's scope to include men, also see T Loenen, 'Het discriminatiebegrip', in A. Heringa et al (eds), *Het Vrouwenverdrag. Een beeld van een verdrag* (Maklu 1994) 3. 'Nothing seems to stand in the way of men invoking CEDAW, *provided that* they are equally disadvantaged by something that qualifies as discrimination against women' (translation RH). Loenen gives the example of granting pensions only to widows, which prevents a change of roles between men and women and as such is also detrimental for women (ie discriminatory for women).

better to prohibit all discrimination on the ground of sex and/or gender, instead of discrimination against women.[19] Rosenblum presents an important argument in favour of such an amendment of the Convention: the word 'sex' might be understood to include not only the male and female sex but all kinds of sexes, including transgender, intersex and other differently-sexed and gendered people.[20] We shall return to this discussion in section IV, where we briefly address some strategic aspects of whether or not to explicitly include LGBTI people's rights under the scope of CEDAW.

II.ii. *Defining discrimination under the Convention*

Article 1 of the Convention defines discrimination against women as:

> Any distinction, exclusion or restriction made on the basis of sex which has the effect or purpose of impairing or nullifying the recognition, enjoyment or exercise by women, irrespective of their marital status, on a basis of equality of men and women, of human rights and fundamental freedoms in the political, economic, social, cultural, and civil or any other field.

The Convention requires that *all forms* of discrimination against women that lead to an infringement of their human rights be eliminated. The words 'distinction, exclusion or restriction' are interpreted in an extensive way.[21] Such a broad interpretation of the non-discrimination principle moves beyond the mere formal equality principle,[22] indicating a human rights approach to combating discrimination.[23] In such an approach, discrimination against women is seen as an instance of their oppression.[24] The notion of oppression goes beyond mere *unequal* treatment, but also includes instances of marginalisation, powerlessness, cultural imperialism, and violence.[25] Byrnes, in this respect, notes that there is no reason why the Convention should not be applied to provide protection for women who are discriminated against because of their sexuality where this 'has been used to subordinate women and reinforce male superiority', for example, where 'a lesbian's right to life is violated when she is subjected to death threats for not conforming to dictated heterosexual norms'.[26] It could therefore be argued that the phrase 'all forms of discrimination against women' in the Convention's title also includes oppression that is related to women's sex, sexuality, gender roles, and/or gender identity.

II.iii. *The objectives of the Convention: space for the inclusion of LGBTI issues?*

The interpretation that the Convention also covers oppression that is related to women's sex, sexuality, gender roles, and gender identity can further be underscored when the overall objectives of the Convention are taken into account. It is now widely acknowledged

---

[19] D Rosenblum, 'Unisex CEDAW, or What's Wrong with Women's Rights' (2011) 20 *Columbia J of Gender and L* 98; B Hernández Truyol, 'Unsex CEDAW? No! Super sex it!' (2011) 20 *Columbia J of Gender and L* 195.

[20] Rosenblum, ibid, 125.

[21] See A Byrnes (n 18).

[22] For such an approach the definition of equal treatment, see Directive 2006/54/EC of the European Parliament and of the Council of 5 July 2006 on the implementation of the principle of equal opportunities and equal treatment of men and women in matters of employment and occupation (recast), *O.J. L* 204,23.

[23] M Winston, 'Human Rights as Moral Rebellion and Social Construction', (2007) 6 *J of Human Rights* 279.

[24] M Winston, ibid, argues that one should keep in mind that all human rights law is meant to put an end to the oppression of certain people or groups of people by their government or by other people.

[25] I Young, *Justice and the Politics of Difference* (Princeton University Press, 1990) from 40.

[26] A Byrnes (n 18) 64 (footnotes omitted).

that CEDAW has three main objectives, which are shortly indicated here as: (a) to realise full legal equality between men and women; (b) to enhance *de facto* equality of women; and (c) to take away the cultural and social roots of gender inequality.[27] The third objective, which is in particular expressed in articles 2(f) and 5a CEDAW, implies that state parties must address gender roles and gender stereotypes that lie at the basis of women's discrimination.[28] According to the CEDAW Committee, article 5a, in conjunction with article 2(f), means that the Convention acknowledges that gender stereotypes and fixed parental gender roles 'affect women not only through individual acts by individuals but also in law, and legal and societal structures and institutions'.[29] Therefore, the Convention not only addresses personal convictions, cultural practices, and traditional values, but also addresses systemic and structural discrimination against women,[30] and – in order to overcome the structural discrimination that results from that inequality – calls for transformative equality or 'equality as transformation'.[31]

The CEDAW Committee has made it clear that a correct implementation of the Convention requires 'the recognition that women can have various roles in society, not only the important role of mother and wife, exclusively responsible for children and the family, but also as an individual person and actor in her community and in the society in general'.[32] In this way, the Convention recognises that all human being are equal, have equal rights and deserve respect for their human dignity, but at the same time may have divergent ideas about the way they want to spend their life.[33] Therefore, the concepts of individual autonomy, freedom, and diversity are crucial for a correct understanding of the content and scope of article 5a and of the Convention as a whole.

Women's sexuality and their reproductive capacity are crucial for the construction of gender stereotypes and fixed parental gender roles. This means that the construction of human sexuality as (exclusively) heterosexual forms part of the construction of patriarchal gender relations.[34] The most blatant transgression of the patriarchal female gender

---

[27]See CEDAW Committee, General Recommendation 25, paras 6 and 7.

[28]An analysis of the scope of the obligation under this article may be found in R Holtmaat, 'Article 5' in M Freeman et al (eds) (n 16).

[29]CEDAW Committee, General Recommendation 25, para 7. See also CEDAW Committee, Luxembourg (2000), A/55/38, CEDAW/C/SR.446 and 447, para 404. Although state parties do have specific obligations under article 5a as such, it is not a standalone article. It forms part of the general provisions of the Convention, thereby offering the general interpretative framework for all substantive articles. See C Chinkin and M Freeman, *Introduction*. In Freeman, Chinkin and Rudof, *CEDAW Commentary* (OUP, 2012) 8.

[30]This means that all laws and legal constructs must be subjected to an in depth gender analysis. See R Holtmaat, 'The Power of Legal Concepts: the Development of a Feminist Theory of Law' (1989) 5 *Int J of the Sociology of L* 481; R Holtmaat, 'Gender, the Analytical Concept that Tackles the Hidden Structural Bias of Law', in Verein ProFri (ed) *Recht Richtung Frauen; Beiträge zur feministischen Rechtswissenschaft* (Dike Verlag, 2001). A methodology for such an analysis has been developed in R Holtmaat, *Towards Different Law and Public Policy; The Significance of Article 5a CEDAW for the Elimination of Structural Gender Discrimination*, research undertaken on behalf of the Ministry of Social Affairs and Employment, the Netherlands (Reed Business Information, 2004).

[31]S Fredman, 'Beyond the Dichotomy of Formal and Substantive Equality. Towards New Definitions of Equal Rights', in I Boerefijn et al (eds) (n 16) at 116.

[32]CEDAW Committee, CO Suriname (2002), A/57/38 (part II), CEDAW/C/SR. 557, 558 and 566, para 48. See also CEDAW Committee, CO Uzbekistan (2001), A/56/38, CEDAW/C/SR.500, 501 and 507, para 169.

[33]L Lijnzaad, 'Over rollenpatronen en de rol van het Verdrag' in A. Heringa et al (eds) (n 18) 57.

[34]See J Butler, *Gender Trouble: Feminism and the Subversion of Identity* (Routledge, 1990) 1 34 and 110 128; J Butler, 'Imitation and Gender Subordination' in D. Fuss (ed.), *Inside/Out: Lesbian Theories, Gay Theories* (Routledge, 1991) 13. See also A Gross, 'Sex, Love, and Marriage: Questioning Gender and Sexuality Rights in International Law' (2008) 21 *Leiden J of Int L* 235. At 251, Gross summarises Butler's position as follows: 'the division in two genders as part of the institution of compulsory heterosexuality, (which) requires a binary polarised gender system since patriarchy and compulsory heterosexuality are only possible in a world built on such a hierarchised division'. Real liberation or emancipation of women and gay and lesbian people, according to this author, requires 'undoing gender', instead of accepting the thus pre fixed gender

identity and her fixed gender role is the lesbian woman who chooses to renounce a male sexual partner and thereby also rejects the protection of the male head of household, and all other forms of male supervision on and control of her life.[35] The obligation to modify gender stereotypes and fixed parental gender roles is also of great importance to men who do not want to conform to their assigned heterosexual masculine identity and male gender role. Beyond that, this obligation is equally important for different from male/female sexed persons (intersex and transgender) and persons with a different from heterosexual sexuality (lesbian, gay, and bisexual).[36] Gender stereotypes and fixed parental gender roles directly affect the lives of all persons who renounce traditional heterosexual and patriarchal feminine and masculine gender identities and gender roles. Through an expansive interpretation of article 5a, all of these situations may be brought under the scope of the Convention.

Violations of LGBTI human rights that are based on gender stereotypes and fixed parental gender roles and sexual roles, therefore, could (at least in theory) be addressed in the framework of the third objective of the Convention, more specifically on the basis of article 5a CEDAW.[37] Examples of such violations that are, in our view, covered under CEDAW and could (and should) be condemned by the Committee are practices such as forced marriages of lesbian, bisexual or transgender persons; taking away their children and placing them under the custody of male relatives or their (former) husbands; denying these persons the right to healthcare, reproductive care, housing, education and employment; and (gang) rape and other forms of violence because of these persons' sexual or gender identity. The Committee's interpretation shows that it, at least partially and cautiously, is going in this direction, at least as far as bisexual and lesbian women and transgender persons are concerned. The question remains whether the Committee does indeed use article 5a for that purpose; ie is it constructing the issue of discrimination against lesbian women (and TBI women) as an issue that falls under the obligation on state parties to change all traditions, practices, and beliefs that somehow contribute to the construction of unequal and oppressive gender relations and heteronormativity?

III. The CEDAW Committee's Position as Regards LGBTI Rights

The CEDAW Committee is the main authority that can interpret the Convention. Its views are not binding, but its monitoring has proven valuable because it allows for dialogue and a critical analysis of the anti-discrimination policies in the various state parties. This section discusses whether the Committee uses the possibility offered by article 5a to interpret the Convention in a way which allows various forms of discrimination against LGBTI persons (either male or female) to fall under the scope of the Convention. Do the Committee's Concluding (Country) Observations and General

---

categories and identities. Another way of expressing this principle is saying that a *transformation* of gender and sexuality needs to take place.

[35] Lesbian women being gang raped in order 'to cure them' from their outrageous 'abnormal' sexual preference, is an example of this kind of 'correction'. See for example, Report of the UN Special Rapporteur on the question of torture and other cruel, inhuman or degrading treatment or punishment, Commission on Human Rights March 2006, UN Doc E/CN.4/2006/6/Add.1, para 180 and 183.

[36] That is, different from the heterosexual norm and other than the binary male female scheme.

[37] It is therefore in our view not necessary to 'unisex' CEDAW, as is argued by Rosenblum (n 19). Rosenblum does mention article 5 of the CEDAW, but does not appear to see the full potential of this provision in relation to enhancing LGBTI rights. See also section III of this article.

Recommendations,[38] its Decisions and Views on Individual Communications submitted under the Optional Protocol, or its Report of investigations under the Protocol's inquiry procedure[39] contain any references to the position of LGBTI-persons and the obligations of state parties of CEDAW with respect to their rights? If so, which rights are being given to LGBTI persons on the basis of the Convention? Or, to put it the other way around: what obligations do state parties to the Convention have to respect, protect, and fulfil the human rights of LGBTI persons, specifically connected to their sexual orientation and gender identity?

III.i. *Quantitative analysis*

For the purpose of this contribution, we carried out a systematic analysis of the Concluding Observations adopted by the CEDAW Committee from 1 January 2010 until 31 December 2014. A total of 110 Concluding Observations were considered in this period. We undertook a full-text search of this material, using the search terms gay, lesbian, transgender, transsexual, LGBT, same-sex, and sexual orientation, in order to determine whether the Committee mentioned (discrimination on the grounds of) sexual orientation or gender identity. In 37 cases, ie in roughly one third of all Concluding Observations included in the analysis, a reference was made to one or more of these categories. Noteworthy examples discussed below include the Committee's Concluding Observations on reports of countries from all continents, for example those of Argentina, Finland, Georgia, Guyana, India, the Netherlands, New Zealand, Norway, Panama, Paraguay, the Russian Federation, Singapore, South Africa, Uganda, Venezuela, and Zimbabwe.[40]

Since 1986, the Committee has also published 29 General Recommendations.[41] Sexual orientation is mentioned in only two of these documents: General Recommendations 27 and 28 (both published in 2010),[42] while General Recommendation 21 [1994] underlines women's autonomy in relation to marriage and family matters, recognising 'various forms of family.'[43] In the Committee's case-law regarding complaints by individuals, sexual orientation is mentioned only once.[44] In the three inquiry procedures that were concluded before June 2015, there was no mention of sexual orientation or any of the other search

---

[38]Under article 18, all states which ratify the Convention must report to the Committee. The Committee examines the report, also relying on information sent in by non governmental organisations, and subsequently publishes Concluding Observations on the state party. Along with offering advice to reporting states in the Concluding Observations, the Committee has the ability to issue General Recommendations on its views on matters concerning the elimination of discrimination against women.

[39]Opened for signature 10 December 1999, 2131 UNTS 83 (entered into force on 22 December 2000). States ratifying this Protocol recognise the competence of the Committee to consider complaints from individuals or groups. In addition, article 8 of the Optional Protocol establishes an inquiry procedure that allows the Committee to initiate an investigation where it has received reliable information of grave or systematic violations by a state party of rights established in the Convention. See also F Isa, 'The Optional Protocol for the Convention on the Elimination of All Forms of Discrimination against Women: Strengthening the Protection Mechanisms of Women's Human Rights' (2003) 20 *Arizona J of Int and Comparative L* 291.

[40]See the qualitative analysis below for references to these Observations.

[41]The Committee's General Recommendations may be found at http://www.ohchr.org/EN/HRBodies/CEDAW/Pages/Recommendations.aspxhttp://www.ohchr.org/EN/HRBodies/CEDAW/Pages/Recommendations.aspx.

[42]CEDAW/C/GC/27, para 13 and CEDAW/C/GC/28, para 18.

[43]CEDAW/C/GC/21, para 16.

[44]In case *Lourdes da Silva Pimentel v Brazil*, CEDAW/C/49/D/17/2008.

terms used in our analysis.[45] From a quantitative perspective, therefore, the attention the Committee devotes to LGBTI issues seems to remain limited in all categories of documents except for the Concluding Observations. As such, in the next section we turn to a detailed analysis that primarily deals with this category of Committee output.

III.ii. *Qualitative analysis: Pre-2010*

Our analysis did not include the period before 2010,[46] but it is important to note that the question whether the term 'sex', as employed in the Convention, covers issues concerning women's sexual orientation or sexuality has been a contentious issue for years, as is the extent to which the Convention provides protection to transgender and intersexual persons.[47] Byrnes, in the leading Commentary on the Convention, holds that 'there is, in principle, no reason why the Convention should not be applied to provide protection for women who are discriminated against because of their sexuality'.[48] However, the Committee's approach to this subject in the years up to 2010 is best characterised as vague and cautious. It has not taken a clear stance, although prior to 2010, the Committee had expressed its concern about the criminalisation of same-sex partnerships,[49] while also mentioning discrimination on the grounds of sexual orientation in the two aforementioned General Recommendations published in 2010.[50]

III.iii. *Qualitative analysis: Post-2010 Concluding Observations*

The following are noteworthy findings resulting from our analysis of the quantitative data. First, lesbian women and transsexual, transgender, or intersex persons are most often mentioned by the Committee in relation to the issue of intersectionality, or mentioned in a list of particularly disadvantaged or vulnerable groups of women who need special protection. The categories of sexual orientation and trans- and intersex are apparently 'special' in the sense that they need to be included in such lists. An example of this approach can be found in General Recommendation 28:

> Intersectionality is a basic concept for understanding the scope of the general obligations of States parties contained in article 2. The discrimination of women based on sex and gender is inextricably linked with other factors that affect women, such as race, ethnicity, religion or belief, health, status, age, class, caste and sexual orientation and gender identity. Discrimination on the basis of sex or gender may affect women belonging to such groups to a different degree or in different ways to men. States parties must legally recognize such intersecting

---

[45]CEDAW/C/OP.8/CAN/1 (summary of the inquiry concerning the Philippines, April 2015), CEDAW/C/OP.8/CAN/1 (report on the inquiry concerning Canada, March 2015) and CEDAW/C/2005/OP.2008/MEXICO. Documentation related to the Committee's Inquiry Procedures may be found at http://www.ohchr.org/EN/HRBodies/CEDAW/Pages/InquiryProcedure. aspxhttp://www.ohchr.org/EN/HRBodies/CEDAW/Pages/InquiryProcedure.aspx.

[46]This period is covered in the analysis of these documents in various chapters of the CEDAW Commentary (M Freeman et al, n 14.). Therefore we have investigated in depth the period after 2010, in order to see whether major changes took place since that time.

[47]A Byrnes (n 18) 60. See also C Chinkin and M Freeman, 'Introduction', in M. Freeman et al (eds) (n 16) 15 16; . Ernst, 'Review Essay: The UN Convention on the Elimination of All Forms of Discrimination against Women: A Commentary' (2012) 13 *Melbourne J of Int L* 890, 906 909.

[48]A Byrnes (n 18) 64.

[49]A Byrnes (n 18) 64, mentions a few pre 2010 examples, such as CO Mexico, A/53/38 (Supp) Part I, 18th session (1998) para 420; CO Kyrgyzstan, A/54/38 (Supp) Part I, 20th session (1999) paras 127 128.

[50]General Recommendations 27 and 28: CEDAW/C/GC/27, para 13 and CEDAW/C/GC/28, para 18.

forms of discrimination and their compounded negative impact on the women concerned and prohibit them.[51]

Secondly, LGBTI issues are often addressed in the section of the Concluding Observations that deals with violence against women. In some of these Concluding Observations, these categories of women are mentioned in the context of violence against women belonging to vulnerable and disadvantaged groups. The Concluding Observations on Venezuela provide a typical example:

> 36. The Committee regrets the lack of effective measures taken to address discrimination and violence faced by disadvantaged groups of women, such as indigenous and Afro descendant women, migrant women, older women, women with disabilities as well as lesbian, bisexual, transgender women and intersex persons, and other women facing multiple and intersecting forms of discrimination.
> 37. The Committee recommends that the State party adopt appropriate measures to address the particular needs of disadvantaged groups of women. The State party should provide com prehensive information and disaggregated data in its next periodic report on the situation of these women and the measures adopted to address their specific needs.[52]

In other Concluding Observations, however, the Committee specifically addresses acts of violence against women on grounds of sexual orientation or transgender identities. The Concluding Observations on Albania are an example of this:

> 42. While welcoming the adoption of the Law on Protection from Discrimination, which expressly prohibits discrimination on the grounds of gender identity and sexual orientation, the Committee expresses concern about discrimination and acts of violence against women on such grounds.
> 43. The Committee calls on the State party to implement fully the Law on Protection from Discrimination in relation to discrimination based on gender identity and sexual orientation by providing effective protection against discrimination and violence against women on such grounds.[53]

Similarly, in the Observations on Georgia, the Committee calls upon the state to take measures, specifically addressing 'violence against and harassment of lesbian, bisexual and transsexual women'.[54] The examples of Albania and Georgia show that the Committee devotes particular attention to the protection of women who are discriminated against on the basis of their sexual orientation or gender identity. This notwithstanding, it should be noted that this attention is still dependent on the Committee's determination to combat violence against women *per se*, rather than on a broader equality-based approach.

Moreover, while mentioning discrimination or violence against LGBTI persons illustrates the concerns of the Committee on this topic, these references remain fairly gratuitous if they are not coupled with recommendations on how to actually end such

---

[51]CEDAW/C/GC/28, para 18.
[52]CO Venezuela, CEDAW/C/VEN/CO/7/8 (2014), paras 36 37; see also CO Argentina, CEDAW/C/ARG/CO/6 (2010), paras 43 44; CO Belarus, CEDAW/C/BLR/CO/7 (2011), paras 41 42; CO Paraguay, CEDAW/C/PRY/CO/6 (2011), para 12; CO Peru, CEDAW/C/PER/CO/7 8 (2014), paras 39 40.
[53]CO Albania, CEDAW/C/ALB/CO/3 (2010), para 42 43; see also CO Georgia, CEDAW/C/GEO/4 5 (2014), paras 34 35; CO Uganda, CEDAW/C/UGA/CO/7 (2010), paras 43 44; CO Russian Federation, CEDAW/C/USR/CO/7 (2010), para 40; CO Zim babwe, CEDAW/C/ZWE/CO/2 5 (2012) paras 23 24.
[54]CO Georgia, CEDAW/C/GEO/4 5 (2014), para 35(e).

discrimination. Most often, the Committee does not offer any such recommendation but merely declares that all women should be able to live without fear of violence.[55]

Even considering the constraints under which the Committee needs to operate (such as the sensitivity of the issues it addresses), and while taking into account the cautious and respectful approach that it normally adopts in its recommendations to the state parties, still, the 'recommendations' seem to have the character of a formulaic recitation rather than specifically tailored to the circumstances of the particular state party. A recurring recommendation relates to the enactment of comprehensive anti-discrimination legislation that includes the prohibition of discrimination on the grounds of sexual orientation;[56] sometimes, the Committee (also) recommends the decriminalisation of same-sex relations as an additional measure.[57]

Such advice is very broad and accordingly less likely to be effective than concrete, tailored and detailed recommendations. More concrete recommendations can, for example, be found in the Concluding Observations on the Russian Federation, Uganda, South Africa, and Zimbabwe. The Committee's (identical) advice in those instances includes 'launching a sensitization campaign aimed at the general public, as well as providing appropriate training to law enforcement officials'.[58] In the Concluding Observations on Panama, the Committee recommends fighting 'gender stereotypes . . . and violence on grounds such as sexual orientation and gender identity' with 'awareness-raising programmes in school curricula, the training of teachers and the sensitization of the media and the public at large, including actions specifically targeting men and boys'.[59]

Other more specific advice can be found in the Concluding Observations on Singapore, where the country is invited to put in place 'a comprehensive strategy to modify or eliminate patriarchal attitudes and stereotypes that discriminate against women, including those based on sexual orientation and gender identity';[60] or in the observations on Norway, where the state is called upon to take 'specific measures to address difficulties faced by lesbian and transgendered asylum seekers'.[61] These examples all go to show that there are indeed Concluding Observations in which the Committee, instead of mentioning only the rights of women who are discriminated against on grounds of sexual orientation or gender identity as a kind of *obiter dictum*, goes some way to provide state parties with specific recommendations aiming at eliminating discrimination on grounds of sexual orientation.

As regards the question of whether the Committee uses the normative framework of article 5a to address the discrimination or violence against LGBTI persons or to clarify

---

[55]See eg CO Argentina, CEDAW/C/ARG/CO/6 (2010), para 44. In the CO on Venezuela (CEDAW/C/VEN/CO/7/8 (2014), in para 37), the Committee asks the state party to adopt 'appropriate measures to address the particular needs of disadvantaged groups of women.'

[56]CO Guyana, CEDAW/C/GUY/7 8 (2012), para 23(f); CO Paraguay, CEDAW/C/PRY/CO/6 (2011), para 13; CO Republic of Korea, CEDAW/C/KOR/7 (2011), para 15; CO Russian Federation, CEDAW/C/USR/CO/7 (2010), para 40; CO South Africa, C/ZAF/CO/4 (2011), para 40.

[57]Eg CO Guyana, CEDAW/C/GUY/7 8 (2012), para 23(f); CO India, CEDAW/C/IND/4 5 (2014), para 11. The Committee also calls on Uganda to decriminalise 'homosexual behaviour': see CO Uganda, CEDAW/C/UGA/CO/7 (2010), para 44.

[58]CO Russian Federation, CEDAW/C/USR/CO/7 (2010), para 41; CO Uganda, CEDAW/C/UGA/CO/7 (2010), para 44; CO South Africa, C/ZAF/CO/4 (2011), para 40; CO Zimbabwe, CEDAW/C/ZWE/CO/2 5 (2012) para 24.

[59]CO Panama, CEDAW/C/PAN/7 (2010), paras 22 23.

[60]CO Singapore, CEDAW/C/SGP/CO/4 (2012), para 21(a).

[61]CO Norway, CEDAW/C/NOR/CO/8 (2012), para 36(d).

the obligations of state parties in this regard, our findings hold that this is rarely the case. We have found six Concluding Observations in which the role of stereotypes in relation to the situation of lesbian women, bisexual, intersex or transgender persons was mentioned;[62] in two of these a reference was made to articles 5a and 2(f).[63] An excellent example may be found in the Concluding Observations on Panama, in which the Committee writes that:

> 23. The Committee urges the State party to increase its efforts to design and strengthen com prehensive awareness raising programmes to foster a better understanding of, and support for, equality between women and men at all levels of society. Such efforts should aim to modify stereotypical attitudes and cultural norms about the responsibilities and roles of women and men in the family, workplace, political life and society, as required under articles 2 (f) and 5 (a) of the Convention. The Committee also urges the State party to transform its recognition of the problem of multiple forms of discrimination into an overall strategy for eliminating gender stereotypes relating to women in general and, in particular, to discrimi nation against women as specified in paragraph 22. This strategy could include awareness raising programmes in school curricula, the training of teachers and the sensitization of the media and the public at large, including actions specifically targeting men and boys.

III.iv. *Preliminary conclusion*

The attention that the CEDAW Committee devotes to LGBTI issues remains scarce in all categories of documents except for the Concluding Observations. Our analysis of the Committee's Concluding Observations since 2010 shows that sexual orientation and some forms of gender identity (most notably transgender) are mentioned in over one third of the documents concerning countries from all continents. The Committee, however, continues its cautious approach and has so far refused to take a clear stance on the question of whether the discrimination ground 'sex' in the Convention includes all identities captured under the LGBTI initialism. This notwithstanding, the Committee has at the same time gradually expanded the protection to lesbian, transgender, transsexual and intersexual persons by means of frequent references to discrimination or violence on these grounds. While many of these references are formulaic recitations rather than specific recommendations, this exploration does however also purport to show that some Concluding Observations do contain concrete recommendations that are specifically intended to help state parties combat discrimination on grounds of sexual orientation and gender identity. Such examples go to show that the Convention, to an increasing extent, is applied by the Committee to provide protection for women who are discriminated against because of their sexuality or gender identity.

Although the Committee rarely mentions article 5a in relation to discrimination or violence against these women, it does occasionally mention that the causes of such discrimination and violence lie in gender stereotypes that assign particular roles to women or that conceive of women as subordinate or inferior to men.[64] However, the Committee could

---

[62] CO Chile, CEDAW/C/CHI/5 6 (2012), para 17b; CO Finland, CEDAW/C/FIN/7 (2014), para 29; CO Netherlands, CEDAW/C/NLD/5 (2010), para 25; CO Panama CEDAW/C/PAN/7 (2010), paras 22 23; CO Serbia, CEDAW/C/SER/2 3 (2013), para 20; CO Singapore, CEDAW/C/SGP/CO/4 (2012), para 21.

[63] Namely the Concluding Observations on the Netherlands and Panama.

[64] See CO Chile, CEDAW/C/CHI/5 6 (2012), para 17b; CO Finland, CEDAW/C/FIN/7 (2014), para 29; CO Netherlands, CEDAW/C/NLD/5 (2010), para 25; CO Panama CEDAW/C/PAN/7 (2010), paras 22 23; CO Serbia, CEDAW/C/SER/2 3 (2013), para 20; CO Singapore, CEDAW/C/SGP/CO/4 (2012), para 21.

make its Concluding Observations and General Recommendations much more persuasive, in our view, by exploring more deeply this link between discrimination against LGBTI persons and gender stereotyping and by developing specific guidelines as regards the obligations that state parties have to 'eliminate' these causes of oppression of and discrimination against LGBTI persons.

The question remains how the Committee could achieve a less erratic and ad hoc approach to this topic. Ernst proposes the adoption of a General Recommendation focusing on discrimination against women based on sexual orientation and gender identity, arguing that the Convention's 'prohibition of discrimination "in any field" ought to apply to their choice of life partner as well, and that they should not be forced by traditional gender roles into having a male partner.'[65] Another suggestion would be the elaboration by the Committee of a General Recommendation on article 5a in which it pays attention to the close link between gender stereotypes and traditional gender roles and the oppression of lesbian, bi-sexual, transgender, intersex and bisexual persons.[66]

IV. Conclusion: Is It Wise to Use the Convention to Enhance LGBTI Rights?

In section II of this contribution, we argued that, from a legal point of view, it is possible to interpret the Convention in such a way that the discrimination and violence against LGTBI persons is brought within its scope. The analysis of the existing 'jurisprudence' of the Committee in section III shows that this possibility has not yet been fully utilised. The choice to use CEDAW (or not) for the purpose of enhancing LGBTI rights is also of a political and ideological nature. It is therefore important to also take the theoretical and strategic perspectives into account. We therefore conclude this article with a brief discussion of the pros and cons, or possibilities and problems, of trying to enhance LGBTI rights by means of bringing these categories under the scope of CEDAW.

IV.i. *Some theoretical considerations*

Although at a theoretical level it is acknowledged that CEDAW covers not only unequal treatment, but all forms of oppression that women experience in life because of their sex and gender,[67] the Convention aims at the elimination of *discrimination* (against women). The term discrimination in CEDAW has a wider meaning than merely *unequal* treatment of women as compared to men. Other forms of oppression, exclusion, and violence that are related to sex (ie to being a woman) are covered as well.[68] However, equality, equal treatment and non-discrimination remain central concepts in the interpretation and application of CEDAW.[69] This means that with any attempt to bring LGBTI rights concerning sexuality and gender identity under CEDAW, implicitly, a choice is being made to conceive of these rights mainly through the prism of 'equality' and 'non-discrimination'.

[65]J Ernst (n 47), 19.
[66]A new General Recommendation on Article 5 is called for because General Recommendation 3 dates from 1987 and does not contain any clarification of States parties' obligations under this provision. See R Holtmaat (n 8), 109.
[67]See I Young (n 25).
[68]See section II of this contribution.
[69]This is illustrated in the text of the Convention where each substantive article stresses that the rights that women have under this Convention should be granted to them 'on a basis of equality with men'. See on this issue A Byrnes (n 18), 61.

The demand for *equal* rights of the LGBTI movement once again shows that equality or the right to equal treatment continue to have a strong appeal to all organisations that strive to emancipate their constituency.[70] For example, the demands for the right to marriage, the right to custody over children or to establish family law ties with children, and the right to protection of private life of LGBTI persons, are often phrased as demands for *equal* rights in that regard. Is non-discrimination law indeed something that 'we cannot *not* want to have'?[71] Many legal theorists have profoundly doubted whether 'rights can be rearticulated outside the traditional liberal legal framework without drawing us back into that framework.'[72] When rights are constructed as equal rights, or rights based on the principle of non-discrimination, regardless of whether legal equality is seen as an anti-classification or an ant-subordination principle, it is most problematic[73] that this law is constructed around the notion of non-discrimination grounds. What then, are the classifications or groups that are thus reinstated and confirmed by this law?

Some considerations concerning 'non-discrimination grounds'

Non-discrimination grounds are so-called identity factors: they refer to characteristics of (groups of) persons that, for various reasons, make these persons particularly vulnerable to oppression and exclusion. In non-discrimination law, the characteristics that are thus protected or that deserve strict (judicial) scrutiny are much debated. Various lists of criteria exist, in which most often the factors 'history of persistent past and present discrimination', 'innate or immutable aspect of personal identity', and 'dignity' are mentioned.[74] In particular, the notion of 'innate or immutable characteristics', like sex, race, colour, sexual orientation, is most problematic. Non-discrimination law, through that criterion, instead of conceiving of differences as features arising out of the inter-group relationships, considers them as inherent characteristics of the non-dominant group.[75] In that way, non-discrimination law is a 'regulatory power' that contributes to the creation of these (often submissive) identities and makes them even more inescapable for human beings.[76]

In regard to LGBTI as a prohibited ground of non-discrimination, it is important to discuss to what extent a distinction can or should be made between sex as a non-discrimination ground and other categories or identities, such as gender, sexuality, and gender identity.[77] Is it at all possible to distinguish between these 'identity factors', or are they in fact so closely related that they are inseparable, in as far as human beings' own experience of their personal identity is concerned? Do the categories of sex, intersexuality, and transgender refer

---

[70] R Hunter, 'Introduction: Feminism and Equality', in R Hunter, *Rethinking Equality Projects in Law. Feminist Challenges* (Hart Publishing 2008), 8.

[71] In relation to claiming rights in the framework of liberal Western legal systems, Brown (n 12), 231 argues that although being a mixed blessing and leading to many paradoxes we cannot *not* want to have rights.

[72] A Gross (n 34), 241.

[73] On this difference between non discrimination as an anti classification and an anti subordination principle, see J Balkin and R Siegel (n 15), from 9. See also A McColgan (n 15).

[74] A McColgan (n 15), chapter 2.

[75] See C Bacchi, 'The Practice of Affirmative Action Policies; Explaining Resistances and how these affect Results', in I Boer efijn et al (eds) (n 16).

[76] W Brown (n 12), 230 231.

[77] In European Union equal treatment law, the categories sex (including transsexuals) and sexual orientation are clearly distinguished and regulated in separate Directives with distinctive scopes of application and possibilities to justify inequality of treatment. Sexual harassment is regulated only in the context of European Union sex equality law, which leaves LGB persons unprotected against this form of discrimination. See R Holtmaat, 'Sexual Harassment and Harassment on the Ground of Sex in EU Law: a Conceptual Clarification' (2011) 2 *Eur Gender Equality L Rev* 4.

to purely biological categories of 'being' of a particular 'kind' (and 'having' particular features like hormones and chromosomes – situated in the body), and does sexuality refer to 'feeling' and 'acting' or 'doing' (ie to behaviour)? Or does this distinction lead us away from the real issue, because all denominations of particular features of human existence are human 'acts' and 'performative', ie continuously contributing to their own (re)construction in a particular social, cultural, and economic context? In that regard, the question must be raised whether this division between *being* and *behaving* is not a false distinction in itself, denying that both categories are the result of and subjected to social and cultural constructions of the categories that are captured under the LGBTI initialism.

The discussion surrounding the construction of LGBTI persons' *equal* rights therefore requires a continuous, critical assessment of the meaning of the words ('grounds') that are central in that discussion, like 'sex', 'woman', 'man', 'sexuality', and 'gender'. How are these concepts constructed in social, cultural, legal, and political life, and in what 'power play' are feminist and LGBTI activists involved in when trying to shift the meanings and workings of these concepts? And, just as discussed above, it is not the case that human beings can never be pinned to just one clearly demarcated 'identity factor', but that subordination, exclusion, oppression, and discrimination, are determined by multiple factors, including wider cultural, social, and economic structures that determine people's life chances?[78]

Some considerations concerning 'comparability', 'disadvantage' and 'justifications'

Apart from these theoretical problems concerning the choice, construction, and delineation of discrimination grounds, the application of existing equality or non-discrimination law also leads to complicated issues regarding the comparability, disadvantage, and possible justification of the unequal treatment. A whole legal doctrine has emerged over the past 50 years in which the 'equality analysis' or 'equality test' is developed in great detail.[79] The application of the equality principle, through the possibility of bringing forward justifications for the unequal treatment, opens the door for a discourse on conflicting rights and often results in the right to equality having to give way to other rights, most notably the right to religious freedom. [80]

Claiming equal rights or, most importantly, the right to non-discrimination, also runs the risk of leading to assimilation to the existing dominant (in this case: heterosexual) norms.[81] As Rubin points out, demands for equal rights of persons with a 'different sexuality', instead of creating real sexual liberty, at best leads to giving them the right to have sex in a safe surrounding of registered partnership or marriage, leaving all sexual relations outside these legal constructions in the categories of 'deviant', 'abnormal', or even

---

[78]On intersectionality see K Crenshaw: 'Demarginalizing the Intersection of Race and Sex: A Black Feminist Critique of Anti discrimination Doctrine' (1989) *Feminist Theory and Antiracist Politics* 139.

[79]See for a detailed analysis of this test J Gerards, *Judicial Review in Equal Treatment Cases* (Martinus Nijhoff Publishers, 2005).

[80]See A Stuart, 'Without Distinction A Defining Principle?', in E. Brems (ed), *Conflicts between Fundamental Rights* (Intersentia, 2008), 102; J Goldschmidt 'Het grotere gelijk: alternatieven voor een destructieve verabsolutering van het gelijkheidsbeginsel' (2004) 29 *NJCM Bulletin* 782. The negative consequences of this discourse of conflicting rights have been examined by R Holtmaat: 'The Head of the Woman is the Man; The Failure to Address Gender Stereotypes in the Legal Procedures around the Dutch SGP', in Eva Brems and Alexandra Timmer (eds), *Stereotyping as a Human Rights Issue* (Antwerp, Intersentia forthcoming 2016).

[81]A Gross (n 34), 246 247, who discusses this problem in relation to demanding same sex marriage.

'criminal' forms of behaviour.[82] This leads to the urgent question of whether it is necessary or desirable at all to use this existing legal equality or non-discrimination framework to enhance the protection of the (already existing!) human rights of LGBTI persons. In other words: why claim that LGBTI persons have an *equal* right to marry, instead of simply claiming that they have the right to marry *as such*?[83] Is it not true that *all* human beings have the right to marry, the right to family life, the right to be free from violence, the right to freedom of expression – including expression of their sexual and gender identity, etc? Why not continue on the road of the Yogyakarta Principles and claim that these existing human rights will finally be applied to all human beings? [84]

IV.ii. *Some strategic issues*

A last, but certainly not least important, dimension of the question of the instrumental value of CEDAW for the purposes of enhancing LGBTI rights is strategic: what are the possible positive and negative effects of such a strategy? Theoretical concepts and constructs like 'gender' or 'gender identity' are developed as tools for a critical assessment of existing unequal power relations between the sexes and of forced heteronormativity and can be used in the context of emancipatory projects. Our main concern at this juncture is that they can also be used by powerful (often religious) groups to organise resistance against any changes in the unequal relationships between the sexes and against changes regarding forced heteronormativity, and thus can become useless or even damaging for these same emancipatory projects. What repression or opposition may be expected, in particular from the religious right in the world, when any such an attempt is made?[85] Would that opposition also damage the enhancement of 'women's human rights' to such an extent that we should not go down this route? Or is it more important that we can escape from the detrimental effects of the asymmetrical approach when we leave the paradigm of 'women's rights' behind us?[86] On the other hand: would a shift to a symmetrical approach not bring us from bad to worse, as this would mean that the m/f comparator model of sex equality is thereby adopted, with all its assimilationist effects? Answering these questions is beyond the exclusive competence of lawyers, and requires an in-depth study from political scientists and other social science disciplines as well. We hope that this article contributes to having this discussion.

We would also like to devote a few final words to the proposals that were made in order to either shift from an asymmetrical to a symmetrical approach ('unisexing CEDAW';

---

[82]G Rubin, 'Thinking Sex: Notes for a Radical Theory of the Politics of Sexuality', in CS Vance (ed), *Pleasure and Danger: Exploring Female Sexuality* (Routledge 1984) 267. See also A Gross (n 34) 246 247, who holds that demanding the equal right to marry 'reinforces the message that marriage is the ultimate form of human relationship, whether different sex or same sex', and that 'this message is discriminatory towards all who do not participate in it.'

[83]Of course, these rights have to be expressly claimed by LGBTI persons because they have historically been, and still continue to be, denied to them in all cultures and all legal systems. There is an important role to be fulfilled by the judiciary and the treaty bodies in interpreting these (universal) rights in such a way that they are truly inclusive, ie are truly granted to *all* human beings. An overview of ways in which courts and treaty bodies have done so can be found in A Byrnes, 'Gender Challenges for International Human Rights', in S Shearan and N Rodley (eds), *Routledge Handbook of International Human Rights Law* (Routledge, 2014) 631 633.

[84]The Yogyakarta Principles have been described in detail in M O'Flaherty's contribution to this issue.

[85]For a discussion of this resistance in relation to the concept of gender, see J Scott, 'The Uses and Abuses of Gender' (2013) 16 *Tijdschrift voor Genderstudies* 63.

[86]The argument was advanced by D Otto (n 10).

Rosenblum[87]) or to explicitly extend the scope of CEDAW to cover the elimination of all forms of discrimination against LGBTI persons ('supersexing CEDAW'; Hernández-Truyol[88]). In our view, Rosenblum's main reason to unisex CEDAW (ie in order to give rights to LGBTI persons), is not a convincing argument to change the non-discrimination ground of the Convention from 'women' to 'sex'. A prohibition of discrimination on the grounds of sex is commonly interpreted in a strictly binary or bipolar scheme in which the (presumably essential) male and female sexes are compared with one another; only when one of the two sexes suffers a certain disadvantage for which there is no objective justification, this non-discrimination norm becomes applicable. The vast (feminist) literature in the area of sex equality rights shows the strong tendency towards assimilation to the male norm that is inherent in any formal sex-equality norm.[89] Besides, a 'gender neutral' sex equality norm suffers from the danger – exemplified in eg the practice of EU sex equality law – that very often men appeal to this norm in order to claim the advantages women might have over them (eg in the area of protection of motherhood).[90] The result of such legal actions then is to water down these entitlements, leaving men and women without these advantages. Apart from this practical problem, there is also the ideological obstacle which holds that changing the understanding of sex to include 'other sexes' and sexualities, as is suggested as the solution to this problem by Rosenblum, might appear to be as difficult and controversial as acknowledging that differences between men and women are culturally and socially constructed instead of 'natural' or 'God-given'.

In reaction to Rosenblum's proposal, Hernández-Truyol suggests the adoption of a second optional protocol to CEDAW in which principles similar to the Yogyakarta Principles are laid down in order to 'super-sex' CEDAW, thereby expressly including the rights of LGBTI persons under the Convention.[91] To our mind, this proposal is also rather unrealistic. Progress in the area of creating international instruments that guarantee the human rights of LGBTI persons is very slow. Like Garvey has demonstrated in his article on the history of the Brazilian Resolution that aimed to enhance LGBTI rights, any such attempt may invoke so much resistance that progress is blocked, instead of enhanced.[92] Garvey therefore argues in favour of enhancing these rights through the slow and piecemeal judicial process, instead of through the creation of new international law documents.

An Optional Protocol to CEDAW would have to be negotiated at the highest level within the UN and would take years and years – if ever – to materialise. More realistic proposals are to adopt a CEDAW General Recommendation on this topic or – perhaps even more feasibly – to adopt a General Recommendation specifically on article 5a and include an analysis of the link between gender stereotypes and gender roles and LGBT-

---

[87]D Rosenblum (n 19).

[88]B Hernández Truyol (n 19).

[89]Critical assessments of the very limited or adverse instrumental value of liberal and formal equality law are abundant. See eg S Fredman, *Discrimination Law* (OUP, 2011), in particular from 8. Increasingly, it is acknowledged that replacing the notion of formal equality with that of substantive equality will also 'not deliver the goods'. See eg R Hunter, 'Introduction: Feminism and Equality' 8; R Hunter, 'Alternatives to Equality', and K van Marle, 'Haunting (In)equalities', all in R Hunter (n 70).

[90]See above in section II, where we discuss the effect of a symmetrical sex equality norm.

[91]B Hernández Truyol (n 19) 220.

[92]T Garvey, 'God v. Gays? The Rights of Sexual Minorities In international Law as seen through the Doomed Existence of the Brazilian Resolution' (2010) 38 *Denver J of Int L and Policy* 659.

discrimination into that document. However, as was testified by former Committee vice chair Neubauer at the Oslo Conference, also within the CEDAW Committee itself, it is very difficult to overcome the strong and persistent resistance against using the concept of gender and, even more so, to explicitly address LGBTI issues. Hence, an adoption of such a General Recommendation will probably also take years. To us, the most realistic (though slow) way forward therefore seems to be to encourage state parties and non-governmental organisations to include discussions of discrimination against LGBTI persons in Country Reports and Shadow Reports to the Committee, thereby inviting the Committee to reflect on LGBTI discrimination. The Committee can (and should) more often and more openly acknowledge in its Concluding Observations that discrimination of LGBTI persons is structurally connected to women's discrimination, in particular through the phenomenon of gender stereotyping and gender roles. Reports of such discrimination can be used by the Committee to address this problem in its Concluding Observations.

One example of how this can be done is a shadow report on Singapore that was submitted to the Committee in 2010. In the report, written by Singaporean gay rights' NGO Sayoni, the problems faced by lesbian, bisexual, and transsexual women were addressed.[93] This resulted in numerous questions by members of the Committee,[94] and, eventually, in the aforementioned call on the country to put in place 'a comprehensive strategy to modify or eliminate patriarchal attitudes and stereotypes that discriminate against women, including those based on sexual orientation and gender identity'.[95] This is just one example indicative of the instrumentality of shadow reports in addressing LGBTI discrimination. Based on such Concluding Observations, the Committee can then in the future prepare a General Recommendation on this topic, along the lines suggested above.

Circling back to our position on the question of whether it is desirable and/or feasible to enhance the human rights of LGBTI persons by means of an extensive interpretation of CEDAW, we tend to be rather cautious. CEDAW does, in theory, offer some possibilities to do so. But the end result of such a strategy might be contra productive or regressive, both in terms of the rights of women and those of LGBTI persons. A step-by-step recognition by the CEDAW Committee that there is a crucial connection between gender discrimination and discrimination of LGBTI persons seems to be the best way forward.

---

[93]This shadow report is available at the organisation's website, see http://www.sayoni.com/index.php?option=com jdownloads&Itemid=97&task=viewcategory&catid=5http://www.sayoni.com/index.php?option=com jdownloads&Itemid=97&task=viewcategory&catid=5.
[94]CEDAW Committee, 39th Session, Summary Record of the 803rd meeting. Consideration of reports submitted by States parties under article 18 of the Convention (third periodic report on Singapore). Cedaw/C/SR.803 (A).
[95]CO Singapore, CEDAW/C/SGP/CO/4 (2012), para 21(a).

The Rights of LGBTI Children under the Convention on the Rights of the Child

Kirsten Sandberg

ABSTRACT

UN treaty bodies have increasingly highlighted the need to end discrimination and violence against lesbian, gay, bisexual, transgender, and intersex (LGBTI) persons. While these recommendations are relevant to children, they take on an adult's perspective and therefore fail to take particular regard to how the situation for children may differ from that of adults. This article provides a children's perspective on LGBTI rights. It presents and discusses relevant articles of the Convention on the Rights of the Child in addition to jurisprudence of the Committee on the Rights of the Child, with a focus on the rights to non-discrimination, identity, self-determination, and health.

I. Introduction

Several issues arise under the UN Convention on the Rights of the Child (CRC)[1] regarding children whose sexual orientation or gender identity differs from that of the majority population. In this context, these include lesbian, gay, bisexual, transgender, and intersex (LGBTI) children. Some of the issues also arise with regard to children of LGBTI parents.[2]

Over the past years, UN treaty bodies have been increasingly active in highlighting the need to end discrimination and violence against LGBTI persons. As early as 1994, in the case of *Toonen v Australia*, the Human Rights Committee held that states have an obligation to protect individuals from discrimination on the basis of their sexual orientation.[3] This statement set the scene, and the same view, in addition to that of gender identity, has been expressed in General Comments by other committees including the Committee against Torture (CAT) General Comment No 2 (2008) on the implementation of article 2,[4] the Committee on Economic, Social and Cultural Rights General comment No 20 (2009) on non-discrimination,[5] and the Committee on the Elimination of Discrimination against Women (CEDAW) General comment No 28 (2010) on core obligations.[6] It has also been reflected in concluding observations by all of these committees.[7]

---

[1] Convention on the Rights of the Child (adopted 20 November 1989, entered into force 2 September 1990) 1577 UNTS 3 (CRC).
[2] Some of what is said below would be relevant to queer and questioning children as well. See M A Fineman, 'Vulnerability, Resilience, and LGBT Youth' (2014) 14(292) *Legal Studies Research Paper*, Emory University School of Law, 101 122.
[3] *Toonen v Australia* Communication No 488/1992 (1994), UN Doc CCPR/C/50/D/488/1992.
[4] CAT, *General Comment No 2 (2008) Implementation of article 2 by States parties*, CAT/C/GC/2, para 21.
[5] CESCR, *General Comment No 20 (2009) Non discrimination in economic, social and cultural rights (art 2, para 2, of the International Covenant on Economic, Social and Cultural Rights)* 2 July 2009, E/C.12/GC/20, para 32.
[6] CEDAW, *General recommendation No 28 (2010) on the core obligations of States parties under article 2 of the Convention on the Elimination of All Forms of Discrimination against Women*, CEDAW/C/GC/28, para 18.
[7] See OHCHR (2011) (n 54 below).

Many of these recommendations are relevant to children; yet, they are written from an adult perspective with little particular regard to how the situation for children may differ from that of adults. The aim of this article is to provide a children's perspective on the human rights issues concerning LGBTI children. In this respect, the CRC and the jurisprudence of its monitoring body, the Committee on the Rights of the Child, are of special interest.

For all these children, discrimination is an issue, and sometimes it is linked to violence. Another prominent issue is the right to be who you are, which is an aspect of the right to identity. Closely related to this is the right to self-determination. For lesbian, gay, and bisexual children, this is about the right not to have a mainstream sexual orientation imposed on you and to have the freedom to decide who you want to be with and to be open about your orientation. For transgender and intersex children, the issue concerns self-determination in relation to one's gender identity, this may or may not include access to medical treatment. Intersex children in addition need to be protected against unnecessary medical intervention with the purpose of deciding their gender, a procedure sometimes performed at an early stage in life before the child is able to express a view.

Children have a right to non-discrimination under CRC article 2; a right to identity under article 8; a right to privacy under article 16; and a right to health under article 24. The implications of these rights for LGBTI children and the issues in question will be developed below. One strand of this article is to review the protection against discrimination and the related right to freedom from violence. The other main strand is a discussion of whether a right to self-determination of gender identity and to medical treatment can be derived from the rights to identity and to health.[8] First, I shall briefly present the CRC and the monitoring of the Convention by the Committee on the Rights of the Child.

II. The CRC and its Monitoring System

The Convention on the Rights of the Child has been ratified by 196 states. It is thus the most widely ratified human rights instrument with only the US not being a party to it.[9] As such, the CRC is a strong instrument, covering most children around the world. It is monitored by the Committee on the Rights of the Child (the Committee), composed of 18 independent experts from all over the world. States which have ratified the Convention are obliged to submit a report to the Committee every five years on what they have done to uphold children's rights. The Committee receives additional information from UNICEF, national human rights institutions, and non-governmental organisations (NGOs), describing the situation of children's rights in the country. Based on all this material, the Committee holds a one-day dialogue with the state in question and thereafter issues its Concluding Observations to the state, consisting of concerns and recommendations. Some of these will be used as examples below.

---

[8] I am indebted to Anders Sondrup for ideas and discussions while I supervised his MA thesis: Sondrup, Anders Skjellerudsv een, *Har barnet en rett til rett kjønn? En vurdering av hvorvidt barnet har krav på pubertetsutsettende og femininiserende eller maskuliniserende hormonbehandling ved kjønnsinkongruens* [Unofficial English translation: Does the child have a right to the right gender/sex?], master thesis, Faculty of Law, University of Oslo (2015), available at: https://www.duo.uio.no/bitstream/handle/10852/45651/232.pdf?sequence=1&isAllowed=y. The thesis only exists in Norwegian.

[9] South Sudan and Somalia both ratified the Convention in 2015.

The Committee also issues General Comments dealing with topics on which the Committee has seen a need for further clarification and where it provides detailed explanations regarding state obligations. Some General Comments will be referred to in the following.

A third Optional Protocol to the CRC,[10] adopted in 2011, gives children a right to submit individual complaints to the Committee concerning violations of the CRC which have taken place after the state in question ratified the Protocol. By December 2015, 22 states had ratified the Protocol. So far, few complaints have been lodged and none of them have been related to the topic discussed here. Thus, there is no case law under the CRC.

Four of the provisions in the CRC have been pointed out by the Committee as being general principles and are commonly referred to as such.[11] As general principles they are cross-cutting norms relevant in the interpretation and application of all the Convention's rights. These general principles are CRC article 2 on the right to non-discrimination; article 3 on the right to have the child's best interests taken into account as a primary consideration; article 6 on the right to life and development; and article 12 on the right to be heard.

III. Non-Discrimination

CRC article 2 holds that states shall respect and ensure the rights in the Convention without discrimination of any kind, irrespective of the child's or his or her parents' or legal guardian's race, colour, sex, language, religion, political or other opinion, national, ethnic or social origin, property, disability, birth or other status.

III.i. General Comments

The expression 'other status' has been interpreted by the Committee to include sexual orientation and gender identity. I have reviewed all the General Comments by the Committee and the results are referred to in the following. The first General Comment mentioning this is No 3 (2003) on HIV/AIDS, para. 8, stating:

> 8. Of particular concern is gender based discrimination combined with taboos or negative or judgemental attitudes to sexual activity of girls, often limiting their access to preventive measures and other services. Of concern also is discrimination based on sexual orientation. In the design of HIV/AIDS related strategies, and in keeping with their obligations under the Convention, States parties must give careful consideration to prescribed gender norms within their societies with a view to eliminating gender based discrimination as these norms impact on the vulnerability of both girls and boys to HIV/AIDS. States parties should, in particular, recognize that discrimination in the context of HIV/AIDS often impacts girls more severely than boys.

It does not elaborate on the issue, and the main focus is on gender with a particular emphasis on discrimination against girls.

---

[10]Optional Protocol to the Convention on the Rights of the Child on a communications procedure, adopted 19 December 2011, entered into force 14 April 2014. UN Doc A/RES/66/138 (3rd Optional Protocol).

[11]Committee on the Rights of the Child, *Treaty specific guidelines regarding the form and content of periodic reports to be submitted by States parties under article 44 , paragraph 1 (b), of the Convention on the Rights of the Child (rev 2015)*, 3 March 2015, UN Doc CRC/C/58/Rev.3, paras 23 27.

According to General Comment No 4 (2003) on adolescent health and development, 'developing an individual identity and dealing with one's sexuality' is one of the challenges of adolescence. After referring to the discrimination grounds explicitly mentioned in article 2, it goes on to say:

> 6. ... These grounds also cover adolescents' sexual orientation and health status (including HIV/AIDS and mental health). Adolescents who are subject to discrimination are more vulnerable to abuse, other types of violence and exploitation, and their health and development are put at greater risk. They are therefore entitled to special attention and protection from all segments of society.[12]

The General Comment further stresses the importance of sexual information, including that on the prevention and treatment of sexually transmitted diseases (STDs). To this end, states parties are urged to develop effective prevention programmes, including measures aimed at changing cultural views about adolescents' need for STD prevention and addressing cultural and other taboos surrounding adolescent sexuality (para 30).

Gender identity was first dealt with in a General Comment by the Committee in 2011. General Comment No 13 (2011) on the right of the child to freedom from all forms of violence holds that states parties must address discrimination against vulnerable or marginalised groups of children.[13] Among children in potentially vulnerable situations, children who are lesbian, gay, transgender or transsexual are mentioned.[14] States have an obligation to 'make proactive efforts to ensure that such children are assured their right to protection on an equal basis with all other children'.[15]

General Comment No 15 (2013) on the child's right to health includes sexual orientation and gender identity under discrimination grounds,[16] whereas No 14 (2013) on best interests does not list any discrimination grounds. Sexual orientation is mentioned in another context,[17] but gender identity is not. In the other General Comments from that year, No 16 on children's rights and the business sector[18] and No 17 on the right to play and leisure, there is no reference to LGBT children. This might have been included in the General Comment on the right to play, as several other groups of children in vulnerable situations are listed,[19] and discrimination grounds or vulnerable situations are altogether absent from the General Comment on business. General Comment No 18 on harmful practices (2014), issued jointly with the CEDAW Committee, simply lists 'sex, gender, age and other grounds' as prohibited categories for discrimination.[20]

---

[12] *General Comment No 4 (2003) Adolescent health and development in the context of the Convention on the Rights of the Child*, 1 July 2003, CRC/GC/2003/4, para 6.
[13] *General Comment No 3 (2003) HIV/AIDS and the rights of the child*, 17 March 2003, CRC/GC/2003/3, para 60.
[14] Ibid, para 72(g).
[15] Ibid, para 60.
[16] *General Comment No 15 (2013) on the right of the child to the enjoyment of the highest attainable standard of health (art 24)*, 17 April 2013, CRC/C/GC/15, para 8.
[17] *General Comment No 14 (2013) on the right of the child to have his or her best interests taken as a primary consideration (art 3, para 1)*, 29 May 2013, CRC/C/GC/14, para 55.
[18] *General Comment No 16 (2013) on State obligations regarding the impact of business on children's rights*, 17 April 2013, CRC/C/GC/16.
[19] *General comment No 17 (2013) on the right of the child to rest, leisure, play, recreational activities, cultural life and the arts (art 31)*, 17 April 2013, CRC/C/GC/17, paras 48 53.
[20] UN Committee for the Elimination of All Forms of Discrimination against Women and UN Committee on the Rights of the Child, *Joint general recommendation/general comment No 31 of the Committee on the Elimination of Discrimination against Women and No 18 of the Committee on the Rights of the Child on harmful practices*, 5 November 2014, CEDAW/C/GC/31 CRC/GC/18, paras 6 and 14.

III.ii. Concluding observations

In several of its Concluding Observations to states, the Committee has pointed to the obligation to prevent discrimination against LGBTI children. For example, to the UK in 2008, the Committee expressed concern that 'in practice certain groups of children, such as . . . lesbian, bisexual, gay, and transgender children (LGBT) . . . continue to experience discrimination and social stigmatization' (para 24). The Committee recommended that the state strengthen its awareness-raising and other preventive activities against discrimination and, if necessary, take affirmative action for the benefit of such groups of children (para 25b).

Concern was expressed briefly to Malaysia in 2007 regarding the insufficient efforts made to address discrimination based on sexual orientation, though no specific recommendation was given.[21] To China, again in 2007, concern was raised about the lack of legislation in Hong Kong specifically prohibiting discrimination on the basis of sexual orientation.[22] Nothing was said about the issue with regard to mainland China. Surprisingly, in the Concluding Observations to China in 2013, the Committee was silent on the issues of sexual orientation and gender identity. In 2011, the Committee recommended that New Zealand strengthen its awareness-raising and other preventive activities against discrimination and, if necessary, take affirmative action for the benefit of children in vulnerable situations, such as, among others, lesbian, bisexual, gay, and transgender children and children living with persons from these groups.[23]

Examining the Concluding Observations of all the 16 states that were reviewed under the CRC in 2014,[24] I found that the issue of discrimination against LGBTI children was raised with six of the states: Hungary, the Holy See, Russia, Kyrgyzstan, Portugal, and Venezuela.[25] The recommendations to the first three states mentioned also covered children living in LGBT families, whereas the latter three did not mention that group of children.

The Concluding Observations to Russia in 2014 were rather strong in this regard. The Committee expressed its concern at:

> the recent legislation of the State party prohibiting 'propaganda of unconventional sexual relationships', . . . which encourages the stigmatization of and discrimination against lesbian, gay, bisexual, transgender and intersex (LGBTI) persons, including children, and children from LGBTI families.

Discrimination was linked to violence, the Committee being:

---

[21] UN Committee on the Rights of the Child, *Concluding observations: Malaysia*, 25 June 2007, CRC/C/MYS/CO/1, para 31.

[22] UN Committee on the Rights of the Child, *Concluding observations: China (including Hong Kong and Macau Special Administrative Regions)*, 24 November 2005, CRC/C/CHN/CO2, paras 31 and 33.

[23] *Concluding observations: New Zealand*, 11 April 2011, CRC/C/NZL/CO/3 4, para 25.

[24] In addition to reviewing reports under the CRC itself, the Committee also reviews reports under the two first Optional Protocols, Optional Protocol to the Convention on the Rights of the Child on the involvement of children in armed conflict; and Optional Protocol to the Convention on the Rights of the Child on the sale of children, child prostitution and child pornography.

[25] *Concluding observations on the combined third, fourth and fifth periodic reports of Hungary*, 14 October 2014, CRC/C/HUN/CO/3 5, paras 19 20; *Concluding observations on the second periodic report of the Holy See*, 25 February 2014, CRC/C/VAT/CO/2, paras 25 26; *Concluding observations on the combined fourth and fifth periodic reports of the Russian Federation*, 25 February 2014, CRC/C/RUS/CO/4 5, paras 24 25; *Concluding observations of the Committee on the Rights of the Child, Kyrgyzstan*, 7 July 2014, CRC/C/KGZ/CO/3 4, paras 18 19; *Concluding observations on the combined third and fourth periodic report of Portugal*, 25 February 2014, CRC/C/PRT/CO/3 4, paras 25 26(a); and *Concluding observations on the combined third to fifth periodic reports of the Bolivarian Republic of Venezuela*, 13 October 2014, CRC/C/VEN/CO/3 5, paras 27 28(c).

particularly concerned that the vague definitions of propaganda used lead to the targeting and ongoing persecution of the country's LGBTI community, including through abuse and violence, in particular against underage LGBTI rights activists.[26]

It was recommended that Russia repeal its laws prohibiting propaganda of homosexuality, as well as ensure that LGBTI children and children from LGBTI families are not subjected to any forms of discrimination by raising the public's awareness of equality and non-discrimination on the basis of sexual orientation and gender identity.[27]

First and foremost, it is considered unacceptable that states have legislation prohibiting so-called unconventional sexual relationships, which may even be seen as encouraging violence against children and others belonging to the groups mentioned in the quote. However, abolishing the law is not sufficient, there is also a need to change the attitude of the public through awareness-raising.

To the Holy See in 2014, the issue of discrimination against these children was similarly highlighted.[28] It was seen as a consequence of past statements and declarations by the Catholic Church on homosexuality, contributing to social stigma and violence. To other states, LGBTI children and children from LGBTI families, if mentioned, were listed together with other children in vulnerable situations, such as children with disabilities or girl children in rural areas.[29]

For as many as 10 states examined in 2014, the Concluding Obsevations failed to mention any concern with regard to LGBTI children, those states being Croatia, Morocco, Fiji, India, Indonesia, Jordan, Saint Lucia, Congo, Germany, and Yemen. It is difficult to imagine that none of these states faces challenges in these areas.

The reasons why the Committee raises the issue with some states and not with others may vary. The questions to the state in the dialogue are usually based on information provided from various sources in addition to the report from the state itself. Most states are not likely to mention the issue of discrimination against LGBTI children in their report, and consequently, the Committee relies on civil society, national human rights institutions, or others in order to be made aware of the situation of this group of children. If there is no information on the issue, members may still ask questions about the situation and how it is dealt with by the state; however, unless the state acknowledges that there is a problem, it is difficult to formulate a concern. It may also be the case that members do not ask a question in spite of information being provided in supplementary reports. The reason for this, in some instances, may be that for some countries there are so many other pressing concerns with regard to children's rights. Practically speaking, there is a word limit to the length of UN treaty bodies' Concluding Observations, and the treaty bodies have been requested by the UN General Assembly to reduce their length further,[30] which inevitably means they will have to prioritise. Also, the issue may be simply overlooked, for which there is no excuse, except that there is a considerable amount of information with which the Committee members are supposed to be

---

[26] *Concluding observations: Russia* (n 25), para 24.
[27] Ibid, para 25.
[28] *Concluding observations: Holy See* (n 25), paras 25 26.
[29] Eg *Concluding observations: Kyrgyzstan* (n 25), paras 18 and 19.
[30] UNGA, *Strengthening and enhancing the effective functioning of the human rights treaty body system*, 9 April 2014, Res 68/268, as a result of the Treaty Body Strengthening process.

acquainted. However, the level of awareness of members on this issue is an important factor and could well be raised.

IV. The Right to Identity

Article 8(1) of the CRC gives the child the right to preserve his or her identity as recognised by law without unlawful interference. Nationality, name, and family relations are explicitly mentioned in the article as included in identity. However, the identity of a person is commonly understood in a broader sense as everything constituting the person's feeling of self and distinguishing the person from others. Gender identity and sexual orientation would be natural parts of identity in that sense.

The issue of including gender identity and sexual orientation within identity under article 8 have not been explicitly dealt with by the Committee. Yet, in General Comment No 14 on best interests, the child's identity is mentioned as one of the elements to be taken into account when assessing the child's best interests under article 3. In this regard, identity is defined, *inter alia*, sexual orientation.[31] Gender identity is not specifically mentioned, but there should be no reason to make a distinction there. In literature on children's rights both are mentioned as aspects covered by article 8,[32] meaning that transgender children have the same right to this aspect of their identity as children who have the traditional identity of male or female.

The article gives a right to 'preserve' one's identity. One may ask whether this excludes a right to have the physical expression of one's gender identity changed, since a change is more or less the opposite of preservation. However, the mental gender identity has already been established at the time when the physical change is sought, and if a physical change is necessary to confirm the child's mental gender, it can be seen as a preservation of the child's gender identity.[33] The right to identity in this sense may at least give a right to legal recognition of the child's new gender identity, a reasoning which is in line with the interpretation of ECHR article 8 in *Goodwin v UK*. Whether it gives a right to treatment in the form of surgery and/or hormonal treatment is less clear.

The obligation of the state is to 'respect' this right. At least, that is to say that one should be able to enjoy one's identity without interference from the state. Today, it is self-evident that this includes the right to be open about sexual orientation and gender identity and not have to live in secret. However, the article does not only imply a passive obligation of non-interference on the part of the state, the state also has positive obligations with regard to preserving the child's identity, such as birth registration. Furthermore, since a right to legal recognition of gender identity as confirmed through physical change may be said to follow from the right to preserve one's identity as mentioned above, it is hard to see how the state could 'respect' that right without performing the actual change in the registry.

Whether the child has a right under article 8 not only to legal recognition of a gender identity confirmation that has already taken place, but to the treatment necessary to achieve that confirmation as well, is another matter. It might seem to be a natural next

---

[31] *General Comment No 14* (n 17), para 55.
[32] Hodgkin and Newell, *Implementation Handbook for the Convention on the Rights of the Child*, CD ROM (UNICEF, 2007) 115; Melinda Jones, 'Adolescent Gender Identity and the Courts', in Michael Freeman (ed), *Children's Health and Children's Rights* (Martinus Nijhoff Publishers, 2006) 121, 148 at 129 regarding gender identity; and Sondrup (n 1) 39.
[33] Sondrup (n 8) 39.

step following from what is said above, and I shall not exclude the possibility that with a dynamic interpretation article 8 might be understood in that way.[34] However, the CRC in article 24 also gives the child a right to health and I would rather say that the right to identity may be used as an argument in a discussion of a right to treatment under this article.

V. Self-Determination of Gender

V.i. Introduction

The right to any sexual orientation, be it heterosexual, lesbian, gay, bisexual, or others, is not a question of 'determination' and decision-making but of being who you are. Naturally, there are decisions surrounding the consequences of one's sexual orientation, such as who to be with, where to go, and how to lead your life. The individual's right to make these decisions is implied in the right to identity under article 8 and the right to privacy under article 16 CRC.

The issue under scrutiny in this subsection is the right to make decisions determining one's gender or sex. The children concerned are trans- and intersex children. Different questions arise with regard to the two groups, and will be dealt with separately below.

The CRC does not give children a general right to self-determination. What it does stipulate is a right of the child to participate in decisions by expressing views and having them given due weight, confer article 12. A certain right to self-determination of gender identity may be implied in article 16 which gives the child a right to protection against interference with his or her privacy. The decisions under scrutiny here regarding determination of one's gender identity, certainly are of a private character and thus protected under article 16. This would probably mean that once children are capable of understanding the consequences of the existing alternatives, ie non-treatment and different forms of treatment with or without surgery that may be offered to them, they should have the final say.

However, to include in article 16 a claim on the state to provide medical treatment would be to take this state obligation a significant step forward. Although the obligation on the state is not merely to refrain from interfering but also to take active measures to protect the child from the interference by others, it is not clear that this would include a right to medical treatment at the expense of the government. I will rather seek the solution in a discussion of the right to health under CRC article 24.

V.ii. Trans-children: A right to medical intervention?

For trans-children the issue of self-determination within our current discussion implies the question of whether they have a right to medical treatment to have their physical sex changed in line with their gender identity. This question only arises if they want to undergo medical treatment in the form of surgery and/or hormonal treatment. Surgery cannot be carried out without hormonal treatment before and after the procedure, whereas hormonal treatment may be used alone, at least as long as the child is less than 18 years of age.

---

[34] According to Sondrup (n 8) 39, the child's right to identity implies a right to treatment, while the content of that right is to be found in the right to health and to development.

For those who do not want a physical change, the issue is the right to have their gender identity formally confirmed in official registries, or not to have a gender registered. The first has been dealt with under the right to identity above; the latter is outside the scope of this article as it is a wider question which is just as relevant for adults.

(a) The right to the highest attainable standard of health

To attempt to answer the question of whether trans-children have a right to medical treatment one has to look at the right of the child to health, which is formulated in article 24 as:

> 1. States Parties recognize the right of the child to the enjoyment of the highest attainable standard of health and to facilities for the treatment of illness and rehabilitation of health. States Parties shall strive to ensure that no child is deprived of his or her right of access to such health care services.
> 2. States Parties shall pursue full implementation of this right and, in particular, shall take appropriate measures: . . .
> (b) To ensure the provision of necessary medical assistance and health care to all children with emphasis on the development of primary health care;

It is hardly debatable that medical treatment of trans-children has to do with health. The WHO provides a wide definition of health as being 'a state of complete physical, mental and social well-being'.[35] In its General Comment No 15 on the right to health, the CRC Committee adheres to this definition, saying that this positive understanding of health provides the public health foundation for the general comment.[36]

Yet, concerning whether each individual child has a right to treatment, the wording of article 24 is not very strong. According to General Comment No 15, the notion of 'the highest attainable standard of health' takes into account both the child's biological, social, cultural, and economic preconditions and the state's available resources.[37] It goes on to say that:

> 24. Children's right to health contains a set of freedoms and entitlements. The freedoms, which are of increasing importance in accordance with growing capacity and maturity, include the right to control one's health and body, including sexual and reproductive freedom to make responsible choices. The entitlements include access to a range of facilities, goods, services and conditions that provide equality of opportunity for every child to enjoy the highest attainable standard of health.[38]

More specifically on 'facilities for the treatment of illness and rehabilitation of health', the General Comment states that children are entitled to quality health services, including treatment and rehabilitation. It adds that secondary and tertiary level care should also be made available, to the extent possible.[39] The services in question here would belong to those levels.

States are expected to provide health services to children to the maximum extent of their available resources (confer CRC article 4), meaning that the requirements would

---

[35]Constitution of the World Health Organization (entry into force 7 April 1948) 9 UNTS 3, § Preamble.
[36]*General Comment No 15* (n 16) para 4.
[37]Ibid, para 23.
[38]Ibid, para 24.
[39]Ibid, para 25.

be higher on a state like Norway in comparison to a developing state with few resources. In Norway, treatment of transpersons in order to obtain a physical confirmation of their gender has already been provided by the public health system for some time and is recognised as part of the health services.[40] Thus, the treatment is attainable and it is hard to see why trans-children should not be entitled to it, if it improves their health in the wide sense. For children in this situation, the right to the 'highest attainable standard' of health would not be realised unless they receive this treatment.

Consequently, in some countries there may a general right to this treatment. It should be made available as a form of medical treatment, and accessible to the individual. The issue then is whether an individual child may claim to undergo this kind of treatment. That is partly a question of who is to decide, and partly on what criteria the decision should be made.

(b) Who should consent?

Possible decision-makers concerning surgery and/or hormone treatment are the child, the parents, and the doctors. I shall come back to the doctors who will need to have a strong say with regard to medical considerations and first deal with the child and the parents.

As already mentioned, the CRC does not provide any clear rules on self-determination of the child. Inherent in the parents' responsibility for the child, they have a right and a duty to make decisions for the child when the child is too young or not sufficiently mature to make the decisions for him- or herself. Under article 12, the child has a right to express his or her views and to have them given due weight in the decision. Since the decision is such a personal one for the child, with great consequences for him or her both at present and in the future, the child's views must be given great weight. It is difficult to defend an intervention being made where the child does not want it. Thus the weight must amount to a right to veto a decision to perform a treatment. Formulated in a more legal way, the treatment cannot be carried out without the consent of the child. This may also be said to follow from the right to privacy under article 16.

If the child wants to undergo treatment, it is a question of whether the child's consent is sufficient or whether the consent of the parents is needed in addition. CRC article 5 holds that states shall respect the responsibilities, rights, and duties of parents to provide, in a manner consistent with the evolving capacities of the child, appropriate direction and guidance in the exercise by the child of the rights in the Convention. It recognises the role of the parents, but also expresses that the role changes over time, with the evolving capacities of the child.

General Comment 15 on the right to health, after referring to the evolving capacities of the child says that:

> States should review and consider allowing children to consent to certain medical treatments and interventions without the permission of a parent, caregiver, or guardian, such as HIV testing and sexual and reproductive health services, including education and guidance on sexual health, contraception and safe abortion.[41]

---

[40]More in Sondrup (n 8) 42 43, with reference to Peleg, Noam (2012), *The Child's Right to Development*, A thesis submitted to University College London for the degree of Doctor of Philosophy, November 2012, http://discovery.ucl.ac.uk/1384778/4/1384778 Peleg The Child Right to Development.pdf, 95 96 on the connection between article 24 and the right to development under article 6.

[41]*General Comment No 15* (n 16) para 31.

Here, the Committee indicates that it should be possible for children to obtain sexual and reproductive health services without parental consent. That would mean not having to ask their parents about the issue, but if the parents are informed and disagree, the idea is that the child's view in certain situations should be allowed to prevail. Medical treatment in order to confirm one's body with one's gender identity is not specifically mentioned, and this kind of rare and far-reaching treatment may not be included without further discussion. Yet, the statement suggests that the area of sexual and reproductive health is special. It concerns very personal and private questions where a child may not want to involve his or her parents, as well as being an area where parents may wish to close their eyes to their child's situation and not support the decision the child would like to make.

Different states offer different solutions for consent to medical treatment of children, and the Committee has not given any explicit preferences to these models, except the following in the General Comment on adolescent health:

> States parties need to ensure that specific legal provisions are guaranteed under domestic law, including with regard to setting a minimum age for . . . the possibility of medical treatment without parental consent. These minimum ages should be the same for boys and girls (article 2 of the Convention) and closely reflect the recognition of the status of human beings under 18 years of age as rights holders, in accordance with their evolving capacity, age and maturity[42] . . .

The highly personal and private character of the issue under consideration for the child speaks in favour of leaving the decision to the child when he or she is mature enough to have a firm desire to undergo treatment, based on an authentic feeling of his or her gender identity being different from his or her physical appearance. The child's right to identity supports the view that the child should have the final word with regard to treatment of a transgender condition.

However, the seriousness of the decision and its short and long term consequences may indicate that the responsibility for the decision should not be carried by the child alone, and that the consent of the parents in addition to that of the child would be needed until the child is sufficiently mature to consent independently. It follows from the General Comment quoted above that an age limit for the child to consent alone to medical treatment should be less than 18 years of age. If parental consent is required up to a certain age as indicated, there would be a need for an exception by law for situations where the parents withhold their consent in spite of the child's wish to undergo treatment and where parental wishes are at odds with the best interests of the child. Legislation would have to specify who should make that consideration. It might be the courts, or it could possibly be left to the doctors or a multidisciplinary team in the first instance to arbitrate the matter, but the process leaves open the possibility for the child and the parents to bring the matter before the courts.

(c) Medical assessment and best interests

Valid consent according to the law of the country in and of itself would still not be sufficient to undertake the treatment. In addition, an assessment would have to be made as to

---

[42]*General Comment No 4* (n 12).

whether a treatment would be medically justifiable in each individual case. This would be the role of the doctors. Doctors would also have to determine whether treatment is in the best interests of the child in accordance with CRC article 3, or, preferably, this determination should be tasked to a multidisciplinary team of professionals as recommended by General Comment No 14 on the best interests of the child.[43] The best interests assessment must comprise the child's own views, with due weight, the child's right to privacy, physical integrity and identity, the health and development of the child with and without the treatment and with different kinds of treatment, the risks implied in the treatment, any particular vulnerability of the child, and other elements that might be relevant for the individual child.[44] In these cases, where there are no legitimate competing considerations, the best interests of the child should not only be *a* primary consideration as stated in article 3 but *the* paramount consideration.

V.iii. Intersex children: The right to non-intervention until the child can consent

Intersex children are born with atypical sex characteristics (including genitals, gonads, and chromosome patterns), making it difficult at birth to determine whether they are girls or boys. For decades, the medical practice largely has been to decide, while the child is still an infant, whether it should become a girl or a boy. Genital surgery would then be administered with parental consent at this very early stage of the child's life and repeated at regular or irregular intervals through childhood. Parents have consented to this because doctors have persuaded them to think that the surgeries were necessary. These genital surgeries, which consist of removal of gonads, ovaries or testicles, are done for cosmetic reasons but are irreversible. Also, children have been exposed to forced excessive genital examinations and other medical treatments, in particular with hormones. Gradually, this medical practice has come under scrutiny due to the realisation that there is no evidence that children benefit positively from this. In fact, it is well-documented that children suffer both physically and mentally from early genital surgery.[45]

There are several problems with the medical practice described above in relation to children's rights. It constitutes an intervention into the physical integrity of the child, from which the child has a right to be protected unless such intervention is medically necessary. Since it has been established that this treatment is not medically necessary, at least at the

---

[43] *General Comment No 14* (n 17) para 94.

[44] Ibid and Sondrup (n 8) 68 78.

[45] L Brinkmann, K Schuetzmann and H Richter Appelt, 'Gender Assignment and Medical History of Individuals with Different Forms of Intersexuality: Evaluation of Medical Records and the Patients' Perspective' (2007) 4(4) *J of Sexual Med*, 964 980; UN Special Rapporteur on the right of everyone to the enjoyment of the highest attainable standard of physical and mental health, *Report to the General Assembly (on informed consent and right to health)* 2009, A/64/272, para 49; Swiss National Advisory Commission on Biomedical Ethics NEK CNE, *On the Management of Differences of Sex Development: Ethical Issues Relating to 'Intersexuality'* (Berne, 2012) 8 and 13; WHO, 'Sexual Health, Human Rights and the Law' (2015), last accessed 2 December 2015 at http://apps.who.int/iris/bitstream/10665/175556/1/9789241564984 eng.pdf, 26, para 3.4.9; Council of Europe, 'Human Rights and Intersex People', Issue paper published by the Council of Europe Commissioner for Human Rights (2015), last accessed 2 December 2015 at https://wcd.coe.int/com.instranet.InstraServlet?command= com.instranet.CmdBlobGet&Instranetimage=2768767&SecMode=1&DocId=2282716&Usage=2, 20 22; UNFE, 'Free and Equal, United Nations for LGBT Equality, Fact Sheet Intersex' (undated) last accessed 2 December 2015 at https://www.unfe.org/system/unfe 65 Intersex Factsheet ENGLISH.pdf; Swiss NGO Report 2014: *Intersex Genital Mutilations. Human Rights Violations of Children with Variations of Sex Anatomy*, compiled by: Zwischengeschlecht.org (Human Rights NGO), Intersex.ch (Peer Support Group) and Verein SI Selbsthilfe Intersexualität (Parents Peer Support Group), the Report was sub mitted as a shadow report to the CRC in 2014; and Katrina Karkazis and Wilma C Rossi, 'Ethics for the Pediatrician: Disorders of Sex Development: Optimizing Care' (2010) 31 *Pediatr*. Rev, e82 e85, e84, 1st column.

early stages of a child's life, the parents have no right to consent to it. Where there is no valid consent in performing the surgery or other forms of treatment, the medical doctors violate CRC article 19, which gives the child a right to be protected from all forms of violence.

Any medical intervention that is unnecessary at a given stage must be postponed as long as possible, preferably until the child understands what the procedure entails and can have a say in the matter in accordance with article 12 of the Convention. For most intersex children, the decision concerning potential medical intervention may be deferred to when the child is of sufficient age and maturity to have a well-reasoned view on whether or not to have treatment and on what kinds of treatment.[46] Indeed, as mentioned in the context of trans-children, the matter is so personal and serious that treatment should not be carried out without the child's consent.

If an intervention is undertaken at the earlier stage, despite the recommendations provided here, it will also constitute a violation of article 3 on the best interests of the child. Additionally, it would impose a gendered identity of the child contrary to article 8.

The practice as a whole also can be viewed as a harmful practice, and it has been termed 'intersex genital mutilations'. This was the position taken by the Committee on the Rights of the Child when for the first time dealing with the issue in its review of a country report.[47] Under harmful practices, to Switzerland, in January 2015, the Committee expressed its deep concern at:

> Cases of medically unnecessary surgical and other procedures on intersex children, without their informed consent, which often entail irreversible consequences and can cause severe physical and psychological suffering, and the lack of redress and compensation in such cases.[48]

The recommendation was as follows:

> (b) In line with the recommendations of the National Advisory Commission on Biomedical Ethics on ethical issues relating to intersexuality, ensure that no one is subjected to unnecess ary medical or surgical treatment during infancy or childhood, guarantee bodily integrity, autonomy and self determination to the children concerned, and provide families with inter sex children with adequate counselling and support.[49]

As appears from the concern, the surgery was still being practised by some doctors on infants and small children. The Swiss National Advisory Commission on Biomedical Ethics previously had made both timely and apt recommendations in 2012 with which the Swiss government did not comply. Adequate counselling and support is what parents need in the first place when their child is born intersex in order to make them understand that, with support, a child can live well with that condition until it is able

---

[46] Jones (n 32); and Swiss National Advisory Commission (n 45) 14. See also other references in previous footnote.

[47] The Committee could have raised this issue with Germany in January 2014 based on the report from the German Institute for Human Rights: *Suggested topics to be taken into account for the preparation of a list of issues by the Committee on the Rights of the Child on the implementation of the Convention on the Rights of the Child in Germany* (2013), last accessed 2 December 2015 at http://tbinternet.ohchr.org/Treaties/CRC/Shared%20Documents/DEU/INT CRC IFN DEU 15945 E. pdf, para 2(b). However, the issue was overlooked, for which the Committee has later been rightfully criticised by the Institute (oral exchange).

[48] CRC Committee, *Concluding observations on the combined second to fourth periodic reports of Switzerland*, 26 February 2015, CRC/C/CHE/CO/2 4, para 42(b).

[49] Ibid, para 43(b).

to make a decision itself. The child needs medical and other forms of counselling during childhood and in particular when a possible decision is to be taken at a later stage.

The human rights of intersex persons were raised by the CEDAW Committee in its Concluding Observations to Germany in 2009; however, the Committee limited itself to expressing regret that the government had not entered into a dialogue with relevant organisations.[50] To Costa Rica in 2011, the same Committee communicated the concern that some intersex women were victims of abuses and mistreatment by health services providers and law enforcement officials, without further specification.[51]

The first time that the practices of routine surgical alterations in intersex children were raised explicitly in a treaty body's review of a state party was by the CAT Committee to Germany in 2011. That Committee made some quite detailed recommendations which may be used for a comparison with those of the CRC Committee to Switzerland:

> a) Ensure the effective application of legal and medical standards following the best practices of granting informed consent to medical and surgical treatment of intersex people, including full information, orally and in writing, on the suggested treatment, its justification and alternatives;
> b) Undertake investigation of incidents of surgical and other medical treatment of intersex people without effective consent and adopt legal provisions in order to provide redress to the victims of such treatment, including adequate compensation;
> c) Educate and train medical and psychological professionals on the range of sexual, and related biological and physical, diversity; and
> d) Properly inform patients and their parents of the consequences of unnecessary surgical and other medical interventions for intersex people.[52]

Not surprisingly, the CRC's Concluding Observations (see above) focus more explicitly on children. They also emphasise more clearly the 'bodily integrity, autonomy and self-determination' of the children concerned.[53] While the CAT Committee's recommendations recognise the need for a properly informed consent, it is less clear who should consent and the role of the child itself. On the other hand, the CRC Committee may well include recommendations like those in (b) and (c) of the CAT Concluding Observations, which hold that a state must undertake investigation of such incidents and provide redress to the victims, including compensation, as well as train medical and psychological professionals on the diversity in this field.

VI. Discussion and Conclusion

VI.i. Recent UN initiatives

The OHCHR, in 2011, submitted a report to the Human Rights Council on violence and discrimination against individuals based on their sexual orientation and gender identity, which was updated in 2015.[54] In July 2013, the High Commissioner launched UN Free

---

[50] *Concluding observations of the Committee on the Elimination of Discrimination against Women: Germany,* 12 February 2009, CEDAW/C/DEU/CO/6, para 61.

[51] *Concluding observations of the Committee on the Elimination of Discrimination against Women: Costa Rica,* 2 August 2011, CEDAW/C/CRI/CO/5 6; *Concluding observations to Costa Rica,* para 40.

[52] *Concluding observations of the Committee against Torture: Germany,* 12 December 2011, CAT/C/DEU/CO/5, para 20.

[53] *Concluding observations to Switzerland* (n 48), para 43(b).

[54] OHCHR, *Report of the Office of the United Nations High Commissioner for Human Rights on violence and discrimination against individuals based on their sexual orientation and gender identity* (2011) A/HRC/19/41; and OHCHR, *Report of the*

& Equal (www.unfe.org), which is a global education campaign to combat homophobia and transphobia.[55] It is estimated that it has thus far reached more than a billion people around the world through events and via traditional and social media.[56]

Two joint statements were issued in 2015, one of them on the recognition and protection of the rights of young LGBT and intersex people, issued by the Committee on the Rights of the Child, several UN Special Rapporteurs, the Special Representative on Violence against Children, and regional bodies for the International Day against Homophobia, Biphobia and Transphobia, in May 2015.[57] The second statement, issued in September 2015 by a number of UN entities including UNICEF, UN Women, OHCHR, UNODC, and the WHO, concerns ending violence and discrimination against lesbian, gay, bisexual, transgender, and intersex people.

The right of transgender persons to self-determination, including a possible right to medical treatment, has received less attention from what I can see. It was mentioned in the OHCHR report 2011:

> In many countries, transgender persons face particular difficulties in their access to health care. Gender reassignment therapy, where available, is often prohibitively expensive and State funding or insurance coverage is rarely available. Health care professionals are often insensitive to the needs of transgender persons and lack necessary professional training.[58]

In 2015, the OHCHR raised the issue in the same way, bar the mention of state funding or insurance.[59]

The following paragraph in the joint statement of May 2015, while general in its formulation may be of particular relevance to transgender children:

> The health and well being of all children and young adults must be protected, including through ensuring access to non discriminatory health services and comprehensive sexuality education, and by protecting the rights of all children and young adults to their identity, autonomy, and physical and psychological integrity.

VI.ii. The Committee on the Rights of the Child – ways forward

In this article, I have highlighted the need for a children's perspective on issues concerning LGBTI children, through an active use of the CRC and with the Committee on the Rights of the child is an important actor. However, my presentation of the Committee's work has shown that it could be more consistent in raising these issues with states. This is not only relevant to the issue of discrimination and violence against LGBTI children, but also regarding violations of intersex and transgender children's right to self-determination. If there is no information in the reports themselves, either from the state or from other actors like NGOs or national human rights institutions, the Committee should raise the

---

Office of the United Nations High Commissioner for Human Rights on discrimination and violence against individuals based on their sexual orientation and gender identity (2015) A/HRC/29/23.

[55]UNFE (n 45).

[56]OHCHR (2015) (n 54), para 6.

[57]Joint statement Discriminated and made vulnerable: Young LGBT and intersex people need recognition and protection of their rights by the Committee and other UN and regional bodies for the International Day against Homophobia, Biphobia and Transphobia, 17 May 2015, http://www.ohchr.org/EN/NewsEvents/Pages/DisplayNews.aspx?NewsID=15941&LangID= E#sthash.aiEvQmvg.dpu

[58]OHCHR (2011) (n 54), para 57.

[59]OHCHR (2015) (n 54), para 54.

issue in the pre-session with the latter actors. It is too late to raise it in the dialogue with the state, because information about the situation of those children is needed in advance as a basis for discussing it in a meaningful way with the state and to possibly make a recommendation.

The Committee might also be more consistent in the way the issues concerning LGBTI children are dealt with in Concluding Observations, when included. True, the concerns and recommendations have to be concrete and specific for each country; on the other hand, if the situation is similar, the recommendations should not differ too much. There is a fine balance to strike between these two considerations; however, the main point is perhaps to be conscious about what we have recommended to other states in this regard.

Concerning intersex children, in addition to recommendations like those made to Switzerland, the Committee may include the training of professionals as well as the need for investigation of violations and redress to the victims. As for transgender children's right to self-determination and a possible right to medical treatment, probably more could be done by the Committee in raising the issue with civil society actors and the states.

LGBTI children have received increasing attention by the Committee on the Rights of the Child recently and more can be done. However, the main responsibility lies with the states, and I shall end with a paragraph from the joint statement of May 2015[60] on what is expected of them:

> We call on States to comply with their obligation to respect, protect and fulfill the rights of all children and young adults without discrimination, to ensure that lesbian, gay, bisexual, trans gender and intersex children and young people are consulted and participate in discussions on policies and laws that impact on their rights. We also call on human rights and child rights institutions to fulfil their mandate and play their part in protecting them from violence and discrimination.

---

[60] Joint statement (n 57).

Legal Gender Meets Reality: A Socio-Legal Children's Perspective

Anniken Sørlie

PhD Candidate, Department of Public and International Law, University of Oslo, Norway

ABSTRACT
Under Norwegian law, the registration of children at birth is regarded as the minimum guarantee for their enjoyment of children's rights. But how does the legal gender assigned at registration impact on gender non-conforming children's and adolescents' experiences? How does the regulation of gender assignment under Norwegian law chime with the human rights of gender non-conforming children, particularly the right to respect for one's private life and non-discrimination? Are there any possibilities for children to change their legal gender? This article gives voice to the experiences, challenges, and wishes of gender non-conforming children. The aim is to show how legal gender intertwines with feelings of recognition, self-confidence, self-respect, and self-esteem.

I. Introduction

> Mum, would you love me if I had short hair? Mum, do you love me no matter what? No matter what I wear? Even though I won't wear a dress any more?[1]

Daniel, who at birth was registered as a girl, asked these questions to prepare his mother for his prospective coming-out – a process which he began by hinting at his gender identity. Daniel was tired of living his life as somebody he was not. If he were to go on living, he needed to live as Daniel. He told his mother this explicitly some years later – at the age of 16. Her unconditional support came as a great relief. From his father, he experienced misrecognition – in his father's eyes, Daniel was still his little princess. When telling his father, he started the conversation by saying 'Dad, please don't hate me. I want to be happy.' This is telling of the fear of misrecognition and rejection many gender non-conforming children and adolescents feel. Unfortunately, largely due to the gender norms of the society in which we live, this fear is often well-founded.

Judith Butler writes that a norm is neither a rule nor a law. 'A norm operates within social practices as the implicit standard of normalization.'[2] It is usually difficult to read. The norm governs the domain of the social, and determines which practices and actions can be recognisable.[3] We live our lives in societies where gender norms, religious

---

[1] Informant 'Daniel', interviewed in 2015. I refer to the informants in accordance with their expressed gender identity. All names are pseudonyms. The translations are my own.
[2] Judith Butler, *Undoing Gender* (Routledge 2004) 41.

norms, and norms on sexuality intertwine. These norms impact on our capabilities and experiences, though norms are neither laws nor rules. Law, however, is never inseparable from prevailing norms. In democracies, law emanates from the citizens who navigate their lives amid these norms. It is within this context that our identities are formed. For transgender people, identity formation takes place alongside provisions on legal gender. The norms on which the provisions are based may influence whether or not transgender children gain parental support, and consequently, their ability to freely shape their identity. Lack of support can lead to disputes between parents and the child, where the former's rights conflict with the rights of the child. Martha Albertson Fineman argues that institutions like the family, school, and community, where children are supposed to build their resilience, are failing young LGBT[4] people. The failure arises from a structural disadvantaging of children, while family privacy and parental rights are valorised. Children are an especially vulnerable group in society. An LGBT child experiences a double vulnerability as both a child and an LGBT person.[5] Being transgender too can be challenging. Transgender people face widespread discrimination and harassment. In 2015, a Swedish inquiry into the health status of transgender people revealed that more than half of the respondents reported that they had been subjected to abusive treatment or behaviour at least once in the last three months.[6]

The legal gender of Norwegian citizens is marked by a gender-specific national identity number, which is assigned shortly after birth. While most Norwegians hardly ever notice that their national identity number gives information about their gender, for those children who experience a mismatch between their legal gender and their gender identity, their legal gender is a challenge. In Norway, as in many other countries, the LGBT movement has demanded an end to requirements for legal gender recognition, which they consider intrusive, such as the diagnosis of transsexualism and the irreversible removal of reproductive organs. In June 2015, the Ministry of Health and Care Services finally published a consultation paper for the first Norwegian law on legal gender recognition.[7] The law proposal suggests abolishing the existing requirements for medical interventions for legal gender recognition.[8] According to the proposal, children over 16 can apply individually to change their legal gender, whereas children between seven and 16 require parental consent.

The aim of this article is to discuss the existing and proposed Norwegian laws and regulations in the light of the lived realities of gender non-conforming children. The article aims to show how certain identities are accepted, while others are misrecognised by law, and how the law thus determines whose identities can obtain full recognition and who can freely shape their identity. It gives examples of how the law's inclusion or exclusion of identities are experienced and perceived by transgender young people. Like Jill Marshall, I see law as a key element in an individual's identity:

---

[3]Butler (n 2) 42.

[4]Lesbian, gay, bisexual, and transgender.

[5]Martha Albertson Fineman, 'Vulnerability, Resilience, and LGBT Youth' (2014) 23 *Temp Pol & Civ Rts L Rev* 307.

[6]Folkhälsomyndigheten, 'Hälsan och hälsans bestämningsfaktorer för transpersoner: En rapport om hälsoläget bland trans personer i Sverige' (2015) 30.

[7]The Ministry of Health and Care Services, 'Høringsnotat: Forslag til lov om endring av juridisk kjønn' (15/2180, 25 June 2015).

[8]The Norwegian government will abolish medical requirements for legal gender recognition. The Ministry of Health and Care Services, 'Ny rapport om juridisk kjønn' (10 April 2015) https://www.regjeringen.no/no/aktuelt/ny rapport om juridisk kjonn/id2405435/.

Law defines; it both includes and excludes entities as human beings to be protected by human rights law. It allows, permits, protects and provides; it also recognises, misrecognises and ignores identities. In doing so, it conditions the formation of certain types of identity. Human rights law does this particularly by purporting to translate moral norms of human freedom and human dignity into legal rights given to human beings by virtue of their species … While somehow believing we are making our subjectivity and freely choosing our identities, we are increasingly being obliged to live in certain conformed ways, pushing out identities that do not fit with what is acceptable.[9]

However, unlike Marshall's book, this article takes gender non-conforming, or transgender, children's lived experiences as its starting point. Drawing inspiration from the feminist jurisprudence developed by Tove Stand Dahl, I approach these experiences through an integrated analysis of philosophical, doctrinal, and legal sources.[10] The narratives give rise to a series of questions regarding the relationship between legal gender assignment and gender non-conforming children's self-confidence, self-respect, and self-esteem. According to the philosopher Axel Honneth, these forms of self-relation are fundamental to the formation of an individual's identity and to self-realisation. These different forms of self-relation are attainable through participation and recognition in the private sphere, the legal sphere, and the social sphere. All are regarded as ontogenetic developmental stages in achieving a good life. The forms of self-relations can only be attained through intersubjective recognition.[11] With this as the theoretical basis for the discussion, I investigate how Norwegian law impacts on the experiences of gender non-conforming children. To do this, I present the stories of three young transgender people. The main research questions are how legal gender assignment and change of legal gender are regulated under Norwegian law. This, consequently, begs the question: how can this regulation fit with the human rights of gender non-conforming children, particularly the right to respect for one's private life and non-discrimination? What are their narratives, and how can we understand their narratives in the light of Honneth's theory? Finally, how can his theory be applied to render experiences relating to legal gender visible, and therefore also to contribute to the human rights discussion?

Following this introduction, section II unpacks the philosophical and legal framework, on which the later analysis builds. In section III, I describe the methodology used in the article. In part IV, I present and analyse the narratives categorised in Honneth's three spheres of recognition: (1) the private sphere, (2) the legal sphere, and (3) the social sphere. This division demonstrates the complexity of recognition, and how the spheres interrelate. In section V, I discuss two alternatives to legal gender by drawing on the analysis in the previous sections.

II. Theoretical and Human Rights Framework

This section provides the backdrop for the analysis of the relationship between empirical sources, describing gender non-conforming lived realities, the philosophical theory of recognition, and international and national law on the right to dignity and gender identity.

---

[9]Jill Marshall, *Human Rights Law and Personal Identity* (Routledge, 2014) 18, 19.

[10]See, eg, Tove Stang Dahl, 'Mot en fortolkende rettsteori' (1988) 101 *Tidsskrift for Rettsvitenskap* 54.

[11]Axel Honneth, *Kampf um Anerkennung: Zur moralischen Grammatik sozialer Konflikte* (Suhrkamp Verlag Frankfurt am Main, 1992).

I start with Honneth's theory of recognition before presenting the human rights framework applied in this article. I then give an overview of Norwegian law and practice on assignment and change of legal gender. In addition, drawing on the presentation in II. ii, I briefly outline how Norwegian administrative practice on legal gender recognition is contrary to the human rights of transgender people.

II.i *Theory of recognition*

Axel Honneth explicates the formal conditions for human self-realisation in his main work *Kampf um Anerkennung. Zur moralischen Grammatik sozialer Konflikte*.[12] In this work, he refines the concept of recognition by reconstructing Hegel's model for recognition by reference to the object-relations theory of psychoanalyst Donald W Winnicott and the social psychology of philosopher, sociologist, and psychologist Georg Herbert Meads.

Human beings are, according to Axel Honneth, dependent on mutual recognition in order to develop their personal identity.[13] The development of self-confidence, self-respect, and self-esteem are necessary for self-realisation and identity-formation. These modes of practical relation to oneself are regarded as ontogenetic developmental stages in the attainment of the good life, or for successful human self-realisation. These positive forms of self-relation correspond to three different spheres in modern societies: (1) the private sphere, (2) the legal or judicial sphere, and (3) the social or solidarity sphere. An individual can acquire the three basic kinds of self-relation – self-confidence, self-respect, and self-esteem – through participation in each of these spheres and by establishing mutual recognition in them. Each sphere consists of intersubjective relations of recognition, where central aspect of our humanness is recognised.

The first form of recognition, love, and development of self-confidence, constitutes the condition for participation in intersubjective relations. This is the first ontogenetic stage. According to Honneth, self-confidence can only be developed in personal relations (that is, the private sphere), such as the relation between parent and child and through friendship. Emotional safety is the foundation and makes the individual capable of developing other forms of self-respect.[14] Secondly, self-respect is, on the other hand, developed through universal rights and the individual's capacity to claim rights. Recognition through rights secures the autonomy of an individual. To be a possessor of rights means that the individual is respected by others. The highest level of self-respect is only attainable when a person is recognised as an individual with an autonomous legal personality.[15] Thirdly, self-esteem can be attained if an individual has the feeling that they are regarded as an important contributor to society, for example because their way of life and individual skills are valued.[16] This is so, according to Honneth: 'For it is only due to the cumulative acquisition of basic self-confidence, of self-respect, and of self-esteem – provided, one after another, by the experience of those

---

[12]Ibid.

[13]Rasmus Willig, *Axel Honneth: Behovet for Anerkendelse: En Tekstsamling* (Mogens Chrom Jacobsen (trs) and Rasmus Willig (ed), Hans Reitzels Forlag, 2003) 12.

[14]Axel Honneth, *Kamp om Anerkjennelse: Om de sosiale konfliktenes moralske grammatikk* (Lars Holm Hansen (tr), Pax Forlag, 2007) 104 116.

[15]Honneth, *Kamp om Anerkjennelse* (n 14) 117 129.

[16]Ibid, 138.

three forms of recognition – that a person can come to see himself or herself, uncon-ditionally, as both an autonomous and an individuated being and to identify with his or her goals and desires.'[17]

II.ii *The right to gender identity and non-discrimination under international human rights law*

The European Court of Human Rights (ECtHR) has played an important role in increas-ing the protection of the human rights of LGBTI persons. In the Court's early case law on the legal recognition of transgender persons' gender identity, a dissenting opinion by Judge Martens points out that:

> The principle which is basic in human rights and which underlies the various specific rights
> spelled out in the Convention is respect for human dignity and human freedom. Human
> dignity and human freedom imply that a man should be free to shape himself and his fate
> in the way that he deems best fits his personality.[18]

Human dignity serves as a common denominator between the theory of recognition and the right of transgender people to legal recognition. Human dignity is the basis of human rights as well as a principle for the interpretation and application of specific human rights.[19] Numerous international human rights conventions refer to human dignity either in specific provisions or preambles, or by referring to other conventions, which explicitly address the dignity of all human beings.[20] Paolo G Carozza asserts that, in the context of how human dignity is applied in international human rights law, human dignity is both an ontological claim and a normative and meta-legal principle, which are interrelated. It is an ontological claim concerning the status of persons. All persons have 'an equal and inherent moral value or worth.' As a normative and meta-legal principle it affirms the entitlement of all persons to have this worth protected or respected by others.

The normative content of human dignity must be seen in relation to substantive rights. Carozza identifies four main principles which sheds light on the normative content of human dignity: (1) integrity, (2) equality and non-discrimination, (3) satisfaction of basic material needs, and (4) personal autonomy.[21] A closer look at select case law from the ECtHR demonstrates how the principles of integrity, non-discrimination, and personal autonomy are essential to the establishment of the right to gender identity. The European Convention on Human Rights (ECHR) applies to everyone – including children. The right to respect for one's private life in article 8 includes the right to recog-nition of one's gender identity, or the freedom to define one's gender. The ECtHR has set

---

[17] Axel Honneth, *The Struggle for Recognition: The Grammar of Social Conflicts* (Joel Anderson (trs), Cambridge, Polity, 1995) 169.

[18] *Cossey v The United Kingdom*, judgment, app no 10843/84, 27 September 1990, dissenting opinion of Judge Martens, [2.7].

[19] Paolo G Carozza, 'Human Dignity', in Dinah Shelton (ed), *The Oxford Handbook of International Human Rights Law* (Oxford University Press, 2013) 346.

[20] See, for example, Universal Declaration of Human Rights (adopted 10 December 1948 UNGA Res 217 A(III) (UDHR) article 1. Convention for the Protection of Human Rights and Fundamental Freedoms (European Convention on Human Rights, as amended) (ECHR) and Convention on the Rights of the Child (adopted 20 November 1989) United Nations, Treaty Series, vol 1577, p 3 (CRC) refer to the UDHR.

[21] Carozza (n 19) 346, 351 356.

forth this right from 2002 onwards.[22] The principles of autonomy, identity, and integrity are essential features of personal freedom.[23]

The struggle for the right to gender identity, or recognition of one's gender identity, began in 1974[24] when the first case was referred to the European Court of Human Rights. The issue remains unresolved, both at the international and national level. Jill Marshall's analysis of case law from the ECtHR shows that article 8 of the Convention has evolved from a right to respect for one's private life into a right to personal identity.[25] Michael O'Flaherty says: 'the cases are not about any effort of states to prohibit forms of gender identity choices. Instead, they address the positive obligation on the state to take the administrative actions, such as amendment of identity documents, that are necessary for the affected individuals to live in their changed gender identity.'[26] According to Marshall, the Court has taken a wide and evolving interpretation of ECHR. Its jurisprudence now provides freedom to identity-formation and to live as one chooses, as long as it does not harm others.[27] When ruling in favour of the applicant in the case of *Christine Goodwin v The United Kingdom*, the Court stated that:

> the very essence of the Convention is respect for human dignity and human freedom. Under Article 8 of the Convention in particular, where the notion of personal autonomy is an important principle underlying the interpretation of its guarantees, protection is given to the personal sphere of each individual, including the right to establish details of their identity as individual human beings ... [28]

In addition, the Court finds 'that society may reasonably be expected to tolerate a certain inconvenience to enable individuals to live in dignity and worth in accordance with the sexual identity chosen by them at great personal cost.'[29] The ECtHR concludes that no significant factors of public interest weighed against the applicant's interest in obtaining legal recognition of her gender identity.[30] Similarly, in the case of *van Kück v Germany*, the Court points out that 'the applicant's freedom to define herself as a female person, [is] one of the most basic essentials of self-determination.'[31] Furthermore, the ECtHR has, in several rulings, addressed the notion that the concept of a private life 'covers the physical and psychological integrity of a person'.[32] Similarly, the Court relies on the principles of personal development, autonomy, and integrity when finding that the refusal by a Turkish court to authorise gender confirmation treatment for the appellant because he was not permanently unable to procreate, constitutes a violation of article 8.[33]

---

[22]See *Christine Goodwin v The United Kingdom*, judgment (Grand Chamber), app no 28957/95, 11 July 2002; *van Kück v Germany*, judgment (Chamber), app no 35968/97, 12 June 2003; *Grant v The United Kingdom*, judgment (Chamber), app no 32570/03, 23 May 2006; *L v Lithuania*, judgment (Chamber), app no 27527/03, 11 September 2007; *Hämäläinen v Finland*, judgment (Grand Chamber), app no 37359/09, 16 July 2014; *YY v Turkey*, judgment (Chamber), app no 14793/08, 10 March 2015.

[23]Jill Marshall, *Personal Freedom Through Human Rights Law?: Autonomy, Identity and Integrity under the European Conven tion on Human Rights* (International Studies in Human Rights, Vol 98, Martinus Nijhoff, 2009) 2.

[24]*X v The Federal Republic of Germany*, app no 6699/74.

[25]Marshall, *Personal Freedom Through Human Rights Law?* (n 23) 103 122.

[26]Michael O'Flaherty, 'Sexual Orientation and Gender Identity', in Daniel Moeckli, Sangeeta Shah and Sandesh Sivakumaran (eds) *International Human Rights Law* (Oxford University Press, 2010) 334.

[27]Marshall, *Personal Freedom Through Human Rights Law?* (n 23) 120 121.

[28]Christine Goodwin (n 22) [90].

[29]Ibid, [91].

[30]Ibid, [93].

[31]Van Kück (n 22) [73].

[32]Ibid, [69].

[33]*YY* (n 22) [122], [102], [57], [65].

Even though the ECtHR has stated that 'the prohibition of discrimination under Article 14 of the Convention duly covers questions related to sexual orientation and gender identity',[34] other human rights bodies have so far addressed the principle of non-discrimination in relation to transgender people more fully than the Court. In 2009, the Committee on Economic, Social and Cultural Rights wrote in General Comment No 20 that 'gender identity is recognized as among the prohibited grounds of discrimination'.[35] The Committee on the Rights of the Child stresses that '[s]tates parties must address discrimination against vulnerable or marginalized groups of children, such as ... transgender or transsexual ... and make proactive efforts to ensure that such children are assured their right to protection on an equal basis with all other children.'[36] Further, the Committee states that gender identity falls within the scope of 'other status' in article 2 of the Convention on the Rights of the Child.[37] The UN High Commissioner for Human Rights recommends that states address discrimination by '[e]nsuring that anti-discrimination legislation includes sexual orientation and gender identity among prohibited grounds, and also protects intersex persons from discrimination'.[38]

II.iii *The legal framework of legal gender assignment at birth and change of legal gender*

Pursuant to article 7 CRC and article 24(2) of the International Covenant on Civil and Political Rights (ICCPR), every child shall be registered immediately after birth. The registration recognises the child's existence, its status under the law, and ensures the full enjoyment of children's fundamental rights.[39] The Human Rights Committee (CCPR) states that the main purpose of birth registration is 'to reduce the danger of abduction, sale of or traffic in children, or of other types of treatment that are incompatible with the enjoyment of the rights provided for in the Covenant.'[40] States are under an obligation to make registration compulsory under domestic law to secure its efficiency. The obligation pertains to both parents and the relevant administrative authorities.[41]

In Norway this registration takes the form of the assignment of a mandatory national identity number for all people resident in the country.[42] The identity number consists of 11 digits, which include the holder's date of birth. The ninth digit differs for legal males and legal females – an even number denotes female and an odd number denotes

---

[34]*Identoba and others v Georgia*, judgment (Chamber), app no 73235/12, 12 May 2015 [96].

[35]UN Committee on Economic, Social and Cultural Rights, 'General Comment No 20: Non discrimination in economic, social and cultural rights' (2009) UN Doc E/C.12/GC/20 [32].

[36]UN Committee on the Rights of the Child, 'General comment no 13: The right of the child to freedom from all forms of violence' (2011) UN Doc CRC/C/GC/13 [60], [72(g)]. For more about the work of the Committee on the Rights of the Child in relation to LGBTI children, see Kirsten Sandberg 'The Rights of LGBTI Children and Children with LGBTI Parents under the Convention on the Rights of the Child' in this issue.

[37]Committee on the Rights of the Child, 'General comment no 15: The right of the child to the enjoyment of the highest attainable standard of health (art. 24)' (2013) UN Doc CRC/C/GC/15 [8].

[38]UNHCR 'Report of the Office of the High Commissioner for Human Rights, Discrimination and Violence Against Individuals Based on their Sexual Orientation and Gender Identity' (4 May 2015) UN Doc A/HRC/29/23 [79(c)].

[39]Rachel Hodgkin and Peter Newell, *Implementation Handbook for the Convention on the Rights of the Child* (United Nation's Children Fund, 2007) 98.

[40]UN Human Rights Committee, General Comment No 17 Rights of the Child (Article 24), (29 September 1989) [7].

[41]Njål Høstmælingen, 'Sivile rettigheter og friheter' in Høstmælingen, Kjørholt and Sandberg (eds), *Barnekonvensjonen: Barns Rettigheter i Norge* (Universitetsforlaget, 2012) 120.

[42]Act No 01 of 16 January 1970 on the Population Register, 4.

male.[43] The number indicates a person's legal gender. The allocation of the national identity number shows that the individual is entered in the legally established Norwegian Population Register.[44]

The Norwegian registration of legal gender is in accordance with the recommendations of the Committee on the Rights of the Child, which identifies sex as one of the basic details that should be registered.[45] Allocation of national identity numbers is based on the information given – normally by a midwife or a doctor – on the Norwegian birth notification form, which offers the options boy, girl, or unknown. Children who are registered with an unclear gender, are assigned female legal gender.[46] On the basis of this assignment, all newborns are assigned a gender-specific national identity number once the Norwegian Tax Administration receives the birth notification form.[47]

Through the allocation of a national identity number, all individuals are categorised at an early stage of life within the binary gender model. One's legal existence begins with this number, and ends with the entry of the identity number in the death register. However, pursuant to Norwegian administrative regulations dating back to 1979, the possibility to change legal gender exists. The national identity number can be changed if 'gender status' is changed.[48] The term 'gender status' is defined by neither law, preparatory work, nor other sources of law.[49] Yet, according to administrative practice, change of legal gender requires complete gender confirmation treatment. Change of legal gender, which is administered by the Norwegian Tax Administration, requires the diagnosis of F64.0 transsexualism, real-life experience of at least 12 months' duration, hormone treatment, and surgical removal of testis or ovaries. During the period of real-life experience, transgender people are required to live full-time as their preferred gender. In 2014, 500 people were registered as patients at the National Treatment Unit for Transsexualism – among them 110 children. The implicit age limit for change of legal gender is 18 years, given the surgical requirement. The old national identity number is kept in the national population register after the new one has been allocated. The old number refers to the new number and vice versa.[50]

Norwegian administrative practice on legal gender recognition is problematic in relation to numerous human rights. In 2013 the UN Special Rapporteur on Torture stated that interventions such as the involuntary sterilisation of transgender people, 'always amount at least to inhuman and degrading treatment ... and they are always prohibited by international law.'[51] To enjoy legal recognition in accordance with

---

[43]Forskrift om folkeregistrering (FOR 2007 11 09 1268) 2 2.

[44]Act No 01 of 16 January 1970, 1.

[45]Hodgkin and Newell (n 39) 101.

[46]See form 'Melding om fødsel'; Act No 7 of 8 April 1981 relating to Children s 1; Act No 64 of 2 July 1999 relating to Health Personnel etc, 35. Email to the author from Harald Hammer in the Norwegian Tax Administration 1 April 2015.

[47]FOR 2007 11 09 1268, 3 1.

[48]Forskrifter om Føringen og Ordningen av Folkeregistrene (FOR 1979 11 26 9) 58; Forskrift om Folkeregistrering (FOR 1994 03 04 161) s 31; Forskrift om Folkeregistrering (FOR 2007 11 09 1268) 2 2.

[49]For a discussion of the legal basis of the requirements, see Anniken Sørlie, 'Retten til kjønnsidentitet som menneskeret tighet: Kan norsk forvaltningspraksis' krav om irreversibel sterilisering ved endring av fødselsnummer forsvares?' (Kvin nerettslig skriftserie nr 90 2013 University of Oslo).

[50]The Norwegian Directorate of Health, 'Rett til rett kjønn   Helse til alle kjønn: Utredning av vilkår for endring av juridisk kjønn og organisering av helsetjenester for personer som opplever kjønnsinkongruens og kjønnsdysfori' (2015) 36, 43 47, 54, 65.

[51]UNGA 'Report of the Special Rapporteur on torture and other cruel, inhuman or degrading treatment or punishment, Juan E Méndez' (1 February 2013) UN Doc A/HRC/22/53 [81], [76].

one's gender identity falls within the core provision of article 8.[52] To be excluded from legal gender recognition because one fails to fulfil the medical requirements, or to be compelled to undergo surgery one does not desire, encroach on this right. As several domestic courts have concluded, medical requirements violate the right to respect one's private life and physical integrity. In 2011, the German Constitutional Court ruled that gender reassignment surgery is in breach of the right to self-determination and physical integrity.[53] Similarly, in 2012, the Swedish Administrative Court of Appeal in Stockholm ruled that the Swedish sterilisation requirement constituted a forcible intrusion into an individual's physical integrity.[54] The interference cannot be justified in light of article 8(2). In addition, as regards the Norwegian case, the practice lacks sufficient legal basis to justify interference with the right to respect for one's private life.[55]

As mentioned in the introduction, to bring Norwegian administrative practice in line with the human rights obligations of the Norwegian state, the legal proposal suggests that a change in legal gender shall be done without medical interventions or diagnoses. Instead, a feeling of belonging to a gender different from that assigned at birth is required. The only 'proof' of this is by self-declaration. The proposal thus suggests that children should be able to change their legal gender. Children over the age of 16 could demand to change their legal gender independently, whereas children between the ages of seven and 16 could demand legal gender change if parental consent is gained.[56] The proposal demonstrates one of the many different ways in which to implement the human rights of transgender people. The different alternatives ensure the fundamental principles of autonomy, dignity, integrity, and non-discrimination for all human beings to varying extents. Drawing on the analysis in section IV, I discuss alternative ways of incorporating human rights principles into Norwegian law in section V.

III. Linking Ethical, Legal, and Empirical Dimensions

As already mentioned, Professor Tove Stang Dahl has provided three main methodological sources for the study of the relationship between gender and law: the ethical, the empirical, and the doctrinal.[57] This approach, which takes the lived realities of women as the starting point for examinations of the relationship between gender-neutral law and gendered realities, has inspired me to give voice to vulnerable individuals at the cutting edge of this dilemma, in being both children and gender non-conforming. To this end, I have conducted interviews with young transgender people and their parents.

---

[52]See part II.ii

[53]Federal Constitutional Court, 1 BvR 3295/07.

[54]Mål nr. 1968 12, Kammarrätten i Stockholm, Avdeling 03.

[55]For an evaluation of the requirement for irreversible sterilisation in Norway, see Anniken Sørlie, 'Tvungen identitet   en vurdering av norsk forvaltningspraksis' krav om irreversibel sterilisering ved endring av juridisk kjønn' (2014) 12(4) *Tids skrift for familierett, arverett og barnevernrettslige spørsmål* 272. See also Sørlie, 'Retten til kjønnsidentitet som mennes kerettighet' (n 49).

[56]The Ministry of Health and Care Services (n 7) 2 and 4 of the proposal.

[57]Stang Dahl (n 10) 61.

III.i *Qualitative interviews, case studies, and legal story telling*

For the purposes of my PhD project, I carried out ten interviews with transgender people or their parents.[58] The interviews form part of a larger qualitative multiple-case study. Robert K Yin defines case study as 'an empirical inquiry that investigates a contemporary phenomenon (the "case") in depth and within its real-world context, especially when the boundaries between phenomenon and context may not be clearly evident.'[59] The case study design was chosen because it facilitates further analysis of the relationship between legal gender and recognition and misrecognition of gender non-conforming children and adolescents. The selection of different cases makes it possible to evaluate the broad phenomenon of legal gender and the relation between law and transgender people, by taking different approaches and perspectives. This approach demonstrates the complexity and paradoxes arising from legal gender as regards transgender people.

Three particular interviews are used in this article because the children involved started to live in accordance with their gender identity as young children and can therefore provide information about their experiences as children, which is the focus of this article. These stories also provide information about parents' experiences. The narratives of two mothers, one father, one child, and one young man form the basis of the three stories about young lives told in this article: the struggles of Paul, Christine, and Daniel for recognition. Paul, Christine, and Daniel live in different cities in Norway and have lived in accordance with their gender identity for at least six months. Paul and Christine are between six and ten years old, whereas Daniel is over the age of majority. They have changed their first names so that they correspond with their gender identity in the national population register. Though they wanted their legal gender to match their gender identity, the gender designated at birth is still listed as their legal gender. They are anxious for a change in Norwegian practice. Paul, Christine, and Daniel have been in contact with their general practitioners and the children's and young people's psychiatric out-patient clinic (BUP) because of their gender incongruence. According to Paul's mother, Paul identifies as a boy and as a transgender person. He has started taking puberty-blockers pre-scribed by his general practitioner. Christine identifies as a girl, and she also defines herself as a transgender person. Daniel identifies as a boy and is undergoing gender confirmation treatment at the National Treatment Unit for Transsexualism, but he says that he does not identify as transsexual. He has started hormone treatment, but apart from that will do as little as possible to his body.

Narrative methods are particularly useful when working with cases. These methods draw attention to why and how a story is told and the social and local context of the stories comes to the fore.[60] Professors Daniel A Farber and Suzanna Sherry point out that: 'legal storytelling ... usually focuses on the narrator's experience of events. Stories supply both the individualized context and the emotional aspect missing from most legal scholarship. Thus "personal narrative" is described as a "feminist method."'[61] John

---

[58]I obtained approval from the National Social Science Data Services (NSD) before I started the data collection. In addition, I applied for a project in TSD (tjeneste for sikker datalagring) before carrying out the interviews in order to ensure the secure storage of information about my informants which could directly or indirectly identified them.

[59]Robert K Yin, *Case Study Research: Design and Methods* (5th edn, Sage 2014) 16.

[60]Catherine Kohler Riessman, *Narrative Methods for the Human Sciences* (Sage, 2008) 12 13.

[61]Daniel A Farber and Suzanna Sherry, 'Telling Stories Out of School: An Essay on Legal Narratives' (1993) 45(4) *Stan L Rev* 807, 811.

Paley and Eva Gail hold that '[a] "narrative" refers to the sequence of events and the (claimed) causal connection between them.'[62] While a story has a plot and character, this is not true of all narratives. Every story is a narrative, but not all narratives are stories as they may lack the organisational structure of a story.[63] As Catherine Kohler Riessman puts it, narratives invite readers 'to enter the perspective of the narrator.'[64] At the same time, the truth of narratives can be questioned. Narrators choose which stories to tell, and by so doing, construct their preferred narratives about themselves. The presence of the researcher, listening and asking questions, also influences what narrators choose to tell, and the researcher thus takes part in the construction of the narrative.[65] In this study, in the case of two of the stories, the narrator was a parent, not the gender non-conforming person himself/herself, which has a bearing on the analysis. In addition, I decided which stories to analyse in this article. The analysis may differ from the informant's own interpretation of the event. The consents from my informants do not include my analysis of their narratives, since the analysis has developed in the course of the project. It is important to bear in mind that my analysis is an alternative way of interpreting the informants' narratives, based on the approach taken in this article.[66]

The theory of recognition serves as a tool for interpreting the narratives. The narratives are categorised and analysed thematically under the three different spheres of recognition: (1) the legal sphere, (2) the private sphere, and (3) the social or solidarity sphere, following Honneth's theory of recognition. Each sphere presents different narratives: coming out to family and coming out to friends, awareness of legal gender and its impact on everyday life, and living openly in a binary society. Though my analysis focuses on content, or what the narrator describes, the analysis also takes note of the societal context in which the narratives emerge.

The narrative approach within this field where biases and transphobia are widespread can help increase knowledge about the role of law within society, and describe and discuss gender non-conforming children's position in law and society.[67] It says something about the narrator's experience of an event, and the narrators' narratives give information about the norms and culture in which the experiences originate.[68] In this way, the narratives can provide information about structures that might otherwise be difficult to unearth.

III.ii *Data collection*

In order to get in contact with potential informants, and at the same time ensure that they did not feel pressured to participate, I contacted the following Norwegian organisations, together with a few key people: the Harry Benjamin Resource Centre, the National

---

[62] John Paley and Gail Eva, 'Narrative Vigilance: the Analysis of Stories in Health Care' (2005) 6 Nursing Philosophy 83, 83 quoted in Yasmin Gunaratnam and David Oliviere (eds), *Narrative and Stories in Health Care: Illness, Dying, and Bereavement* (Oxford University Press, 2009) 2.

[63] Gunaratnam and Oliviere (n 62) 2.

[64] Kohler Riessman (n 60) 9.

[65] Ibid, 7, 9, 50.

[66] Tove Thagaard, *Systematikk og innlevelse: En innføring i kvalitativ metode* (4th edn, Fagbokforlaget Vigmostad & Bjørle AS, 2013) 132 133.

[67] See Norman Anderssen and Kirsti Malterud (eds), *Seksuell orientering og levekår* (Uni Helse/Uni Research, 2013) on, *inter alia*, attitudes towards transgender persons in Norway.

[68] Thagaard (n 66) 152 155.

Association for Lesbians, Gays, Bisexuals and Transgender Persons (LLH), Queer World, the Association for Transgender People and Stensveen Resource Centre. They circulated my information letter and request for participants to their members and contacted people they thought might be interested in taking part. Anyone interested in participating was asked to contact me either directly, or, if they did not want me to now their identity, through the person who contacted. My involvement in the LGBT movement, both as an activist and as a researcher, could have made potential informants feel pressured to participate. This strategy, however, ensured that participants consented freely, which was crucial for my chosen recruitment method.

Amongst those who responded, I selected 10 families or individuals with different gender identities, of different ages and ethnicities, in order to ensure as much diversity amongst the informants as the response allowed. The youngest informant is between six and 10 years old, and the oldest between 70 and 80. Asking potential informants to contact me might have led to a bias, in the sense that my informants might be more comfortable speaking about their life than would be the case for transgender people in general. However, the interviews revealed differences between the informants, though they all hoped that their participation would contribute to a better life for transgender people in Norway. In that respect, their participation was based more or less on a sort of activist agenda.

The interviews used in this article were conducted in 2015. The informants were interviewed face to face, at a place of their choosing. Beforehand, every informant received an information letter in which the project was explained. Before starting the interview, I provided further information about the project and encouraged the informant to ask questions. Each informant gave written consent. In addition to interviewing Christine's parents, I had a short conversation with Christine, whose mother consented on her behalf. She was informed about the project before we met, and her mother took part in our conversation. The main part of Christine's story is based on the interviews with her parents, but during my conversation with her she confirmed her parents' narrative, when her mother referred to things they had said.

The interviews were semi-structured. Each informant was invited to speak freely on matters such as identity, coming out, feelings of recognition, school, meetings with health care institutions, legal gender, legal name, and positive and negative experiences in different situations. Follow-up questions were asked to a varying degree, depending on the specific conversation. The interviews lasted from around one hour to up to four hours, and were recorded on two devices: a smart phone and a Dictaphone. After the interviews, I transcribed the data and deleted the audio files to ensure that any information which could be used either directly or indirectly to identify the informant or their child was destroyed.

IV. The Struggle for Recognition

> [E]very individual is dependent on the possibility of constant reassurance by the Other; the experience of disrespect poses the risk of an injury that can cause the identity of the entire person to collapse.[69]

---

[69] Axel Honneth, 'Integrity and Disrespect: Principles of a Conception of Morality Based on the Theory of Recognition' (1992) 20(2) *Political Theory* 187, 189.

In this part, I present the narratives and analyse them in the light of Honneth's theory of recognition. First, I introduce and analyse the narratives I have categorised as being within the private sphere. Secondly, I turn to the legal sphere, before going on to present the narratives relating to the social sphere.

The informants used many of the same terms, such as acceptance, normal, self-confidence, to shield, the state, the system, vulnerability, role models, fear, to protect, and to feel safe. At the same time, one word can describe and summarise their narratives: strategy. In each sphere of recognition, the informants tell stories about how they or their children navigate amongst binary gender norms and prejudices and develop strategies to deal with them. Their strategies concern, *inter alia*, coming out, building self-confidence, dealing with negative attitudes, and confronting lack of resources, and unwillingness to change structures at school. The parents describe feeling of constantly fighting the system, feelings of inadequacy, and how they must contend with negative attitudes and the fear of doing something wrong. The narratives portray structural disadvantages and binary gender norms, which challenge their everyday life.

IV.i *The first step towards recognition: The fear and strategies involved in coming out in the private sphere*

The first pattern of recognition, love in the private sphere, is the first step towards self-realisation. By love, Honneth means a strong emotional connection between a few people, such as parents and children, or strong friendship. The experience of mutual recognition makes individuals realise that they are dependent upon each other.[70] In this part, I focus on the child-parent relationship and on relationships with other family members. Coming out is not a one-off experience. For the purposes of presenting the narratives, I identify the coming out experience as having two main parts for the youngest informants: the child's coming out to the parents, and the next step: the shared coming out of the child and parent.

Gender spectrum

Before I present the coming-out stories, some background on the parents' conception of gender is useful. Christine and Paul's mothers describe their children's childhood as gender-neutral. According to them, their children were free to choose their toys and to wear whatever clothes they liked. The mothers recall that they did not pay much attention to this. This is in tune with their conception of gender. Christine's mother says: 'It's not just men and women and transgender. It's a great human spectrum.' This quote also illustrates Paul's mother's view of gender. In addition, she emphasises that gender and its variations can change throughout life. This implies that they situate themselves within a post-structural understanding of gender.

Aloofness – I didn't know anything about it

Nevertheless, Christine and Paul had to come out to their parents – an experience their parents describe as difficult, both for their child and for themselves. The process can be described as involving uncertainty, lack of knowledge, anguish, and a situation where

---

[70]Honneth, *Kamp om anerkjennelse* (n 14) 104.

one's child takes the lead – either coming out to the parents or when coming out at school. The childhoods of Christine and Paul, which had been free from gender stereotypes, suddenly changed. Their freedom was restricted. Christine's parents limited her gender expression, and both Paul and Christine's parents were reluctant to their expressed wish to live in accordance with their gender identity. Though the parents describe themselves as pro-gender neutrality and gender fluidity, it would appear that society's gender norms and prejudices were of great concern to them at the beginning of their child's coming-out process.

Coming out to parents is narrated as being a lengthy process, which started with hints that eventually led to an explicit expression of the need to live as a girl or a boy. Paul's mother says:

> I tried to say the right things, such as you [Paul] know that we will always love you and you know that it is possible to do something about it [your body] when you get older ... [I said this] given my limited knowledge at the time, I did not know and had not heard that such small children [could experience this] ... So, we decided to delay [the transition] until later. I believe that he took this as a bit of a rejection, even though, formally, it was an acceptance [from me].

The Norwegian TV series 'Born in the Wrong Body'[71] was the trigger for Paul's coming out to the rest of his family. Paul had already made his parents aware of his gender identity, but everything had been put on hold due to his parents' uncertainty. Then Paul used the series to illustrate what his life was like. When his mother asked him why he was unhappy, he was able to refer to the series without needing to elaborate. The programme thus provided Paul with a language and his parents with knowledge. From then on he started to live openly as a boy. His parents told his family, school, and local community.

The two mothers spontaneously speak of their subsequent regrets. It appears evident to me that the way they reacted to their child's coming out causes them great unhappiness. Christine's mother recalls: 'It wasn't nice of me, but I did it because I thought it was healthier for her ... Afterwards I've felt very ashamed.' Paul's mother says: 'In retrospect, I've regretted that I took so long and postponed it. At the same time, I think that if I'd just immediately said "of course", then maybe later I would have been asking myself whether I pushed him.'

Both children told their parents relatively early in life. Coming out to other family members, however, took some time – for one thing, because the children needed time to develop a language to 'convince' their parents, and their parents needed to get information about the matter. In both cases, coming out to grandparents, aunts and uncles, etc is described as a pretty smooth process. Most family members accepted the child's wish, but both families have broken contact with a few family members who harbour negative attitudes against the child's transition so as to shield their child.

Christine took charge of her own coming out to her friends and the local community by wearing dresses and asking her friends to call her Christine from then on. She recalls that she was a bit surprised because no one actually seemed to care, but she says that now and then children ask her about the clothes she is wearing and whether she is a girl or a boy. At

---

[71] A Norwegian documentary of six episodes directed by Petter Vennerød broadcast on TV2 in 2014. It follows 14 people and their experiences during the process of gender confirmation.

home her parents try to give her as much reassurance as possible to help her handle these situations.

According to Paul's mother, he changed a lot after he started to live openly as Paul. She describes it as 'getting [her] child back,' but the positive changes lasted only a short time. School children soon started to use the wrong pronoun and some parents complained to the school. 'It goes against my faith', one parent said.

I want to be a boy in my next life because I can't be a boy now

Daniel used to think that he could not live as a boy in this life, but might do so in another. After many years he came to the following conclusion:

> I felt that either I had to receive my new life now or I had to create something of it myself, if you understand what I mean. Either I have to end it, be over and done with it, or I had to face it straight on and be honest about what it was and try to find help ... The hate [that I had] became greater and greater and I became even more tired. It was a vicious circle; it felt really good to be honest and to see that things got better.

Unlike the two mothers, Daniel does not speak of a trigger, but of an ever-increasing struggle to live. The question about whether to be open turned into a life-and-death matter. He speaks self-confidently about it without directly saying that he was contemplating suicide. His suffering is similarly implied in many of his narratives, without being directly expressed. As mentioned in the introduction, Daniel experiences recognition and support from his mother, but misrecognition from his father. While he openly speaks about coming out to his mother, it is only in response to my question that he discusses coming out to his father:

> I just think it's so comical ... I said, 'please, don't hate me, I want to feel good'. And he responded, 'no, no, but you are my child.' Then I became so happy and I thought that he had accepted and understood me. Then, two months later, he says, sorry, but you will always be my little girl and my little princess ... Since then, I have tried to talk to him about this on a regular basis, but I don't believe he is capable of understanding it, so I just stopped going over there [to his house]. I'll go back [over there] when I have a beard and then we can see who the little princess is.

Before telling his parents, Daniel told some of his friends. He describes this as a trifling, and says that this revealed a lot about himself as a person to his friends.

Fear is a feature of the coming-out narratives. Daniel expresses his own fear, whereas the two mothers' narratives express parents' fears towards the attitudes that their child will meet in everyday life. In subsection IV.iii, which deals with the social sphere, I explore further how the informants strategically try to avoid or deal with these attitudes, and will also relate their fears to surveys on transgender peoples' quality of life.

The importance of participation and recognition in the private sphere is illustrated by Daniel's fear of coming out, and the mothers' description of how their children changed when they and other people accepted them. This change in their self-confidence squares well with Honneth's emphasis on this sphere as a determinant of identity formation. When children feel confident about their parents' love, they will develop a self-confidence that enables them to be alone and independent.[72] In the case of the informants, they are

---

[72]Honneth, *Kamp om anerkjennelse* (n 14) 113.

made capable of facing society and other people, thanks to their devoted parents and their unconditional love. A parent's acceptance of a gender non-conforming child, and the fact that the parent regards transgender and gender fluidity as normal and something positive, are great demonstrations of parental love. The development of self-confidence is, according to Honneth, the psychological condition for the development of any other kind of self-relation or form of recognition.[73] As children, without the support of their legal guardians, who in most cases are their parents, they exhibit a limited ability to enjoy their rights. In this way, Honneth's ontogenetic 'stairway' to recognition matches children's steps towards recognition. The next subsection looks at the legal sphere and demonstrates how children have no access to recognition without the support of parents.

IV.ii *The legal sphere*

> Many think that such a record [birth record] is needed to comply with a person's human rights to know who they are. This implies that who they are exists at birth.[74]

As demonstrated above, human rights, as well as domestic law, form and create subjects of law through legal provisions regarding legal gender assignment at birth and legal gender recognition. To be excluded from the legal system, in the sense of being excluded from certain rights, can impact on a person's psychology and on how one perceives one's identity.[75] Several scholars have criticised the role of medicine in determining what, for legal purposes, gender is. Julia Greenberg, among others, stresses that 'the legal community must question its long-held assumptions about the legal definitions of sex, gender, male, and female.'[76] Depending on how laws and regulations are applied in reality, laws can create a set of norms which clearly define the gender borders of a society. Existing Norwegian legislation requires early assignment to either male or female legal gender on the basis of a medical conception of gender. For legal gender to be changed later in life, there has to be an absence of reproductive organs. This constitutes biological determinism and the construction of a dualistic gender regime within the legal system.[77]

Transgender children and adolescents are protected against discrimination on the grounds of gender identity and gender expression.[78] In this regard, they are entitled to the same protection as everyone else when it comes to matters of gender identity and gender expression. According to Norwegian law, children who have their parents' permission have the right to change their legal name.[79] The change is supposed to require only the individual's own statement that he or she belongs to a different gender, or is transgender, but the administrative circular letter is unclear when it comes to children.[80] Change of legal gender on the other hand, is open only to a small number of people in Norway – and definitely not to children.[81]

---

[73] Ibid, 116.
[74] Marshall, *Human Rights Law and Personal Identity* (n 9) 7.
[75] Ibid, 12.
[76] Julia A Greenberg, *Intersexuality and the Law: Why Sex Matters* (New York University Press, 2012) 292.
[77] See subsection II.iii.
[78] Act No 58 of 21 June 2013 prohibiting discrimination on the grounds of sexual orientation, gender identity and gender expression s 5. See also subsection II.3.
[79] Act No 19 of 7 June 2002 on names, 12.
[80] Administrative circular on names of 15 November 2002 (G 2002 20).
[81] See subsection II.ii.

What experiences of legal gender do gender non-conforming children and adolescents – or their parents – narrate, and what can we generalise from these narratives? The narratives are reported and analysed in the context of existing Norwegian administrative practice. Does legal gender matter and if so, in what way? Does it impact on young people's feelings of self-respect and recognition?

Change of legal gender – 'we will do everything we can to show our support'

Daniel, Paul, and Christine live with a legal gender that does not match their gender identity, but their knowledge of their legal gender varies. Daniel became aware of his legal gender as a teenager, whereas Paul is still ignorant of his. Christine, on the other hand, is fully aware of the information given by national identity numbers. However, she does not know that her passport has a separate gender marker, in addition to carrying her national identity number.

Christine and Paul's mothers would have changed their child's legal gender if the age restriction were lower and if no surgery or other medical interventions were required. However, they regard the change of name as more important to their children. Christine's mother says: 'Her name has been very important to her. I don't think it [the legal gender] matters to her because she's so young. She doesn't understand the significance of it.' At the same time, Christine has been very focused on undergoing gender reassignment surgery. Her mother says: '[w]e're wondering if [Christine] would have changed the way she's thinking because she's very focused on surgery ... because the state requires that to let her be a woman.' Christine and Paul's mothers speak of changing legal gender and legal names as proof of their support and respect for their children. This is thus a part of the child/parent relation and an expression of the parents' love for their child, which is necessary for the child's enjoyment of his or her rights. Changing their name was possible for Paul, Christine, and Daniel because they had supportive parents.[82]

The discrepancy between the rules regarding change of name and change of legal gender enables children to obtain partial recognition of their identity in the legal sphere. They are thus not able to obtain the greatest possible self-respect. In addition, they are dependent upon recognition in the private sphere to develop any form of self-respect. This creates young identities which do not match with their legal gender and gendered legal names. It leads to a risk that their gender history will be disclosed in public situations like travelling.

The liberal narratives on legal changes coincide with the two mothers' view of gender presented above. Paul and Christine's mothers present their children, rather than themselves, as experts on their own identities and oppose medical authority. By letting their children decide, and by regarding as insignificant the possibility of a future change back, they break away from the biological, dualistic gender regime embedded in medicine, law, and Norwegian society. They thus situate themselves within the more theoretical conception of gender as being social and historically constructed.

The power of the Norwegian state – the creation of abnormal citizens

The formation of a person's identity takes place within a social context, which is determined, among other things, by the capacity for choice provided by law and legal

---

[82]Act No 19 of 7 June 2002, 12.

regulations. The narratives speak of the repressive effect of Norwegian law. The informants emphasise state authority and express anger towards the system. Even though I did not ask any direct questions about the medical requirements for changing legal gender, their narratives on legal gender centre around the requirement of sterilisation and the power of the Norwegian state and the National Treatment Unit for Transsexualism. They describe current practice as an assault, shameful, incomprehensible, and unfair.

Daniel felt marked when he realised that he had a legal gender. He says: 'the state has told me who I am the whole time and I didn't even know.' He elaborates on the medical requirements:

> I don't want the state to take my reproductive organs because they should be there and because, as I said, it's my body and I have to figure out how to live with it. This upsets me a lot, especially when I think about how they [the state] want to take away my ability to have kids. As if I'm something abnormal, an abnormal human being who has special needs. I'm not. I just want to live like everyone else.

Daniel's narrative – as well as those of the mothers – sees the requirements as symbols of their 'abnormality'– or society's judgement of normality. They make transgender people 'the other', or as Alex Sharpe puts it, monsters.[83] Their narratives clearly demonstrate that they feel that the state treats them differently and values them less than other citizens because of the requirements. Drawing on Marshall, we can see this as an example of how law excludes identities, on the basis of social norms. The feeling of being 'the other' or of less value due to lack of rights, weakens the feeling of self-respect, according to Honneth.[84] Both the fact that they lack the right to change legal gender, and the requirements currently needing to be satisfied before change can take place, hinder the development of self-respect. Birth registration, that was supposed to ensure their rights, results in the erosion of their dignity and integrity. They are not free to shape their identity, and this interferes with their right to personal identity. They are not treated the same way as cisgender[85] people in Norway since cisgender people's gender identity has full legal recognition without any requirements as to what their body should look like, or whether or not they are able to procreate.[86] Yet, in the case of transgender people, their bodies are strictly controlled if they are to acquire a legal gender different from the one they were assigned at birth.

In a modern society, transgender people should anticipate the same treatment as cisgender people and to have dignity and rights. Structural denial of legitimate expectations of equal rights leads to a feeling of disrespect. According to Honneth: 'the person is deprived of that form of recognition that takes the shape of cognitive respect for moral accountability.' Being denied rights may lead to loss of self-respect and self-esteem.[87] Discrimination against whole groups of people is an example of disrespect that can influence or damage our self-respect.[88]

---

[83] A Sharpe, *Foucault's Monsters and the Challenge of Law* (Routledge 2010).
[84] Honneth, 'Integrity and Disrespect' (n 69) 190 191.
[85] *Cisgender* refers to people whose experience of their gender align with the gender they were designated at birth.
[86] In 2014, the Norwegian Equality and Anti Discrimination Ombudsman decided that the Ministry of Health and Care Ser vices had discriminated against the appellant   a woman whose birth designated gender was male   when she was refused to change her legal gender because she did not meet the medical requirements. Case 14/840, 9 September 2014.
[87] Honneth, 'Integrity and Disrespect' (n 69) 190 191.
[88] Mogens Chrom Jacobsen (trs), 'Mellem Aristoteles og kant: En Skitse til Anerkendelsens Moral' in *Axel Honneth: Behovet for Anerkendelse: En Tekstsamling* (Mogens Chrom Jacobsen (trs) and Rasmus Willig (ed), Hans Reitzels Forlag 2003) 88.

IV.iii *The social sphere*

Heteronormative dominance can result in suppression of one's gender identity and therefore hinder positive development or formation of identity. This lack of support in the social context can lead to poor mental and social health.[89] According to Honneth, self-realisation presupposes social value – or self-esteem. As self-confidence and self-respect presuppose intersubjective relations, this form of recognition presupposes an intersubjective horizon of values. Individuals can only value each other if they share values, which is a sign that their qualities matter or contribute to the other person's life. The conditions for the social value of individuals are, however, determined by society's cultural self-realisation. The social value of qualities and skills are rendered concrete by cultural interpretations. Honneth considers as very significant the role interest organisations play in the struggle to ensure that certain groups are valued more highly, but he points out that the struggle for social value is a permanent fight.[90] It is exactly this constant fight for acceptance that the informants narrate.

The transparency of identity documents versus passing – like winning a marathon

I hold my breath when I show it [my bank card] because I think that everyone understands what the third from last digit means, because I know what it means, and so I think that every one else knows it as well. What if they see it?[91]

Exclusion from rights can expose transgender people to harassment and fear. The informants point to passports and other identity documents as especially problematic because their legal gender is revealed in those documents and they cannot be changed. They feel that the passport explicitly discloses their own or their child's gender history, and that it is impossible to hide this information from strangers. Daniel says:

I think it's a shame to get that knowing look when I show [them] my passport. ... It's a very unpleasant reminder. It's not simply an innocent three year old photo ... it does hurt to see it. Although the sex of my reproductive organs is not written on my face, it is in my passport. I don't think this is cool. And everyone can see it. Everyone who sees my passport can see it as well. I might as well just be stripped naked.

Daniel compares the information on his passport to being naked. It exposes intimate information and puts him in situations of indignity and insecurity. He expects to experience non-passing. Daniel explains his fear of non-passing:

I usually think it's okay to go to the men's loo. I don't usually think about it, but then I get these waves of dysphoria. I don't have dysphoria constantly, it just comes in waves and then it gets bad, bad, bad. And then it gets better. But when a wave comes and I have to go to the loo, then I feel as though everyone is looking at me and that, in their eyes, I don't belong there. Will I be beaten up now? I want to go home. Or to sit there with the door locked until I hear that everyone has left, and then run out.

In these situations he tries to focus on all the times he has experienced passing, when he had not expected to. Daniel describes the feeling of passing like this:

I don't think there are words to adequately describe this [feeling]. I have found the meaning of life and the happiness that comes with having found this meaning ... It's as though I've run a marathon that I never thought I would manage to finish and I have finished in first place.

---

[89]Sam Larsson and others, 'Vem får man vara i vårt samhälle? Om transpersoners psykosociala situation och psykiska hälsa' (Statens folkhälsoinstitut, 2008) 236 237.
[90]Honneth, *Kamp om anerkjennelse* (n 14) 130 138.
[91]Daniel.

Anthropologist Jason Cromwell writes:

> Within transsexual discourses, passing means blending in and becoming unnoticeable and unremarkable as either a man or a woman. Blending in as normal means that one has succeeded and become a 'real' man or woman. With 'realness' an individual is no longer a member of the stigmatized group of transsexuals; she or he has completed 'transition' and is now 'just a woman' or 'just a man.'[92]

The narratives from Paul and Christine's mothers tell the story of children who mostly pass in accordance with their gender identity. Yet, their narratives show that the children are tremendously afraid of their gender history being disclosed and feel that their bodies are their greatest enemy in this regard. Swimming is singled out as the most challenging issue, and is something Paul and Christine try to avoid. They feel exposed. Christine's father talks about an experience at the beach:

> It took her an hour and a half   two hours before we managed get her changed … While you would have been running around naked without thinking about putting on your swimming costume, she couldn't take off her clothes. She had to build a house with a fence around it and two safety guards outside in order to change her clothes … But there is nothing. Nobody can see it. There's not much difference between [girls' and boys' bodies at that age].[93]

Zowie Davy criticises Thomas Kando in his suggestion that passing is impossible in relation to people who knew the transsexual before transitioning. According to Davy, whether a transsexual person passes or not depends on the person who is passing their opinion, and on the transsexual's bodily aesthetic.[94] The narratives imply that Paul, Christine, and Daniel regard their bodies as markers of their difference from cisgender people and as symbols of their trans identity.

The children's fear of non-passing can be interpreted as meaning that they do not expect to pass and that they expect other people to think that they – because of their bodies – break Norwegian norms. They fear to be discovered and feel that other people regard them as 'less worthy'. Passing, on the other hand, releases them from their fear of being devalued and of being subjected to transphobia. It increases their self-esteem.

Construction of a self within a social and legal construction of abnormality

> I think I would get by just fine on an island by myself. I would be able to come to terms with this in a very different way versus when people are around me. I do not believe that I am cause of my shame. Rather, other people are the cause of this.[95]

In a Norwegian inquiry of 2013, a minority of respondents reported negative attitudes to transgender people (men 20 per cent, women 9 per cent).[96] Amongst the male respondents, 49 per cent supported the statement that human variation is a good thing, such that there are women, men, transgender, and other people, whereas 65 per cent of the female respondents supported this statement.[97] However, 55 per cent of the male respondents and 52 per cent of the female respondents expressed negative attitudes towards the kissing in public by people who do not fit within the two gender categories.[98] Though a

---

[92] Jason Cromwell, *Transmen and FTMs: Identities, Bodies, Genders and Sexualities*, (University of Illinois Press, 1999) 39.
[93] Rewritten to protect anonymity.
[94] Zowie Davy, *Recognizing Transsexuals: Personal, Political and Medicolegal Embodyment* (Ashgate, 2011) 59.
[95] Daniel.
[96] Anderssen and Malterud (eds) (n 67) 130 131.
[97] Ibid, 135.
[98] Ibid, 136.

minority of respondents expressed negative attitudes towards transgender people, the survey shows that prejudice against transgender people is present in Norwegian society.

Alex Sharpe demonstrates that cisnormativity and transphobia are embedded in law and society by discussing criminal cases where transgender men are convicted for sexual offences because they do not disclose their gender history to their female cisgender partner prior to sexual intimacy.[99] These cases are good examples of damaging prejudice transgender people may face in society and how the legal system is not free from prejudice, cisnormativity, or transphobia. Social values are not detached from law. The law embodies social values that impact our identities.[100] Norwegian administrative practice regarding legal gender recognition is an example of this.

According to the mothers, their children express unhappiness at being born the way they were. Christine's mother recalls Christine asking: 'Mum, why wasn't I just born a girl? Can I ever be a girl?' Paul's mother says: 'He thinks it's madly unfair that he's born the way he is. He's unhappy and hurt because he has to experience this ... He just wants to be normal, and most of all, to just be a boy. He wishes he had been born a boy so he was spared from all this.' Daniel puts it this way: 'I don't want trans to be a big part of me. I try to just be a boy like everyone else.' The mothers describe their children's wish to be 'normal' and like everyone else. The children focus on gender reassignment treatment, such as puberty suppression hormones, hormones, and surgery. At the same time, Christine connects gender reassignment surgery with legal gender recognition. This might imply that surgery and change of legal gender will eradicate her view of herself as 'abnormal'. This cannot be detached from the gender borders under Norwegian law, which define gendered legal bodies in terms of the presence or lack of testis or ovaries. Possibly, Christine and Paul would have regarded their bodies as less 'abnormal' if the legal categories of gender were open to all bodies and identities, so that their bodies would have caused them less fear and prejudice and allowed them to have higher self-esteem. This demonstrates the interrelation between the social and legal spheres.

Self-confidence strategies

The devaluing of some life-styles in the way the narratives suggest, can, as Honneth puts it, lead to:

> loss of self esteem   that is, he is no longer in a position to conceive of himself as a being whose characteristic traits and abilities are worthy of esteem. [T]he person is deprived of the form of recognition that is expressed in society's approval of a type of self realization that the person had only been able to acquire through an arduous process involving encouragement in the form of group solidarity.[101]

Self-confidence strategies developed to meet prejudice can take the form of empowerment from parents, through others and from oneself. The first of these can be seen when, faced with their children's unhappiness at being born the way they were, the two mothers try to convince them that they are special and that they can use their difference for something positive. They try to strengthen their self-confidence so that they can deal with the prejudice they are most likely to meet in Norwegian society today.

---

[99] Alex Sharpe, 'Sexual Intimacy, Gender Variance and Criminal Law' in this issue.
[100] Marshall, *Human Rights Law and Personal Identity* (n 9) 18.
[101] Honneth, 'Integrity and Disrespect' (n 69) 191 192.

The second option is building self-confidence via other people. Daniel describes how much it means to him to help and support other transgender people. He also emphasises the importance of supportive comments from strangers and how these empower him. In addition, all the informants emphasise the importance of normalisation through the media and TV series like 'Born in the Wrong Body'. The mothers say that role models have helped both their child and themselves to feel confident that what they are doing is right. Paul's mother says:

> I believe that both given that the focus was on this [issue], and the fact that it was normalised, that those who watched the series could see that they [the cast] were normal people. They were not freaks, they were completely normal. For us and not least for [Paul], this was extre mely important. I doubt whether he otherwise would have dared [to be open with us].

The presence of supportive people, and the feeling of being important and valued strengthen their self-esteem.

The third option is self-empowerment, the importance of which Daniel emphasises. He tries to focus on feeling good about himself and his positive experiences, rather than on the harassment and fear he has experienced. However, he says that he feels that other people respect him for who he is, but that he is not quite sure what he needs in order to feel respected and he does not search for recognition. He says:

> Lately, I've actually tried not to feel accepted because if I have to go and wait for everyone's recognition, then I feel that I will be too dependent on it in order to feel good. So, I try to forget about it and just try to be happy with myself instead, if you get what I mean. It sounds strange because it's good to get recognition, but the problem is what if you don't?

I see this as his strategy to overcome the prejudice he meets, which he talks about too. Negative comments about transgender people make him wonder whether there is something wrong with him, but in order to overcome prejudice, he focuses on empowering himself. According to Daniel, people are more likely to recognise him if he feels good about himself.

IV.iv *The struggle for recognition: How the three spheres interrelate*

Honneth's theory and the categorisation of the narratives into the three spheres show that the spheres intertwine. It becomes clear that, for example, recognition by one's family alone is not enough if recognition is otherwise lacking. The struggle for recognition, though Daniel says he does not actively seek recognition from others, is common to all three stories. Except for the misrecognition Daniel experiences from his father, the narratives portray children whose emotional needs are mostly met in the private sphere by recognition from family and friends. This makes possible the development of self-confidence. The experience of recognition was a precondition for Christine, Paul, and Daniel to be open outside their closest family. But due to their gender identity, they cannot follow the ontogenetic developmental stages to reach full self-realisation. No matter how supportive their parents are, none of them can obtain the maximum amount of self-respect available through equal rights. Denial of their rights and the feeling they are devalued by the state, make it impossible for them to obtain recognition in either the legal or the social spheres. The law itself subordinates their bodies by limiting their ability to freely shape their identity. Their dignity and autonomy as human persons are not recognised. Their struggle for recognition fails here. This lack of recognition in the social sphere and their struggle to develop self-esteem are influenced by the exclusion of their identities in the legal sphere. They fear misrecognition from others if they disclose their gender history, because of prejudice and gender norms embedded in Norwegian society. At the same time, the normalisation of being transgender and the dissemination of information through, for example, TV series, impacted on the feeling of recognition in the private sphere. The narratives demonstrate how social recognition cannot be obtained without recognition in the legal sphere, but also that being open in the private sphere is influenced by social values. In this sense, Honneth's theory of recognition as an ontogenetic developmental stage to achieve a good life, seems to coincide with the narratives, but all spheres seem to interrelate and do not merely function as stages.

V. Increased Self-Determination or Abolition of Legal Gender?

In the following, I present two alternative scenarios which could improve Paul, Christine, and Daniel's self-relation: (1) allowing children to change their legal gender, or (2) abolishing legal gender. I discuss the alternatives with regard to Paul, Christine, and Daniel and their right to privacy and non-discrimination.

A growing number of states have abolished medical requirements for a change of legal gender.[102] As mentioned in the introduction to this article, Norway is in the process of adopting its first law on changing legal gender, which will not require any medical interventions for legal change. For that reason, I omit medical requirements in the following discussion.

V.i *Granting minors the right to change legal gender and maintaining two legal genders*

Up until now, the implicit age limit of 18 years has been justified on the basis of medical requirements. The abolition of the medical requirements therefore removes the justification for the age limit for change of legal gender. The legal proposal suggests an age limit of 16 for changing legal gender without parental consent; children between the ages of seven and 16 would need parental consent.

The suggested age limit of seven would mean that Paul and Christine could change their legal gender. Both of them have parents who support them and believe that they are capable of making this decision themselves. The first option outlined above complies with their right to respect for a private life as enshrined in article 8 of ECHR and article 16 of CRC and to protection against discrimination in accordance with article 14 in conjunction with article 8 of ECHR and article 2 of the CRC. This option ensures their right to privacy and enables them to control whether or not other people can acquire information about their gender history. Unwanted disclosure of gender identity can violate the right to respect for one's private life under article 8 if the requirements prescribed in article 8 (2) are not fulfilled. They will be able to freely shape their identity. This option means they can have the legal gender that corresponds with their gender identity, and therefore not be subjected to different treatment from cisgender people.

---

[102] Among others: Sweden, Denmark, Malta, Argentina, and Germany.

Daniel, who does not want to undergo a complete gender confirmation treatment, would also be able to obtain legal recognition of his gender identity. He is over the age of majority, but the first option means that he could have changed his legal gender at the age of 16, even though he lacked the support of his father. This alternative gives minors over the age of 16 self-determination on matters of legal gender. This matches the general rule regarding self-determination from the age of 16 on health care matters.[103]

Some would argue that minors below the age of 16 are not competent to make the decision to change their legal gender at such an early stage of life. This objection implies that changing legal gender is a more serious decision than the child's decision to be open about their gender identity and break gender norms. This line of argumentation is based on a misconception. A Swedish inquiry dismisses the objection as follows:

> The difficulty of a decision taken about a person's legal gender is, in legal and formal terms, minor because it only concerns a change of personal identity number. The difficulty could rather be said to lie in a young person actively choosing to go against the norms and ideas that dominate in a heteronormative society.[104]

In Norway, legal gender has little bearing on having specific rights or duties. Indeed, the Nordic countries have a tradition of making the wording of acts gender neutral.[105] General conscription, retirement age, and criminal legislation are all gender neutral. Legal gender, on the other hand, is very visible in everyday life. Legal gender is shown in identity documents such as driving licences, passports, and bank cards, which may mean that the holder risks falling prey to discrimination or hate crime if there is a mismatch between the ID card and gender expression.

A similar objection is the risk that children might change their minds, either while going through puberty or later in life. This objection can also be dismissed. Since the legal implications of a change of legal gender is minor, changing one's mind after the fact will be of little significance, as long as the law is open to further changes of legal gender. Further, the risk of the exploitation of rights is minor. Few rights or duties are gender specific, and as mentioned above, going against the heteronormativity of society is probably more difficult than what is involved in changing legal gender. Lack of this possibility could mean that the child's life is put on hold, with the suppression of gender identity and negative implications this could have on their health.[106]

At first sight, lowering the age limit seems to be a good solution since it encompasses children's rights to a greater extent, but this option excludes children who lack the support of their parents. Lack of parental support precludes legal gender recognition. The narratives presented in this article are not representative of all transgender children. Many children experience lack of understanding and support from their parents. Some run away from their homes or break with their parents.[107] The consent of these parents or legal guardians is difficult to obtain.[108]

---

[103] Act No 63 of 2 July 1999 relating to Patients' Rights (the Patients' Right Act) 4 3 para 1b.

[104] Juridisk kön och medisinsk könskorrigering (SOU 91:14) 29 30.

[105] Ragnhild Hennum, 'Kjønnslikestilling på ville veier kan kjønnsnøytrale krisesentre forsvares?' in Beatrice Halsaa and Anne Hellum (eds), Rettferdighet (Universitetsforlaget, 2010) 137.

[106] Larsson and others (n 89) 237.

[107] Frida Darj and Hedvig Nathorst Böös, 'Är du kille eller tjei?' en intervjustudie om unge transpersoners livsvillkor' (2008).

[108] In the Norwegian law proposal, it is not suggested that consent from a third party be introduced as an alternative to parental consent. The Ministry of Health and Care Services (n 7) para 7.2.1 and 7.2.2.

One may ask whether it is in accordance with the rights of a gender non-conforming child not to be able to change legal gender – or whether parental consent is a justifiable requirement for legal recognition of the gender identity of children under 16. As demonstrated in subsection II.ii, according to the ECtHR's jurisprudence, gender identity falls within the scope of a private life under article 8 of the ECHR. The provision gives, at the outset, the right to be legally recognised with dignity and integrity, in accordance with one's gender identity – in other words, the legal entitlement to personal freedom. Marshall argues that the Court's conception of freedom can be understood as self-creation or self-determination, meaning 'the freedom to be and become the person one chooses, while acknowledging that this happens in a societal context and must not harm others.'[109] In the case of gender non-conforming children and adolescents, their rights must be weighed against the rights of their parents or legal guardians. This tension between these conflicting rights is problematic for gender non-conforming children, as well as for every other child, since parental rights can trump the interest of the child. Martha Albertson Fineman argues that all children face the structural disadvantage 'that parents are privileged in the organization of the family and children's interests, both as children and as future adults, and are sometimes compromised as a result.'[110] According to Fineman, this cannot be justified if the state has a responsibility to all its citizens and an interest in the adults the children are likely to become.[111] At the same time, the narratives presented in this article, and Honneth's theory of recognition, show that children are dependent upon support from their parents – both in terms of receiving their rights and forming their identity. Children will face difficulties in forming their identity if their self-confidence is not strengthened with the help of their parents – or others with whom they feel a similar intersubjective emotional relation.

The Convention on the Rights of the Child does not give children a right to self-determination. It does, however, assure children the right to express their views and to be heard, which is vital for the recognition of children as autonomous human beings.[112] The Committee on the Rights of the Child has expressed concern, and urged states to end the categorisation of citizens based on religion and ethnic origin in passports and other identity documents. The committee has also emphasised that children's right to privacy and non-discrimination can be violated by such categorisation.[113] Similarly, legal gender can violate children's right to privacy and non-discrimination. As demonstrated in part IV, children may face discrimination and harassment because of their legal gender.

In addition, the increased self-determination scenario implies a reconstitution and continuation of a dualistic and biological gender regime in Norwegian law. Each person's life will start with the biological determination of gender for legal purposes. This reconstitutes gender as fixed and innate, rather than fluid and performative and goes against the fact that these legal categories embrace performativity and fluidity at a certain prescribed age when change of legal gender is allowed. Demanding recognition by the state could lead to new social hierarchies, and new social outcasts could emerge.[114] An open, but

---

[109]Marshall, *Personal Freedom Through Human Rights Law?* (n 23) 121.
[110]Fineman (n 5) 122.
[111]Ibid.
[112]Kirsten Sandberg, 'Barns rett til å bli hørt' in Høstmælingen, Kjørholt and Sandberg (n 41) 91; Lena R L Bendiksen and Trude Haugli, *Sentrale emner i barneretten* (Universitetsforlaget, 2014) 42.
[113]Hodgkin and Newell (n 39) 204.

dualistic, gender regime would exclude those who identify as neither man nor woman, or both, or fluid etc. In a Swedish inquiry conducted in 2014, 206 out of 798 respondents reported that they could not change their legal gender because the gender they preferred did not exist in Sweden.[115]

V.ii *Abolish legal gender?*

In order to avoid discriminating between children who have the support of their parents and those who do not, as well as differential treatment on the grounds of age, the abolition of legal gender could be a solution, but is abolition feasible? Moreover, would it be a good solution?

This begs the question: what are the reasons behind introducing gender for legal purposes? In Norway, the national identity number was introduced because the increased number of taxpayers required a new method to differentiate between taxpayers.[116] It has also been argued that legal gender is significant for the purpose of statistics.[117] Both of these arguments can be dismissed. Today, decades after its introduction, new and better methods for identification have been adopted. Norwegian passports of people over twelve contain the holder's fingerprints.[118] In addition, it can be argued that legal gender, as a tool for identifying individuals is rather unreliable. Since an increased number of jurisdictions are abolishing medical requirements for changing legal gender, legal gender becomes somewhat moot for the purpose of identification. The different legal genders will include a multitude of bodies and identities and therefore add little information. Citizens of a state can also be identified by the use of gender-neutral identity numbers.[119] As far as statistics are concerned, arguably statistical reliability would increase were the data based on the respondents' gender identity or social gender rather than legal gender.

As mentioned above, under Norwegian law, a limited amount of rights are gender-specific.[120] To mention one more example, in 2008, the Norwegian Marriage Act was amended to include same-sex couples.[121] It appears paradoxical that the law in one area liberates itself from dualistic gender categories, while at the same time reconstituting the dualistic gender regime for the youngest and most vulnerable individuals in society. With regard to this, retaining legal gender may mean that the law itself leads to infringement of the right to privacy of children below the age limit and of those who lack parental support. This is difficult to justify when the necessity for legal gender seems to be slight or non-existent. As mentioned above, the national identity number could be gender-neutral, while a third gender could be introduced for Norwegian passports.[122]

---

[114]Judith Butler, 'Is Kinship Always Already Heterosexual?' (2002) 13(1) *differences: A Journal of Feminist Cultural Studies* 14, 26.

[115]Folkhälsomyndigheten (n 6) 25.

[116]Skatteetaten, *Konseptvalgutredning: Ny Personidentifikator i Folkeregisteret* (30 June 2014) 23.

[117]Letter from the Directorate of Health to the Ministry of Health and Care Services (1 October 2012) 15.

[118]Forskrift om pass (FOR 1999 12 09 1263) p 5. See also Council Regulation (EC) 2252/2004 of 13 December 2004 on standards for security features and biometrics in passports and travel documents issued by member states, article 1(2), which requires fingerprints in EU passports.

[119]This has been suggested in Norway. Skatteetaten. 'Konseptvalgutredning: Ny personidentifikator i Folkeregisteret' (Version 1.0. 30 June 2014).

[120]With the upcoming abolishment of medical requirements for change of legal gender, both legal men and legal women will hold rights concerning pregnancy and birth. This will not be limited to legal women.

[121]Act No 47 of 4 July 1991 on marriage, 1.

[122]See the International Civil Aviation Organization standards for passport. A passport must include either M (male), F (female) or X (unspecified).

VI. Conclusion

Norwegian laws and regulations are to a great extent gender-neutral, but the approach taken in this article has demonstrated how the heteronormativity of laws nevertheless influences transgender children as possessors of rights and their everyday life. Legal gender determines which identities and bodies are included or excluded from Norwegian society. These gender borders impact on transgender young people's everyday life. As demonstrated, it is impossible for gender non-conforming children to follow the ontogenetic developmental stages to achieve full self-realisation in accordance with Honneth's theory of recognition. The three stories show how the three spheres of recognition interrelate, and how Honneth's theory can be useful in showing that interrelation is important for a feeling of recognition in gender non-conforming children's everyday life and for the formation of their identity. Children with supportive parents and family can attain self-confidence but not self-respect. A lower age limit for change of legal gender could change this, but it would be necessary for their parents to give their consent. A legal gender in accordance with their gender identity would render their gender history less visible to strangers and society. This could have an effect on the level of harassment and discrimination they suffer and increase their chance of achieving self-esteem. Full self-realisation and a good life would be attainable for some gender non-conforming children, but not for all children. Abolishing legal gender might be a good solution by removing the differences legal gender creates between children who have supportive parents and those who do not, but the question is whether society is ready to diminish the presence of gender. Removal of legal gender will not necessarily mean that gender non-conforming children would reach full self-realisation in accordance with Honneth's theory. Removal of legal gender would however mean there was one less obstacle. If the law does not exclude certain identities or create otherness, this may change attitudes in society and may improve children's feeling of self-esteem, eventually opening the way to full self-realisation for gender non-conforming people in accordance with their right to respect for their private life and non-discrimination.

Sexual Intimacy, Gender Variance, and Criminal Law

Alex Sharpe

Professor of Law, Keele University, UK and Adjunct Professor, Queensland University of Technology, Australia

ABSTRACT
This article considers a series of recent cases where young transgender men have been successfully prosecuted for sexual offences in circumstances where their female cisgender partners claimed to be unaware of their gender histories. The article will (i) detail the legal background to these cases, (ii) offer a critique of the claims that non-disclosure of gender history serves to vitiate consent, constitute harm and provide evidence of deception, and (iii) provide three arguments as to why criminalisation is inappropriate in any event. The arguments against criminalisation that will be advanced are that prosecution (i) produces legal inconsistency and is potentially discriminatory, (ii) unduly valorises the sexual autonomy of cisgender people, and (iii) is contrary to good public policy. In developing these arguments, the article will highlight how the 'intelligibility' of prosecution proceeds from a prior cisnormative framing of events.

It's now against the law to suck dick if you have a dick and you don't tell the dick you're sucking that you have a dick. Or if you used to have a dick. Or if you have a pussy when they think you have a dick. Or a pussy. Or something.[1]

You are about to enter another dimension. A dimension not only of sight and sound, but of mind. A journey into a wondrous land of imagination. Next stop, the Twilight Zone![2]

Introduction

This article is a developed version of a paper presented at the *Sexual Freedom, Equality & the Right to Gender Identity as a Site of Legal & Political Struggle* conference held in Oslo in December 2014.[3] It considers one specific and important human rights issue, generally neglected within legal scholarship, namely, the successful prosecution of young transgender[4] men for sexual offences based on 'gender fraud.' In all cases, judicial

---

[1] P Lees, 'Should Trans People have to Disclose their Birth Gender before Sex' *Vice* 2 July 2013 https://www.vice.com/en uk/read/should trans people have to disclose their birth gender before sex.
[2] Opening narration, Series 1: *The Twilight Zone* (1959) Fremantle Home Entertainment DVD (2011).
[3] The conference was organised by the Department of Public and International Law, University of Oslo http://www.jus.uio.no/ior/english/research/projects/transgender/events/conferences/2014/gender identity conference/program/.
[4] The term transgender has become something of an umbrella term for all trans identified people (see K Bornstein, *Gender Outlaw: On Men, Women and the Rest of Us* (Routledge, 1994); M Bruce Pratt, *S/He* (Firebrand Press, 1995); L Feinberg, *Transgender Warriors: Making History from Joan of Arc to RuPaul* (Beacon Press, 1996); J. Cromwell, *Transmen and FTMs:*

conclusions of 'fraud' have involved translation of apparently consensual and desire-led intimacy with cisgender[5] women into non-consensual relations on the basis of non-disclosure of gender history.[6] With few exceptions, convicted defendants have received custodial sentences and have been placed on sex offenders registers for life, with all the additional implications for liberty and surveillance that this entails.[7] While this criminal (in)justice scenario has been replicated in the US[8] and Israel,[9] the article will focus on the UK where there has been a recent spate of prosecutions. The article is important, not only because it casts light on the plight of a highly marginalised group of people, now rendered especially vulnerable to prosecution due to legal preoccupation with non-disclosure of gender history as the ultimate deal breaker in sexual relations, but also because it lends itself to broader criminal justice, human rights, and ethical debates concerned with the concepts of non-consent, harm, deception and their limits.

The article comprises three parts. Part 1 will preface discussion of the wisdom of criminalisation of non-disclosure of gender history by providing some background and detail concerning criminal prosecutions brought against young transgender men in the UK. Part 2 will highlight a number of important features of sexually intimate scenarios involving cisgender and transgender people that tend to be lost in wider discussions of the issues.

Identities, Bodies, Genders & Sexualities (Chicago University Press, 1999). For the purposes of this article, it is used in the more limited sense to refer to people who feel incongruence between their gender identity and anatomy. The term trans sexual is often used in this respect. However, the term transsexual fails to exhaust this group because many transgender people refuse the transsexual label because of its medical history and pathologising effects (see A Sharpe, *Transgender Jurisprudence: Dysphoric Bodies of Law* (Cavendish, 2002) Ch 2).

[5]'Cisgender' is a term coined by Julia Serrano (*Whipping Girl: A Transsexual Woman on Sexism and the Scapegoating of Fem ininity* (Seal Press, 2007)). It refers to people who are comfortable with gender expectations and practices that follow normatively from sex designation. 'Cissexual' refers to people who are comfortable in their sexed bodies. While these two terms normally align, some cissexual people are not cisgender. Queer people, in particular, tend to refuse the term cisgender. In this article, the term cisgender will be used to refer to complainants because it is the fact that they are cisgender, rather than cissexual, that is more pertinent to the bringing of prosecutions.

[6]The reader might question this claim, at least in the English context, given the recent decision of the Court of Appeal in *R v McNally* [2013] EWCA Crim 1051. In this case, the court distinguished between *non disclosure* and *active deception*, emphasising that criminal liability attached only to the latter. However, in this case, and others, the distinction tends to unravel in trans contexts as, 'mere' non disclosure is readily translated into active deception. For a critique of the dis tinction see A Sharpe, 'Criminalising Sexual Intimacy: Transgender Defendants and the Legal Construction of Non Consent' (2014) *Criminal Law Review* 207. It should be recognised that the obligation to disclose gender history is not confined to criminal law. For example, under English law, failure to disclose gender history prior to a marriage ceremony provides a ground for annulment of the marriage (see A Sharpe, 'Transgender Marriage and the Legal Obligation to Dis close Gender History' (2012) 75(1) *Modern Law Review* 33).

[7]In the UK context, sex offenders have to register with the police every year, inform the police of any change of name or address, and disclose any intention to travel outside the UK. The police can apply for orders that bar offenders from certain activities and areas associated with children. In the UK, a custodial sentence of 30 months or more leads to inde finite detention (Sexual Offences Act 2003 (Notification Requirements) (England and Wales) Regulations 2012).

[8]*State of Colorado v Clark* (Sean O'Neill) No 1994CR003290 (Colo Dist Ct 16 February 1996) (on file with Harvard Law School Library). The defendant received a custodial sentence of three months and a period of probation after being convicted of the rape of four young women, each of whom he had dated (J Green, 'Predator?' *San Francisco Bay Times*, 22 February 1996). For discussion of the case see J L Nye, 'The Gender Box' (1998) 13 *Berkeley Women's L J* 226; P Califia, *Sex Changes: The Politics of Transgenderism* (2nd edn, Cleis Press, 2003) 234 237. *State of Washington v Wheatley* No 97 1 50056 6 (Wash Superior Ct, 13 May 1997). Christopher Wheatley was sentenced to prison for 27 months after being convicted of third degree rape. Both O'Neill and Wheatley identified as transgender men.

[9]*Israel v Alkobi* [2003] IsrDC 3341(3). Hen Alkobi, who acknowledged some gender confusion and self described as a 'girl boy,' was convicted of false impersonation of a man and attempting to penetrate the complainant's genitalia with an object and was sentenced to six months in prison, commuted to six months of community service and 24 months' proba tion. For a discussion and critique of the case see A Gross, 'Gender Outlaws Before the Law: the Courts of the Borderland' (2009) 32(1) *Harvard J of L and Gender* 165. Amit Pundik has noted that prosecutions for sexual fraud generally appear to be extremely limited within continental legal systems (A Pundik, 'Coercion and Deception in Sexual Relations' (2015) 28 *Canadian J of L and Jur* 97, 98). Certainly, prosecutions for 'gender fraud' appear confined to Anglo American common law systems, or legal systems like Israel which are based substantially on the common law.

In particular, it will highlight how liberal legal and wider discourses surrounding such cases abstract their facts from the ideological context in which they are constructed. Part 3 will present three arguments as to why criminalisation is inappropriate in the present context. It will do so on the basis of a series of assumptions which present the case for a cisgender right to know at its strongest. While these assumptions are hugely problematic, as Part 2 of the article will demonstrate, they are likely to register with state prosecutors interpreting events through the lens of cisnormativity. Therefore it is essential, in making the case against criminalisation, to show its weakness even when we concede the ground that otherwise ought not to be conceded in legal and political struggle.

I. The Legal Background

Over the last three years, a series of successful sexual offence prosecutions for 'gender fraud' have been brought in the UK.[10] While all convicted defendants have expressed some 'gender confusion,' at least three appear to be transgender men or, at least, considered themselves to be so at the time of the alleged offences. This article will focus on these three cases and the argumentation offered will relate specifically to instances of trans-cis sexual intimacy. This should not, however, be taken to imply the appropriateness of prosecution outside this scenario. On the contrary, prosecution of gender queer[11] people and/or lesbians for 'gender fraud' constitutes significant criminal law overreach. Nor should it be assumed, in such cases, that desire-led intimacy is non-consensual and/or that queer or lesbian gender performances are necessarily deceptive.

In the first of the three recent cases involving transgender defendants, Christopher Wilson was convicted by a Scottish court of two counts of *obtaining sexual intimacy by fraud*[12] and sentenced to three years' probation and 240 hours of community service.[13] The facts of the case are that the defendant, then aged 20, met two cisgender girls on separate occasions. In relation to the first girl, who was either 15 or 16 at the time (there is uncertainty on this point), sexual contact was limited to kissing. Two years later, the defendant commenced a relationship with the second girl. She was aged 15 at the time, but told

---

[10]*R v Mason* [2015] (unreported) *The Telegraph* http://www.telegraph.co.uk/news/uknews/law and order/11959495/ Woman posed as a single father to con Facebook friend into sex.html; *R v Newland* [2015] (unreported) http://www.theguardian.com/uk news/2015/sep/15/woman convicted of impersonating man to dupe friend into having sex; *R v Wilson* [2013] (unreported) *BBC News* 9/4/13 http://www.bbc.co.uk/news/uk scotland north east orkney shetland 22078298; *R v McNally* [2013] EWCA Crim 1051 http://www.telegraph.co.uk/news/uknews/crime/9946687/18 year old woman masqueraded as boy to get girl into bed.html; *R v Barker* [2012] (unreported) *The Daily Mail Online*, 6/3/ 13http://www.dailymail.co.uk/news/article 2110430/Gemma Barker jailed Vctims girl dressed boy date speak anguish. html. There is also the much earlier case of *R v Saunders* [1991] (unreported) Pink Paper, 196, 12 October 1991. For a discussion of the *Saunders* case see A M Smith, 'The Regulation of Lesbian Sexuality through Erasure: the case of Jennifer Saunders', in J Kay (ed) *Lesbian Erotics* (New York University Press, 1995) 164 179. To my knowledge, no prosecution of this kind has ever been brought against a transgender woman in the UK or elsewhere. In relation to potential cisgender male complainants, this is perhaps due to more unilateral and extra legal responses to 'discovery' of the fact that one's object of desire is not cisgender. Mason, Newland and McNally were all convicted of *sexual assault by penetration* under s 2 of the Sexual Offences Act (SOA) 2003. This is a sister offence to rape under English law, covering non penile forms of non consensual penetration. Wilson was convicted of two counts of *obtaining sexual intimacy by fraud* under the Scottish Sexual Offences Act 2009. One count covered non penile penetration, the other non penetrative sexual touching. Barker and Saunders were convicted of *sexual assault* and *indecent assault* respectively, both being offences of non penetrative sexual touching under s. 3 SOA 2003 and legislation repealed by the 2003 Act.
[11]J Nestle, et al, *GenderQueer: Voices from Beyond the Sexual Binary* (Alyson Books, 2002).
[12]This is an odd choice of words given that there is no such offence under the Scottish Sexual Offences Act 2009. The most appropriate charges would appear to be s 2 (sexual assault by penetration) in relation to use of a prosthetic device and s 3 (sexual assault) in relation to kissing.
[13]*R v Wilson* [2013] (unreported).

Wilson she was 16.[14] This relationship culminated in penetrative vaginal intercourse by means of a prosthetic device. In the second case, Justine McNally[15] was convicted of six counts of *sexual assault by penetration*[16] and sentenced to three years in prison. The facts of this case are that the defendant met a cisgender girl via social media and developed an online relationship with her over three years. At this point, the defendant, then aged 17, met the girl, who was then aged 16, on several occasions. On two of these occasions the defendant digitally and orally penetrated the girl's vagina. In the third and final case, Kyran Lee (Mason) was convicted of *sexual assault by penetration* and received a suspended sentence of two years. The facts of this case are that the defendant met a cisgender woman via social media. The parties subsequently met in person and the defendant penetrated her vagina, both orally and by means of a prosthetic device.[17]

All three defendants were born and remained female-bodied at the time of the offences. Chris Wilson and Kyran Lee (Mason) identified and presented as men prior to, at the time of, and subsequent to the offences. Justine McNally identified and presented as male prior to and at the time of the offences. However, at the time of the trial and subsequent appeal, she asserted a female gender identity. It is unclear whether her disavowal of a male gender identity is authentic or whether it represents a retreat into womanhood, precipitated by criminal prosecution and media persecution of the 17-year-old. Certainly, like Wilson, McNally, prior to reasserting a female identity, indicated a desire to undergo gender reassignment surgery in the future.[18] In any event, two of the three convicted defendants identify as transgender men, while the third genuinely did so at the relevant moment of criminal liability. Further, and as apparent from the facts detailed, the convictions have not proved dependent on the vaginal penetration of complainants. Rather, and as the *Wilson* case demonstrates, kissing proved sufficient to trigger criminal prosecution.[19] It seems especially problematic that kissing, without coercion of any kind, can meet the threshold for criminal prosecution.

Of course, the reader might think this to be appropriate, given the value we place on sexual autonomy and its relevance to determining consent.[20] In Part 3 of the article, the view that sexual autonomy should be considered an absolute right will be taken to task. For now, it is worth noting that, excepting the example of transgender, non-disclosure of information pertaining to group identity does not serve to vitiate consent under English or Scottish law,[21] even in circumstances of penetration where concern over

---

[14]It should be noted that no charges of sex with a minor were brought. Moreover, the English Crown Prosecution Service does not recommend prosecution in cases of youthful sexual exploration, at least not in the absence of any evidence of coercion or other aggravating factors (http://www.cps.gov.uk/news/fact sheets/sexual offences/index.html).

[15]*R v McNally* [2013] EWCA Crim 1051.

[16]Section 2 SOA 2003.

[17] *R v Mason* [2015] (unreported).

[18]*R v McNally* [2013] EWCA Crim 1051, at [10].

[19]Use of this minimal, and problematic, prosecution threshold is also apparent in some non trans cases, for example, *R v Barker* [2012] (unreported).

[20]In the English criminal law context, this view is most associated with Jonathan Herring ('Mistaken Sex' [2005] Crim LR 511). However, it is also supported by analytical philosophers (S Schulofer, 'Taking Sexual Autonomy Seriously' (1992) 11 *Law and Philosophy* 35; D Archard, *Sexual Consent* (Westview Press 1998); A Wertheimer, *Consent to Sexual Relations* (Cambridge University Press 2003). T Dougherty, 'Sex, Lies and Consent' (2013) 123(4) *Ethics* 717). For criticism of this approach to sexual fraud, see H Gross, 'Rape, Moralism and Human Rights' [2007] Crim LR 220; M Bohlander, 'Mistaken Consent to Sex, Political Correctness and Correct Policy' (2007) 71(5) *J of Crim L* 412; Sharpe n 6 above; K Laird, 'Rapist or Rogue? Deception, Consent and the Sexual Offences Act 2003' [2014] Crim LR 492.

[21]However, see the Israeli case of *Kashur v State of Israel* (published in Takdin, 25 January 2012). In this case, the court convicted an Arab man of rape by fraud on the basis that he failed to disclose his Arab status to his Jewish female

sexual autonomy might be considered especially important. Accordingly, the prosecution of transgender people might be viewed as a dramatic example of criminal law overreach, both in terms of setting such a minimum threshold for prosecution and in terms of an exclusive focus on a single identity group. It also, perhaps, serves to call into question the tendency of some, including feminist, advocacy groups to rely uncritically on the criminal law as the means through which to address perceived human rights abuses.[22] Certainly, in the present context, the punitiveness of such an approach is laid bare. Moreover, and as we will see, the distinction between, and the intelligibility of, the categories 'victim' and 'perpetrator,' tend to unravel in the context of desire-led cis-trans intimacy. Having provided some legal background to sexual offence prosecutions brought against transgender people in the UK, the article will now provide a broader ideological context to the cases, as well as some important caveats regarding state and wider cultural representation of the 'facts.'

II. Sexual 'Misadventure': Through the Looking Glass of Cisnormativity

This part of the article will tease out and challenge three cisnormative assumptions that confer apparent legitimacy on prosecution. These assumptions always appear to be present in actual cases and in wider cultural discourses surrounding them:

i. gender history is a material fact, non-disclosure of which serves to vitiate consent ('the consent claim')
ii. inadvertent sexual intimacy with transgender people is harmful ('the harm claim')
iii. non-disclosure of gender history is deceptive ('the deception claim')

Those who favour prosecution[23] do so because they readily make these three assumptions. And yet, if one pauses to consider what is at stake in each of these claims and to recognise how they proceed, somewhat effortlessly, from a cisnormative worldview, then the legally and culturally self-evident emerges as a highly edited and partial account of intimate moments, one that fails to consider the perspectives and experiences of transgender people. Let us turn to the claims made about consent, harm and deception. First, what does it mean to say that the consent of a cisgender person is lacking in the context of desire-led intimacy because the transgender party did not share in advance information

---

sexual partner. While the case needs to be situated within the specific cultural and religious context of the Israeli state in order to be properly understood, the conviction remains problematic in terms of the precedent it sets. However, it should be appreciated that the defendant pleaded guilty to this charge as part of a plea bargain and there appears to have been evidence of a violent rape and prosecutorial concern that the victim was too traumatised to testify http://www.bbc.co.uk/news/world middle east 11329429. For a critique of the case see A Gross, 'Rape by Deception and the Policing of Gender and Nationality Borders' (2015) 24 *Tulane J of L and Sexuality* 1.

[22] This is especially problematic in relation to feminism because reliance on criminal law requires the mobilisation of the carceral state and therefore teases out tensions that exist with basic tenets of feminism (D L Martin, 'Retribution Revisited: A Reconsideration of Feminist Criminal Law Reform Strategies' (1998) 36 *Osgoode Hall L J* 151; A Gruber, 'Rape, Feminism, and the War on Crime' (2009) 84 *Washington L Rev* 581). This problem of undue resort to criminal law has been described by Janet Halley et al as 'governance feminism' ('From the International to the Local in Feminist Legal Responses to Rape, Prostitution/Sex Work, and Sex Trafficking: Four Studies in Contemporary Governance Feminism' (2006) 29 *Harvard J of L and Gender* 335, 340 342). I am not suggesting here a direct relationship between governance feminism and the pro secution of transgender men. Rather, I am suggesting that such prosecutions become more likely in a world in which women's sexual autonomy is utterly juridified.

[23] See, in particular, Herring above n 20.

about his/her past? The claim being made here is that consent is premised on the right to sexual freedom or autonomy and that this right requires consent to be informed. However, given that no scholar would suggest that this requires total transparency to the world, informed consent emerges as requiring only disclosure of facts considered material or important, either to the complainant or in general normative terms.

A key difficulty here is that the sexual autonomy argument is mobilised not simply in the service of knowledge acquisition. Rather, behind the rhetoric of a right to know lies a legally sanctioned right to define others against their will. Thus, when cisgender people claim, and law confers, a right to 'know,' what is glossed over is the obvious fact that contestation exists over the nature of the facts that are capable of being known. In my view, 'apparent consent' should be viewed as legally valid because the important fact, namely 'authentic' gender identity,[24] is already in the open and there ought not to be a right to know other personal facts about the body and its history. To claim otherwise is, of necessity, to imbue other facts with a weight they ought not to bear, at least not if we wish to take self-determination of gender identity seriously. In the cases that have come before the courts, the 'fact,' upon which all complainants insist, is that the defendant is not a man. Accordingly, from a transgender perspective, the right to know is less about knowledge than its refusal. In short, the legal creation of this right constitutes nothing less than the ontological degradation of transgender people.

In relation to *harm*, I think there is something offensive in the claim that desire-led cis-trans intimacy is harmful to cisgender people. This issue of harm will be addressed more fully in Part 3, given the centrality of harm to the criminalisation question. However, for present purposes, it should be noted that establishing harm, sufficient to justify criminal intervention, is unlikely to be an easy task. Moreover, it should be recognised that 'harm,' in this context, involves the retrospective reconstruction of pleasurable acts and that subsequent distress, disgust, and/or revulsion are emotional responses conditioned by systemic transphobia[25] and/or homophobia. For both these reasons, we should be cautious about concluding that a threshold of harm, justifying criminalisation, has been met. In relation to deception, we should not confuse the claim with the claim about consent. The claim here relates, not to whether the complainant would have consented had she known all the relevant 'facts,' but to whether the defendant appreciated that she would not have consented had he disclosed his gender history. The difficulty here is that transgender people are confronted by the powerful cisnormative assumption and conceit that no cisgender person would knowingly become intimate with a transgender person. It is precisely this assumption that enables fanciful claims of ignorance, on the part of cisgender people, to be entertained by the courts. The assumption also serves to constitute transgender people as presumptively knowledgeable with regard to the consent question and

---

[24]In placing emphasis on 'authentic' gender identity, I am not suggesting an essentialist understanding of identity. Rather, while all identities are, in various senses, socially constructed, they have a reality in lived experience. This is no less true for transgender people than it is for cisgender people. This is important to emphasise because, for transgender people, 'realness' proves to be especially fragile and contingent as both criminal prosecution and disclosure discourse demonstrate.

[25]'Transphobia is an emotional disgust toward individuals who do not conform to society's gender expectations . . . The "phobia" suffix is used to imply an irrational fear or hatred, one that is at least partly perpetuated by cultural ideology' (D Hill and B Willoughby, 'The Development and Validation of the Genderism and Transphobia Scale' (2005) 53 *Sex Roles* 531, 532).

therefore low in the 'hierarchy of credibility'[26] should we claim to have believed in the other party's consent to the desire-led intimacy that occurred. Apparently, the transgender person who believes that a cisgender person might actually want to have sex with him/her even if aware of his/her transgender status is by definition a fraud. It would seem then that low self-esteem and self-loathing are the affective signs of the truly ethical transgender person as legally constructed. In other words, the accusation of knowledge regarding consent contains, implicitly, a view of transgender as abject.[27]

This issue of knowledge requires further consideration because we should not assume cisgender complainants to be unaware of the gender histories of transgender men. While this assumption tends to be triggered automatically, cisgender claims of ignorance should not be accepted so readily. After all, they require a massive exercise in the suspension of disbelief. None of the transgender defendants in the cases detailed above had, at the time of the relevant sexual acts at least, undertaken gender reassignment surgery or commenced hormonal treatment. The latter is especially significant because none of the defendants would have benefited from the significant masculinising effects of testosterone.[28] Accordingly, we are expected to believe that in the context of repeated sexual intimacies, cisgender female complainants remained unaware of their partners' female bodies. Somehow, the belief that the defendants were cisgender men survived intact despite physical contact with bodies that were vaginaed, breasted and which had relatively high-pitched voices. Moreover, my suggestion that we (bracket) claims of cisgender ignorance is not based only on common sense, but also on evidence actually presented in some of the cases under consideration. Thus, for example, in *McNally*, the defendant claimed that the complainant had discovered the facts about gender identity over a year before they physically met.[29] It was also claimed that the complainant commented on McNally's breasts and 'high pitched voice.'[30] In these respects, the bringing of complaints may have had less to do with consent obtained by fraud and more to do with repressed lesbian desire and/or parental pressure informed by homophobia. This concern is also supported by the earlier case of *Saunders*, where evidence was presented that the complainant had asked Saunders to 'pass as her boyfriend as she did not want [her parents] to know the "truth" about her sexuality.'[31]

The assumption regarding deception also proves to be an effect of a focus on, and a misunderstanding of, 'confusion' over gender identity. Thus, in *McNally*, gender identification proved inconsistent.[32] It is important, however, not to deny masculine gender identity simply because of apparently inconsistent or ambiguous testimony. After all, 'gender confusion' is not uncommon among transgender youth and should not be viewed as

---

[26]H S Becker, 'Whose Side are We on' (1967) 14(3) *Social Problems* 239.

[27]J Kristeva, *Powers of Horror: An Essay on Abjection* (Columbia University Press 1984).

[28]In terms of changes likely to be visible, transgender men prescribed testosterone typically experience increases in muscle, body, and facial hair, as well some degree of deepening of the voice (World Professional Association of Transgender Health, *Standards of Care for the Health of Transsexual, Transgender and Gender Nonconforming People* (7th edn, WPATH, 2012) 36).

[29]*R v McNally* [2013] EWCA Crim 1051, at [12].

[30]Ibid, [42].

[31]Gross above n 9, 173. It should also be noted that it may, at least in some cases, be 'gender dissonance' that lies at the heart of attraction (J Butler, *Gender Trouble* (Routledge, 1990) 122 123). While beyond the immediate concerns of this article, we should perhaps consider, as Gross urges us to, 'the extent to which uncertainty about identity, blurring of gender lines, and loss of control over all the information are part of the world of desire' (203).

[32]*R v McNally* [2013] EWCA Crim 1051, at [47].

evidence of gender inauthenticity. Moreover, and as noted earlier, McNally may have retreated into womanhood consequent upon police prosecution and media persecution. The idea that McNally might have sublimated masculine identity and desire in the face of a legal and cultural world in which transgender and deception are viewed as synonymous,[33] is one that finds support in medical evidence dealing with rates of gender persistence. Thus, while many young children exhibiting gender variant behaviour do not go on to identify as transgender as adults, those insisting on non-birth-designated gender identities after adolescence have a very high rate of persistence into adulthood.[34] Certainly, we should not overlook the enormous pressure cisnormativity exerts on vulnerable transgender youth. In any event, McNally appears to have genuinely identified as male at the time of the offences. Therefore criminal liability ought not to have been founded on 'gender fraud.'

It is also important to recognise how a focus on stable binary gender identity can produce injustice beyond the treatment of transgender defendants. That is, there is a real danger here that cisnormative understandings of gender, identity, and authenticity will expand the net of criminalisation beyond the example of transgender, even on the limited question of gender identity 'fraud.' Thus, for example, a woman who identifies as gender queer might perform gender in a masculine way. However, her performance is not deceptive. She does not act inauthentically, nor is she motivated by a desire to deceive. On the contrary, gender queer is precisely the gender identity position that she occupies and lives. She should not be punished because a sexual partner mistakenly assumes her to be male. Crucially, we should recognise the very real danger of coupling truth with gender performances that faithfully and consistently replicate the gender binary, a binary which is, after all, more ideological than real.[35]

III. Responding to the Punitive State

In this Part of the article, we turn to arguments against criminalisation. It will be argued that the argument in favour of criminalisation is not clinched even if we concede cisnormative assumptions concerning consent, harm, and knowledge. This is because justification of criminalisation depends not only on establishing a consent-based right to know, but also on a degree of harm and culpability. It is also necessary to demonstrate that the case for criminalisation is not outweighed by other considerations. I shall argue that criminalisation of non-disclosure of gender history is inappropriate for at least three reasons:

1) it produces legal inconsistency and is potentially discriminatory,
2) sexual autonomy should not be viewed as an absolute right,
3) there are compelling public policy reasons against criminalisation.

---

[33] T M Bettcher, 'Evil Deceivers and Make Believers: On Transphobic Violence and the Politics of Illusion' (2007) 22(3) *Hypatia* 43.

[34] B Wren, 'Early Physical Intervention for Young People with Atypical Gender Identity Development' (2000) 5 *Clin Child Psychol Psychiatry* 220; K J Zucker, 'Gender Identity Disorder', in D A Wolfe and E J Mash (eds), *Behavioral and Emotional Disorders in Adolescents: Nature, Assessment, and Treatment* (Guilford Press, 2006) 535 562; K J Zucker and P T Cohen Kettenis, 'Gender Identity Disorder in Children and Adolescents', in D L Rowland and L Incrocci (eds) *Handbook of Sexual and Gender Identity Disorders* (John Wiley & Sons, 2008) 376 422.

[35] J Butler, *Bodies That Matter: On the Discursive Limits of Sex* (Routledge, 1993).

Objection 1: Prosecution produces legal inconsistency and is potentially discriminatory

The young transgender men convicted of sexual offences were all convicted on the basis of fraud. Yet, convictions for sexual offences on the basis of fraud are rare under English law as they are within Anglo-American and European legal systems more generally. In the absence of coercion they are rarer still. The forms of non-disclosure that do not serve to vitiate consent for the purposes of sexual offences under English law range widely from false declarations of love to HIV+ status.[36] They are likely to include non-disclosure of facts concerning racial or ethnic status, disability, past sexual experience, drug addiction, religious faith and criminal convictions. The list is potentially endless. All of these facts may be ones sexual partners wish to know.

Yet, in all these and many other circumstances law views consent as legally valid. Of course, one might argue that consent provisions should be interpreted so as to include these and/or other forms of non-disclosure. In other words, it might be said that the problem is one of under-regulation. Nevertheless, the problem of inconsistency remains. Moreover, the targeting of gender history, as opposed to other types of historical information, and the fact that it is only the gender histories of transgender people rather than people at large (for we all have gender histories) with which law appears to be concerned,[37] points to the possibility that prosecution might constitute discrimination under article 14 of the European Convention on Human Rights coupled with article 8. Of course, it might be argued that knowledge concerning gender history is likely to be more important to sexual partners than other facts. This might be so, though it is properly an empirical question. It may be, for example, that race or religion is just as important, at least for some people. However, what we need to remember is that this type of argument is not really about a right to know the truth, but a right to define truth. If gender identity has special importance, as claimed, it is because cisgender people insist on defining us in terms of birth-designated sex, and/or on erecting hierarchies of men and women. In terms of developing international human rights jurisprudence, we must draw a clear and non-negotiable line in relation to self-determination of gender identity.

Objection 2: Sexual autonomy should not be viewed as an absolute right

In this section, it will be argued that we should not view sexual autonomy as an absolute right. In relation to cisgender women's right to choose with whom they have sex, this is, for many, tantamount to feminist heresy. In relation to cis-trans intimacy, however, challenging orthodoxy is not merely an act of rebellion, but one of necessity. This article will highlight privacy and/or human dignity as limits to sexual autonomy. However, we should recognise that transgender people also value and have an interest in sexual autonomy. This is a point often overlooked in discussion of the present issue. And yet, surely, it cannot be said that control of personal information concerning administration of

---

[36]Under English law, non disclosure of HIV+ status may lead to a successful prosecution for non fatal assault, but not for a sexual offence where consent is presumed to be present: *R v Dica* [2004] EWCA Crim 1103; *R v Konzani* [2005] EWCA Crim 706.

[37]The exclusive focus on the gender identities of transgender as opposed to cisgender people is an effect of cisnormative ideas about gender realness and artifice (Serrano above n 5).

hormones, the undertaking of surgeries, and earlier coerced gender performances are divorced from this right. After all, informational privacy concerning the body, its history and surgical alteration impact on both the context and the experience of sexual intimacy. Of course, it might be said that 'in the context of sexual intimacy, the right not to associate trumps the right to associate.'[38] In the context of rape-by-force, this claim is unarguable. In the context of 'sexual fraud' the matter is much more complicated as we will see, and this is especially so in the case of non-disclosure of information. Thus, state emphasis on the protection of sexual autonomy does not necessarily justify criminal prosecution. But even if cisgender autonomy were found to trump transgender autonomy in the context of sexual intimacy, a legal requirement to disclose gender history provokes other rights conflicts.

The legal obligation to disclose gender history to sexual partners requires the disclosure of highly personal and private information. Accordingly, it might be viewed as breaching rights to privacy[39] and/or human dignity.[40] If so, it becomes necessary to balance rights[41] and the harms likely to flow from disregarding them. Indeed, criminalisation ought to be preceded by a balancing of harms even where no conflicting right can be identified, as harm minimisation ought to be a key consideration in such calculations. Accordingly, in order to conclude that a right to sexual autonomy requires the disclosure of gender history, it should be demonstrated, by those who favour prosecution, that potential or actual harm suffered by cisgender people is (a) significant and (b) outweighs the harm to transgender people associated with disclosure. Without the possibility of significant consequential harm it is difficult to see why an informational right to know gender history should operate as a trump card.

According to the testimony of complainants in cases that have come before the courts, harm suffered appears to consist in feelings of distress, disgust or revulsion. Thus in *McNally*, and according to prosecuting counsel, the complainant felt 'literally sickened' upon discovery. A question arises here as to whether we are actually in the territory of harm, as opposed to mere offence.[42] If not, then a further objection to criminalisation has been identified. If we are in the territory of harm, and if harm minimisation is our goal, it remains necessary to balance such harms against those likely to be suffered by transgender people. Disclosing gender history is not an act undertaken without risks. Coming out as transgender exposes a person to considerable and well-documented physical risks.[43] We need only think of the tragic case of Brandon Teena, so graphically illustrated in the film, *Boys Don't Cry*. This concern is perhaps intensified in relation to transgender youth and therefore in relation to all defendants prosecuted so far.

In addition to the not inconsiderable physical risks, we need to recognise the psychological and emotional impact of disclosure. For many transgender people, having to

---

[38] S Colb, 'Is There a Moral Duty to Disclose that You're Transgender to a Potential Partner?' *Verdict* 18 June 2015, https://verdict.justia.com/2015/06/18/is there a moral duty to disclose that youre transgender to a potential partner.

[39] Article 8, European Convention on Human Rights.

[40] Article 1, EU Charter of Fundamental Rights; Article 1, Universal Declaration of Human Rights. These provisions emphasise the 'intrinsic worth' of persons and the 'respect and concern' that should be afforded them.

[41] In relation to article 8, para 2 alludes to this balancing act in justifying state infringement of the right to privacy in specified circumstances.

[42] J Feinberg, *Harm to Others: The Moral Limits of the Criminal Law* (vol 1, Oxford University Press, 1984).

[43] In the UK context, Whittle et al found that 'in every sphere of life' transgender people 'are subject to high levels of abuse and violence' (S Whittle et al, *The Equalities Review: Engendered Penalties: Transgender and Transsexual People's Experiences of Inequality & Discrimination* (Press for Change, 2007) 23).

disclose their chromosomal status, present and/or past genital and/or gonadal condition as well as a history of coerced gender performance is a source of pain and trauma. Finally, a balancing of harms requires recognition of the fact that complainant distress, disgust and revulsion are emotional responses conditioned by systemic transphobia and/or homophobia, and for this reason also should not be viewed as sufficient in meeting a threshold of harm justifying criminal intervention, and especially not to target a vulnerable minority group.

Objection 3: A public policy objection

In thinking of prosecution in broader public policy terms it is necessary to develop the theme of transphobia and the state's interest in reducing it. It is instructive here to draw on the analogy of race because once we shift our attention from non-disclosure of gender history to non-disclosure of racial status our concern for, and law's interest in, sexual autonomy tends to wane. The point here is not to redraw attention to the inconsistencies of law, which formed the basis of objection 1. Rather, it is to highlight state complicity in generating precisely what the state is committed, at least ostensibly, to overcoming in public policy and anti-discrimination law terms.

Consider the following example:

> A white woman and a man of mixed race, who outwardly appears white, meet in a wine bar. They flirt with each other. The woman invites the man to her apartment where mutually satisfying sex takes place. Subsequently, the woman discovers the mixed race background of the man and claims to feel violated. She reports the matter to the police and requests that the man be charged with rape on the basis of his failure to disclose his racial background.

There are people who would consider a rape charge an appropriate outcome on these facts, and certainly in circumstances where the man was aware in advance of the woman's racist feelings. However, for the rest of us, such a suggestion seems not only counterintuitive, but offensive. Fortunately, such a prosecution would never get off the ground and, if it did, would certainly fail to secure a conviction under English law. Yet, in the context of cis-trans intimacy, the legal position is obviously quite different. It would seem that the intolerance that we rightly bring to expressions of racism in our society deserts us when we are asked to accommodate the fact of gender variance. If you are a racist, the legal message appears to be: *do not go around assuming people to be of a particular race or ethnicity.* For, if you do, you might be disappointed. Conversely, if you are a transphobe, the legal message is: *assume everybody to be cisgender and if your unreasonable assumption fails to accord with reality, feel free to channel your sense of outrage through the criminal law.*

The view that it is appropriate to prosecute transgender men for non-disclosure of gender history is one that takes the sexual autonomy of cisgender people too seriously, viewing it in near absolute terms. Such a conclusion requires us to trump a public policy concern to counter transphobia. In view of the mixed race example above, it might be objected that equating transphobia with racism in this context only works if minding about gender history is as transphobic as minding about race is racist. This is precisely my argument. The fact that it provokes resistance reveals not the falseness of the argument but society's failure to take transphobia as seriously as it does racism in this specific context of sexual intimacy. Resistance to this argument ultimately resides in the view that while a black man is both black (though not necessarily visibly so) and a man, a transgender man is not a man. It is precisely this view of transgender people as artificial men and women that must be resisted, not replicated by law. Of course, we should all be free to choose with whom we become sexually intimate, though we might want to work-shop an aversion to a particular class of people. But once a desire-led choice has been acted upon, the actor should not be able to disown it or be permitted to reframe an ensuing plea-surable sexual exchange as the rightful object of criminal law, at least not when gender presentation accords with gender self-identity.

Moreover, the fact that a cisgender person minds about gender history, should not translate into the assumption that a transgender person must have appreciated this fact. There is no reason to assume knowledge here, or indeed that transgender people would want to have sex with a transphobe. The fact that this assumption tends to be readily made points not to deceit, but to an unacknowledged, and empirically false, conceit that no cisgender person would knowingly become intimate with a transgender person. For all these reasons, and especially where society is being asked to accommodate preju-dice, we should perhaps give full reign to *caveat amator* or let the lover beware.

Conclusions

This article has considered a series of recent cases where young transgender men have been successfully prosecuted for sexual offences in circumstances where their female cis-gender partners claimed to be unaware of their gender histories. These prosecutions have been based on the assumptions that in these circumstances, consent is lacking, harm is occasioned, and deception is present. The article teased out how each of these legal and cultural assumptions is deeply problematic and an effect of a cisnormative interpretation of the 'facts.' The article argued that even if contested claims around consent, harm, and deception were conceded, the case against criminalisation would remain overwhelming. Ultimately, prosecutions of this kind demonstrate the need to limit the right to sexual autonomy. To see this right in near absolute terms is an act of hubris.

What we ought to scrutinise is not transgender reticence to disclose highly personal information, but cisgender demands to know. For the demand to know is not simply an invasion of privacy for the purposes of discovering objective facts. On the contrary, cis-gender demands to know presuppose an already constructed set of facts which rob trans-gender people of self-definitional agency. The likelihood of further prosecutions will remain as long as transgender continues to be understood as a synonym for duplicity, sub-terfuge, and dissimulation. It is precisely this legal and cultural view to which criminal pro-secutions contribute. Therefore, what we need to confront as scholars and activists is not simply the concrete fact of prosecution, urgent though that obligation is, but the view that non-disclosure of gender history is unethical. Future research in this area needs to con-sider sexual ethics, the question of what we owe to each other in our sexual relations. And in exploring this question, we need to strip away our cisnormative and heteronorma-tive assumptions that might otherwise appropriate the place of the ethical.

Index